THE UNIVERSITY OF GOOGLE

Dedicated to those who have taught with me, and those who have taught me.

Mostly, they are the same people.

Special thanks to Kevin Brabazon, Doris Brabazon, Steve Redhead, Leanne McRae, Mike Kent, Debbie Hindley, Angela Thomas-Jones and the Popular Culture Collective.

The University of Google

Education in the (Post) Information Age

TARA BRABAZON
University of Brighton, UK

ASHGATE

Published by
Ashgate Publishing Limited
Gower House
Croft Road
Aldershot
Hampshire GU11 3HR
England

Ashgate Publishing Company
Suite 420
101 Cherry Street
Burlington, VT 05401-4405
USA

Reprinted 2008

Ashgate website: http://www.ashgate.com

British Library Cataloguing in Publication Data
Brabazon, Tara
The university of Google : education in the
(post) information age
1. Google (Firm) 2. Internet in education 3. Internet
research 4. Learning and scholarship 5. Web search engines
I. Title
371.3'344678

Library of Congress Cataloging-in-Publication Data
Brabazon, Tara.
The University of Google : education in the (post) information age / by Tara Brabazon.
p. cm.
Includes bibliographical references and index.
ISBN 978-0-7546-7097-1 (alk. paper)
1. Education, Higher--Effect of technological innovations on. 2. Internet in higher education.
3. Teaching. I. Title.

LB2395.7.B73 2007
378.1'7344678--dc22

2007025289

ISBN-13: 978-0-7546-7097-1

Printed and bound in Great Britain by TJ International Ltd, Padstow, Cornwall.

Contents

Introduction Living (in the) post 1

Section One – Literacy

1 BA (Google): graduating to information literacy 15

2 Digital Eloi and analogue Morlocks 51

Section Two – Culture

3 Stretching flexible learning 71

4 An i-diots guide to i-lectures 103

5 Popular culture and the sensuality of education 131

Section Three – Critique

6 Exploiting knowledge? 155

7 Deglobalizing education 179

8 Burning towers and smouldering truth: September 11 and the changes to critical literacy 193

Conclusion The gift: why education matters 215

Select bibliography *223*
Index *225*

Introduction

Living (in the) post

> With the public sector, education, the welfare state – all the big, 'safe' institutions – up against the wall, there's nothing good or clever or heroic about going under. When all is said and done, why bother to think 'deeply' when you're not being paid to think deeply?[1]
>
> Dick Hebdige

> Face it: You're always just a breath away from a job in telemarketing.[2]
>
> Douglas Coupland

University teaching is a special job. It is a joy to wake up in the morning knowing that during each working day, an extraordinary event or experience will jut out from the banal rhythms of administration, answering emails and endlessly buzzing telephones. Students, in these ruthless times, desperately want to feel something – anything – beyond the repetitive and pointless patterns of the casualized workplace and the selection of mobile phone ring tones. This cutting consumerism subtly corrodes the self. These students follow anyone who makes them feel more than a number, more than labour fodder for fast food outlets. I believe in these students, and I need to believe that the future they create will be better than the intellectual shambles we have bequeathed them. Being a teacher is a privilege to never take for granted. The bond between students and educators is not severed when a certificate is presented. We share a memory of change, of difference, of feeling that we can change the world, one person at a time.

In 2002, I wrote about teaching in a rage. *Digital Hemlock*[3] was an angry book, howling at the economic decisions and choices made by our university administrators, prioritizing technology over people, and applications over ideas. I was frustrated and amazed at the ignorance and ineptitude that was dismissing the expertise of teachers, and ignoring the outstanding range of educational literature urging caution in unstintingly embracing technological change over more nuanced theories of learning. The response to this embittered book from readers was immediate, powerful and embracing. Letters flooded my mail box. Emails deluged my in-box. It was as if neglected and concerned teachers had been seething with anger – waiting to express critique and ask the difficult questions

1 D. Hebdige, *Hiding in the Light* (London: Comedia, 1988) p. 167.

2 D. Coupland, *Microserfs* (London: Flamingo, 1996), p. 17.

3 T. Brabazon, *Digital Hemlock* (Sydney: UNSW Press, 2002).

– but felt isolated and limited in their ability to counter the forces of managerialism and technological determinism.

It felt good to be part of a group of educators again, a community concerned at the economic neglect of our beautiful but crumbling universities. While *Hemlock* changed my life, it did not change our universities. No book can. Since it was written, the sector is in a worse state than when I finished the final proof. The imperative for flexible learning, i-lectures and internet-mediated education continues, while staff are suffering more than I have ever seen. A senior colleague, a man I looked up to enormously through my teaching career, died just after *Hemlock* was published. Other university friends have had minor strokes and heart attacks. Perhaps such attacks are more than metaphorically appropriate: administrative decisions about hardware purchases and software licences have cut the heart out of education.

Through the techno-celebrations, the failures of the e-ducation initiatives are mounting. In 2000, the then Education Secretary in the Blair Government, David Blunkett, launched UKeU, the British-based e-university. Only able to recruit 900 students worldwide, the Higher Education Funding Council for England (HEFCE) closed it. This failure occurred after an estimated £20 million had been spent on developing an online platform with Sun Microsystems. The financial situation was so dire that, on 30 July 2004, the creditors voluntarily agreed to accept a settlement of 18p in the pound. All the universities who had supported the scheme were treated as unsecured creditors. The University of Central Lancashire was owed £117,500, Nottingham £82,250, Ulster £61,437 and Leeds Metropolitan £7,050. Considering these losses and the inability of UKeU to meet its student target of 5,600, it is a piquant footnote to this story that the former Chief Executive of the organization, John Beaumont, collected a bonus of £45,000 above his £186,000 salary.[4] Such a narrative not only confirms the continual failure of dot.com logic when applied to higher education, but that administrators have neither the expertise nor knowledge to be making predictions about curricula success. The morbid attraction to this digital Medusa, even through the virtual deaths and bloody bankruptcies, remains seductive. Even after this failure of UKeU, Liverpool University announced – on April Fool's Day 2004 – that it was entering a ten-year deal to deliver online degrees. They justified this commitment because Liverpool is not actually funding the scheme, with the money being provided by Sylvan Learning Systems Inc, a company based in the United States that runs campuses through Latin America and Europe. That an 'Inc' could so easily provide degrees is troubling. That Liverpool University could so freely trade its reputation for the potential of a virtual pound, with the digital carcasses lining the superhighway, is brave if not foolhardy. The

4 An outstanding review of the failure of UKeU is Donald MacLeod's 'E-university creditors make net loss', *The Guardian*, 2 August 2004, http://education.guardian.co.uk/elearning/story/0,10577,1274438,00.html, accessed on 3 August 2004.

siren's call to e-learning is still heard by Manchester and Open Universities who aim to use the digital environment to 'sell' their degrees overseas.[5]

There is one great absence from this story of e-failure. What of our students? Through all the marketing plans, strategic initiatives, corporate capital and generic competencies, no one seems to ask the students about their ideas and hopes for a university education. Late in 2004, I received an email from one of my (ex) students who shared a story. I started reading her words – inquisitive to see how she was faring in life. She was a fine student when I taught her – working at a distinction level – and I hoped, as we all do, that her life was happy, satisfying and productive. By the end of the email, I was in tears.

To: t.brabazon@murdoch.edu.au
From: Cheryl
Subject: Hi
Date: Sat, 18 Sep 2004 05:54:32 +0800

Dear Tara,

I am an ex-international student of Murdoch university and I attended two of your classes during my time there – namely Intro to Communications Studies and Cultural Difference and Diversity.

I graduated in 2001 and returned to Singapore to work. I recently landed a job as a 'lecturer' at a commercial school here offering distance-education courses accredited by 'High-end' Universities such as Monash, Deakin, and University of Oklahoma.

I've recently started reading your book, 'Digital Hemlock' (I'm merely at the first chapter) and I decided to drop everything and share my story with you.

After two months teaching, I decided to quit as I had realised that I did not agree with the entire educational system of the school I worked for, and my efforts to change things were met with stern warnings and evaluations which made me feel ambushed and even more stressed than I already was.

5 D. MacLeod and L. Ford, 'On the brink of a revolution', *Education Guardian*, 28 February 2006, p. 12.

The job required me to have 48 hours of contact time with students, which meant that ALL of my time at work was spent teaching. Any prep work HAD to be done at home, often into the wee hours in the morning.

I started to realise that the school did not care if the teachers were prepared, but rather, they were looking for a warm body, ANY body, to stand in front of the class and pull tricks out of their arses.

Unlike 'real' universities, classes were held in 3-hour-blocks, which meant that both lectures and tutorials had to be delivered in one session.

My technique was straightforward (and at the time, I thought, effective). You see, I went in to my classes teaching the way *I* was taught at Murdoch, (especially by you), and at the National University of Singapore, where I did my Master's degree.

I brought in loads of examples, videos, magazines, books, and following from your example, I even played music in my classes. (I find that music helps to ease them into the classes as well as keeps time very well, so if we have a 10 minute break, I would play two 5-minute songs and instinctively resume class after the songs had finished.).

After delivering a 45–50 minute lecture, I would normally call for a 15 minute break, after which we would begin discussions on topics related to the unit.

Unfortunately, many students (there are about 30–40 students per class!) would leave right after the lectures, choosing to just attend for the sake of copying down the notes, being entertained for a bit, and then leaving. Only an enthusiastic few would stay behind to contribute to discussions. I felt that discussions were necessary as I wanted to learn as much from them (and from each other) as they did from me.

Much to my horror, when the evaluations were held, I received many complaints, mostly to the tune of 'she should just speak more and tell us which readings are important and discuss less'.

The management promptly sat me down and said that students had paid 'a lot of money' for the courses and expected to get their money's worth. So in not-so-many words, I was told to just point them to the right readings, give them tips on how to write their essays, and summarise readings for them. I was also told that I was supposed to deliver my lectures for at least 2 hours, which meant that I was doing the talking for the most part.

I could not believe what I was hearing. There we were, promising potential students that they would be getting the 'same quality' of education as their on-campus counterparts, and yet behind closed doors we were practicing the exact opposite.

This is not to say that I do not understand time and money constraints on off-campus students, particular part-time and working adults, but I was completely disgusted by the way the school chose to educate its students.

I promptly sent in my resignation the next day.

As I sat and thought about it, I realised that I did not want to be a part of an organisation that chose to behave more like an 'educational mall' as you call it, and I certainly did not want to perpetuate the kind of educational experience that the school was asking of me.

In the introduction of your book, you mentioned Socrates. I really felt like Socrates at that point, and I felt like I was being condemned for fighting for social justice and cultivating a sense of critical thinking in my students. NONE of my efforts were acknowledged nor appreciated, and I was blatantly told 'this is the way we work, you are part of the system, and there is nothing you can do about it'.

Students came in thinking they could buy their degrees instead of actually working for it. I have even had students disrupt classes, demanding for 'tips' on how to 'write' their essays. When I asked if they had any questions in particular, they just said, 'everything. tell us how to start'.

I am now without a job, and I know that I am the better for it.

My experience with the school may have been a Samson-and-Goliath one (sic), and I would have most likely been fired if I had spoken up

> any more than I already did, but I just want you to know that there are people out there (i.e, me!) who share your vision and passion for education, and we will not stop fighting for what we believe is true and just.
>
> I continue to reminisce about my good ol' days at Murdoch (despite some of its shortcomings) and I often tell people about 'The best lecturer I have ever had by the name of Tara Brabazon'.
>
> I thank you for the mark you have made in my life and the encouragement you have given to all your students to 'keep on rocking'.
>
> Here's wishing you all the best in everything that you do, and I look forward to someday having the chance to inspire future students the way you have inspired me.
>
> Best Wishes,
>
> Cheryl

This story bent my body in confusion and anger. This was not my intention in *Digital Hemlock*: to remove a clearly brilliant and committed teacher from the classroom. A bright, fascinating young woman – principled and compassionate – is without work because she could not abide by the rules of this new system. I did not deserve her praise. She has more courage than I could summon. Upon reading this email, I made a decision that anger and rage is not enough. *Digital Hemlock* failed. I needed to write again, this time with solutions and resolutions to the traumas and triage facing higher education. I am not teaching the best and brightest of their generation to excel and be all they can be, to have them crushed by a system that is confusing interactivity with learning. I do not want other Cheryls to lose their livelihood and dreams of teaching students and inspiring the next generation of scholars.

The University of Google is the result of this desire to restart the computer, activate the hard drive and return the sensitive touchpad to education. In the chapters that follow, I place particular attention on literacy, popular culture, information management and the knowledge economy. The aim is to find a way to revalue reading, writing and thinking to demonstrate not only social, but economic and political, benefits. I unpick the assumptions of a mass higher education system, supposedly facilitating lifelong learning and contributing to the competitiveness of nations and individuals in a global marketplace.[6] The rapid increase in student numbers, not only in the post-1945 period but particularly in the last 20 years, poses challenges for universities operating within restrictive administrative parameters and dense dependencies on governmental policy. The push to managerialism means that many more men in shiny polyester suits – arbitrarily given 'vanity' titles like Professor on the basis of position not scholarship – pace around our university campuses. Not surprisingly, words like diversity and flexibility weave through their footsteps. Transferable skills, strategic plans, cross-sector synergies and generic competencies bounce along for the ride.[7] Through this mudslide of management-speak, it has become acceptable to minimize the importance of scholarship and academic expertise when leading a university.

> Mr Allen, who is registrar and secretary at Exeter University said: 'Clearly you've got to understand academics, but why do you have to have the T-shirt? There are plenty of people in universities who are excellent leaders and managers but who are not members of the academic tribe.'[8]

David Allen is Chair of the Association of Heads of University Administration in the United Kingdom. Obviously, his career profile and ambition is circumscribed by the demand that the best *academics* run *academic* institutions. He has confused – and conflated – management and leadership. Allen could manage a university, sans metaphoric T-shirt. But he could not offer teaching or research leadership, as he has not demonstrated ability in the writing of curricula, the delivery of course materials, or an intricate understanding of how to balance a portfolio of teaching and research. These are not tribal activities. They are components of scholarship. His selection of metaphor brings into question his capacity to lead academics, but this honest disclosure from an administrator that academic expertise is over-rated creates a space for clear-headed debate. Now is the time for academics to confirm their worth and why the life we have lived, the students we have taught and the research we have conducted has mattered, and continues to matter. By living (in the) Post – postmodern, postindustrial,

---

6 I particularly acknowledge the diverse interpretations and meanings of lifelong learning. Most of the definitions in this chapter are derived from the United Kingdom, United States of America and Australia. However, I note the diversity of the term when applied to particular nations. I am assisted in this discovery by Hans Schuetze and Maria Sloweys' edited monograph, *Higher Education and Lifelong Learners: International Perspectives on Change* (London: Routledge, 2000).

7 An outstanding analysis of the rationale for these phrases is Joshua Powers, 'R&D funding sources and university technology transfer: what is stimulating universities to be more entrepreneurial?' *Research in Higher Education*, Vol. 45, No. 1, February 2004, pp. 1–23.

8 David Allen, cited in Anna Fazackerley, 'Allow non-academics to lead, urges registrar', *The Times Higher*, 28 July 2006, p. 5.

postcolonial and post-Fordist[9] – new critical and reflexive spaces are created to build a post-information society, one that can take the first unsteady steps to knowledge and wisdom.

This book investigates the struggles, problems and responsibilities of learning, teaching and working in the contemporary education system. My goal is to probe assumptions and offer productive and positive alternatives and solutions to the difficulties punctuating our classrooms and curricula. The interdisciplinary sources and research material deployed from media studies, library studies, information studies, creative industries' policies, popular cultural studies and education studies aligns, jars and resonates. This mix of styles and paradigms is productive, yet through all the research cited, there is one article – indeed one paragraph – that presents a core challenge for me as an educator. Geoff Pugh, Gwen Coates and Nick Adnett, in their analysis of performance indicators in the UK education system, made a profound statement:

> Students from under-represented groups may require more extensive support or more radical changes in teaching and learning strategies if they are to approach completion rate norms. Thus, HEIs [Higher Education Institutions] need to consider both the support and the teaching and learning cultures and strategies they offer to students from disadvantaged backgrounds, rather than merely concentrating upon the application and entrance process … a priority should be to find ways of ensuring more students succeed in completing their course and qualification rather than intensifying the marketing effort to expand recruitment.[10]

The goal of *The University of Google* is to accept Pugh, Coates and Adnett's challenge. Instead of assuming that 'technology' can solve educational 'problems', attention is placed on 'more extensive support' through curriculum, methods and literacy. Three sections structure my argument and the project of this book. The first part, *Literacy*, introduces the Googlescape with the aim of developing an information scaffold in

9 There are many interpretations of the 'post' prefix. It can be synonymous with antagonism – anti-modernism, anti-structuralism – or it can refer to a reflexive questioning of totalizing histories. Gianni Vattimo described this usage of 'the post' as 'taking leave of modernity'. Please refer to *The End of Modernity* (Oxford: Basil Blackwell, 1988), p. 3. Another interpretation, where the post refers to critique and challenge, has often been deployed by Robert Hewison. Please refer to *Future Tense* (London: Methuen, 1990). Throughout my book, both these deployments of 'the post' are activated.

10 G. Pugh, G. Coates and N. Adnett, 'Performance indicators and widening participation in UK higher education', *Higher Education Quarterly*, Vol. 59, No. 1, January 2005, p. 33. Such a challenge was also suggested by C. Macdonald and E. Stratta, 'From access to widening participation: responses to the changing population in higher education in the UK', *Journal of Further and Higher Education*, Vol. 25, No. 2, 2001, pp. 249–58 and M. Yorke, 'Outside benchmark expectations? Variations in non-completion rates in English higher education', *Journal of Higher Education Policy and Management*, Vol. 23, No. 2, 2001, p. 147–58.

curriculum. The goal is to integrate an information system into a social system. The second section, *Culture*, problematizes the concept of 'flexible learning', demonstrating the costs to student achievement and teachers' credibility. Instead of the band aid panacea of 'web literacy', the sensuality of popular culture in education is revealed. The final part, *Critique*, situates the changes to education into wider political changes. Phrases like 'creative industries' and the 'knowledge economy' are contextualized within the political manifestations of deglobalization and terrorism. The focus is on learning cultures and the strategies through which they can be developed and nurtured, even in difficult times.

The computer is not the fount of educational troubles. Google is not the facilitator for neoliberalism. The goal of this book is to embed computer-mediated communication and applications into other media and social structures. I look for continuities and alliances between the analogue and digital, past and present. The ideological boundaries encircling computers are permeable and morph with the changes to literacies. Particularly it is important to focus on the relationship between media. The links and qualitative differences between older and emerging cultural formations are displayed through attention to screen and sound, visual and aural sources. It is timely to remember that the internet is not a physical entity, but a system of communication and data transfer. Placing attention on inclusion and exclusion, social justice and sharp inequality, computers are more than a product to be bought, but a cultural artefact and information system to be embedded into social structures.

Books about teaching are often dull. Stephen Brookfield described these texts as being 'written in a disembodied tone of bloodless asceticism'.[11] This coldness in language and interpretation is odd, considering the heat, passion, confusion and energy that explodes from the best of classrooms. It is almost as if the dullness of academic meetings has saturated the literature in the field. This is not the time for teachers and scholars to be complacent, quiet, complicit or dull. There are so few voices and documents affirming the importance of educating the citizens of a nation, not only because it improves economic efficiency and development, but also forges relationships between people in different places and times. To enact this goal, I open up my classrooms for readers, noting there is nothing special about me as an educator. This ordinariness is important, as it is a reminder how revelation emerges from the smallest incident, event or moment. Yet each day, an email arrives in my in-box that cuts away or dissolves another pillar of education. Recognizing the consequences of Brookfield's words, *The University of Google* returns the sweaty beauty to education, so that if we are to lose what most of us have worked a lifetime to build, at least we have some word pictures, monuments and memories for our efforts.

---

11 S. Brookfield, *Becoming a Critically Reflective Teacher* (San Francisco: Jossey-Bass Books, 1995), p. xv.

A primary goal for the humanities and social sciences is to create better citizens, to facilitate the development of creative, provocative and passionate thinkers who challenge those around them to do better and be better. The three sections of this book link text and context so as to develop curriculum with consciousness. My classrooms, experiences, fears and hopes are thrown open for scrutiny. Only by diagnosing and interpreting our new classrooms can informed pedagogical and policy decisions emerge.[12] Our lived experiences of teaching intersect with the intellectual history of education to create an evocative landscape of problem solving. In mapping value judgments in an empirical way, [13] theories of technology, information and education are made meaningful. The challenges of teacher research pepper the pages. I probe methods to think about and through teaching and learning. Through the difficult silences that emerge, the most important point made in this book is that technological changes and initiatives in internet and web-based education have been framed and fanned by the managerial transformations of universities. Quality teaching and learning strategies or outcomes have not been the cause or impetus. The goal has been to save money and be efficient. The problem is in the political framework and policy agenda, not the platforms, software and hardware. Internet education and e-learning arrived at a time when words like competency, efficiency and flexibility were accepted by teachers and administrators, seemingly without question.

Technology is central to the project of capitalist modernity.[14] Yet as modernity is shaken through the deglobalizing world crises of war, terrorism and 'natural' disasters,

---

12 Such practices are discussed and validated by Elizabeth van Es and Miriam Sherin in 'Learning to notice: scaffolding new teachers' interpretations of classroom interactions', from *Journal of Technology and Teacher Education*, Vol. 10, No. 4, 2002, pp. 571–96. Particularly, they wished teachers to 'learn to develop skills in interpretation that can then be used to inform pedagogical decisions', p. 575.

13 Peter Strauss has provided an effective model of qualitative research in teaching. He stated, 'How can I as a researcher come to terms with the feelings of despair that an inquiry into my own practice is likely to generate? … One of the most troubling things I have discovered is that I am not the teacher I thought I was', from 'No easy answers: the dilemmas and challenges of teacher research', *Educational Action Research*, Vol. 2, No. 2, 1995, p. 30.

14 I wish to note the scale and scope of the debates encircling terms like critical and capitalist modernities. From Anthony Gidden's *The Consequences of Modernity* (Palo Alto, CA: Stanford University Press, 1991) through to Peter Drucker's *Post-Capitalist Society* (New York: HarperCollins, 1994) and Teresa Brennan's *Exhausting Modernity* (London: Routledge, 2000), debates about modernity as an era and project are volatile, exciting and extremely important. While conducting the research for this book, I have been strongly influenced by the recent writings of Zygmunt Bauman, particularly *Liquid Modernity* (Cambridge: Polity Press, 2000). By utilizing the term 'capitalist modernity', I am not suggesting that modernity is singular. Instead, I am making the more obvious point that modernity has not only emerged and developed in and through capitalism, but also in other modes of production.

education must assume another function, beyond 'giving' civilization and culture, beyond maintaining a market economy. In a time of such change and turmoil, the views of John Tiffin become even more inexplicable.

> Academics answer the same questions that students ask generation after generation. What if artificial intelligence could take care of these questions? You don't get a good education if you're part of a 1:20 ratio rather than 1:10 – and student numbers are rocketing.[15]

Tiffin is simply wrong in his judgments. Students are not asking the same questions, because the identity of students attending universities in the last ten years – let alone generation after generation – has changed. Mature-aged students shape scholarship distinctly from those who have just left school. The role and proportion of international scholars has also increased. Similarly the relationship between universities and the workplace has also altered. Students deserve better than generic answers to specific and individual questions. If the problem is staff and student ratios, then that issue should be addressed directly and not masked by 'gee wizz' technological 'solutions' of 'artificial' intelligence.

The radical change to our campuses, students, regulatory policies and curriculum after September 11, the second Iraq War, the South Asian Tsunami and the bombing of the London Underground are vast.[16] It is tougher to teach, and it is tougher to learn. Neo-conservative morality tempers the range and mode of our ethical questions. Neo-liberal market agendas sell our knowledge to the highest corporate bidder. Yet our time – and through the history we are writing around us – demands more. As the waves lashed the coasts of Sri Lanka, India, Thailand and Indonesia after the seaquake in December 2004, the world appeared on the edge of destruction with almost immeasurable suffering, death and grief. Concurrently, a war in Iraq – unsanctioned by the same United Nations that was summoned to coordinate global health and relief strategies in Asia – demonstrated the brutal military thrust of demodernizing forces. In such an environment, education generally and universities specifically have never been more important, but less valued. Few politicians have time for the complex, long-term challenges of reading, writing and thinking. Indeed, an informed citizenry able to probe the spin, untruths and propaganda is not useful for the contemporary workforce or political system.

Twenty years ago, Dick Hebdige asked why we should think deeply if we are not paid to think deeply.[17] The 1990s and 2000s have provided an answer to his question.

---

15 J. Tiffin, 'When computers become our tutors', *Guardian Weekly*, 8–14 January 2004, p. 22.

16 Even before September 11, Peter Magolda recognizes the complex nature of the contemporary university in 'Border crossings: collaboration struggles in education', *The Journal of Educational Research*, Vol. 94, No. 6, July/August 2001, pp. 346–58.

17 Hebdige, *Hiding in the Light*, p. 167.

Pied Pipers have called our tune for too long. It is time to hear an alternate refrain. We need to read against the grain. We need to write from the shadows. We need to push against the tide. In battling modernity, Fordism, fact and fiction, the information age will not provide all the skills required for these struggles. Only when our aim is the building of knowledge, not the gathering of data, may we move forward. Learning to think – critically, expansively and with humility towards scholars from the past – is the most effective guide through 'the post'. My words offer alternatives, plans and strategies for our educational institutions. The goal is to transform a fetish for information into a desire for argument, debate and knowledge. Without schools and universities, we are living (with) a terrorism, in our minds.

Section One
Literacy

Chapter one

BA (Google): graduating to information literacy

> Academic research involves three steps: finding relevant information, assessing the quality of that information, then using appropriate information either to try to conclude something, to uncover something, or to argue something. The Internet is useful for the first step, somewhat useful for the second, and not at all useful for the third.[1]
>
> Beth Stafford

A problem has emerged in my teaching during the last few years that requires attention. As each semester progresses, a greater proportion of my students is reading less, referencing less and writing with less clarity and boldness. There will always be the top 25 per cent of the class who are rigorous and committed scholars in the making. They require little overt assistance, but can operate in models of student-centred learning. Increasingly the middle fifty per cent, who require greater guidance, attention and commitment from teaching staff to pass a course, is producing inadequate work. This group invariably writes assignments in the days before they are due, runs a spelling checker through the document rather than drafts it, and relies on the internet for research material rather than refereed course readings. These problems are not caused by Google. Instead, the popularity of Google is facilitating laziness, poor scholarship and compliant thinking.

An example of this problem emerged in 2006 after the second lecture in my first year course. As I walked away from the auditorium to my office, a student asked why they were having problems accessing the course readings from home. I replied in a concerned tone, 'Haven't you been able to buy a reader?' I was referring to the collection of articles and book extracts photocopied for the students. With an agitated voice she stated that she had the reader, but wanted to access the material on the further reading lists online. She had telephoned the library 'and everything'. When, with raised eyebrow, I stated that the further readings were books and articles sitting on the shelves of the library, she became exasperated: 'You mean I have to go into the library and get them?'

1 B. Stafford, 'Information for people or profits?' in S. Hawthorne and R. Klein (eds), *CyberFeminism: Connectivity, Critique and Creativity* (North Melbourne: Spinifex, 1999), p. 145.

Such a statement would be funny at any time from a university student. That these words were uttered as we were *walking adjacent to the library* only added aromatic spice to the intellectual sauce. This is our current environment. We provide readings for students. They are on paper so they ignore them. We provide further reading lists for the students. These books are sitting on library shelves so they ignore them. Instead, poor quality online materials are used as an avoidance strategy to dismiss important scholarly work. Clicking replaces thinking.

In response to this context, the first chapter of *The University of Google* conducts a thought experiment by localizing 'a problem', probing the insights of contemporary literacy theory, and then offering possible solutions. I need to find a way to encourage focused reading, sharp writing and effective thinking to ensure that learning outcomes are strongly tethered to my set assignments and marking criteria. Mobilizing approaches from theorists of critical literacy,[2] I offer explanations and a context for my current concerns. I then try to solve my problem – and quickly – so that not another cohort googles their way through a course. The aim is to develop a functional information scaffold, attempting to align learning goals and expectations with the assignments submitted by students. These methods trigger an incisive and informed intervention.

Google time

Google, and its naturalized mode of searching, encourages bad behaviour. When confronted by an open search engine, most of us will enact the ultimate of vain acts: inserting our own name into the blinking cursor. This process now has a name: googling. This is a self-absorbed action, rather than outward and reflexive process. It is not a search of the World Wide Web, but the construction of an Individual Narrow Portal.[3]

It is important to be completely honest about the internet – let alone the web – that is being searched by Google. The web is large, occasionally irrelevant, filled with advertising, outdated ghost sites and is increasingly corporatized. It seems appropriate

2 While many theories and theorists of literacy are deployed in this book, I acknowledge the sharp definition deployed by Mitzi Lewison, Amy Seely Flint and Katie Van Sluys: 'We reviewed a range of definitions that appeared in the research and professional literature over the last 30 years and synthesized these into four dimensions: (1) disrupting the commonplace, (2) interrogating multiple viewpoints, (3) focusing on sociopolitical issues, and (4) taking action and promoting social justice. These four dimensions, which guided this study and the interpretation of data are interrelated – none stand alone', from 'Taking on critical literacy', *Language Arts*, Vol. 79, No. 5, May 2002.

3 Tim Dowling describes the impact of the Google Search Engine on his online habits: 'At last I am able to type my own name into a box and at the press of a button receive an instant assessment of how many people in the world think I am a prick', from 'Back page', *The Guardian*, 8 August 2006, p. 36.

that Google is ubiquitous at the moment when teachers and librarians are overworked and less available to see students. David Loertscher confirmed that,

> Search engines such as Google are so easy and immediate that many young people, faced with a research assignment, just 'google' their way through the internet rather than struggle through the hoops of a more traditional library environment.[4]

There are consequences for the proliferation of Google, which is the most popular search engine, but not the best for all searches. AltaVista has distinct features and search capabilities particularly in languages other than English.[5] Google's origin in the United States of America creates a blinkered world view. There is a reason for the limited vista of this virtual landscape. Google is a business and a brand.[6] Two recent books about the company describe it as 'the hottest business, media and technology success of our time'[7] and that the firm 'rewrote the rules of business and transformed our culture'.[8]

Larry Page, one of the founders of Google along with Sergey Brin, developed the technology while a doctoral candidate in engineering at Stanford University.[9] The word Google is derived from the mathematical term googol, a one followed by 100 zeros. This etymology is important, as founding ideologies invariably frame the meaning of structures in the long term. The cultural orientation of the search engine was engineering and mathematics, not education, library, internet or media studies. The aim of Page's initial study at Stanford was to understand 'back linking', or the 'BackRub project' as he termed it. His goal – modelled on citation practices – was to find a way to count the number of backlinks on the World Wide Web. PageRank was the algorithm created that recognized and measured the number of links into a particular site, and the number of links into these other sites.[10] This equation determined the order of the Google returns.

---

4 D. Loertscher, 'The digital school library', *Teacher Librarian*, Vol. 30, No. 5, June 2003, p. 14.

5 AltaVista searches both the web and Usenet, but its interface is not open for the casual user. Complex searches are possible, but the options must be mastered. In 1995, AltaVista indexed 16 million pages. One decade later, Google indexed 8 billion pages.

6 Naomi Klein, in *No Logo* (London: Flamingo, 2000), stated that 'it is online that the purest brands are being built: liberated from the real world burdens of stores and product manufacturing these brands are free to soar, less the disseminators of goods and services than as collective hallucinations', p. 24.

7 D. Vise, *The Google Story* (New York: Bantam Dell, 2005), front cover.

8 J. Battelle, *The Search* (London: Nicholas Brealey, 2005), front cover.

9 Page came from a family of computer innovators. His father was a computer science professor at Michigan State.

10 John Lanchester described Larry Page and Sergey Brin's 'big idea': 'It was based on one of the most widely mocked areas in academia, that of bibliometrics: assessing the importance of any given article or piece of information purely by measuring how often other people in the field mention it. This never-mind-the-quality-feel-the-width approach sounds like a ridiculous way of

AltaVista and Excite ranked on keywords: Google initially searched the words in titles, then developed full-text searches. Frequent upgrades, updates and improvements have emerged after the initial release. There is a suite of Google products, including the image search, a Usenet discussion service and Froogle – a virtual shopping mall. In November 2003, a new software package – the Google desk bar – was released, which allowed the user to access the search engine without opening a new web browser. The software was released free of charge because of the exposure granted to the logo.[11]

The key to understanding Google is to grasp PageRank, which is an 'objective' measurement of the importance of web pages by assessing the number of links that point to them. As Russell Brown described,

> Google embodied a simple, brilliant idea. It was, effectively, to ask us what we thought was important. If a website had many links to it, or its key people were name checked elsewhere, it was considered to be a trusted part of a community, and its ranking reflected that. In doing a Google search, we could draw on the knowledge, experience and good taste of everyone else.[12]

Google ranks their search results via the popularity and number of links and hits to that site. For example, when 'Tara Brabazon' is entered into Google, the number one returned search is my Home Page, the site developed (by me) to promote my career. The links with less hits, but perhaps more critical information, are far lower on the ranking. My personal web page has so many hits because a link is presented at the bottom of each email I send from my work computer. Not surprisingly, hundreds of curious undergraduates with a bouncy index finger click to their teacher's profile. Yet this is the site that a Google search returns when clicking 'I'm feeling lucky'. This is one example, from one person. Ponder the more serious consequences when students click onto highly ideological sites that are assessed by popularity, not qualitative importance or significance. There are many other ways that this ranking could be assembled, particularly with intervention by librarians and information managers. The assumption of Google is that the popularity of sites is a validation of quality. Google is the internet equivalent of reality television: derivative, fast and shallow. In an era of the supposedly 'long tail' of niche markets and plural interests, Google's top return receives 42.1 per cent of click throughs, with the second listed link gaining 11.2 per cent.[13]

---

assessing the importance of intellectual work but it is, I am told, a surprisingly powerful tool', from 'Engine trouble', *The Guardian*, 26 January 2006, p. 7.

11 'Searching without browser, Google-style', *Australasian Business Intelligence*, 11 November 2003, npn.

12 R. Brown, 'Information Entrepreneurs', Public Address.net, 2 September 2005, http://publicaddress.net/print,2494.sm, accessed on 9 September 2005.

13 C. Arthur, 'Top of the heap', Technology Guardian, *The Guardian*, 31 August 2006, p. 1.

A persona is constructed and summoned through Google that is not a neutral avatar, but configures a self on the basis of popularity. It is strangely riveting to see how an identity is constructed through Google. For example, Paul Morley, one of the most iconoclastic and talented of popular cultural writers, put his own name into the blinking cursor.

> I decided to … punch my name into the Google search engine to see how I have been gathered, collected, framed, defined on the World Wide Web. Who am I on the net? I figured that this would be a pretty good description of who I was, or who I have been. It would be accurate, neutral, and would sum up my achievements inside the media, as a writer, as a personality, as some kind of operator in arts and entertainments. The Google search engine raked in versions of myself from across the virtual universe, and from the results you could piece together a version of me that is as good a biography as anything. What you could see straight away, from the very first mentions, is that I did become famous as a rock-and-roll writer of all time. I say this, without believing it, while knowing it to be fairly true, and would say that, on various occasions, during the late seventies and early eighties, while writing for the New Musical Express, I did materialize now and then as the greatest but overall, in the lists of greats, I would just about put myself inside the top twenty. Well, inside the top ten. About seventh. Or sixth. All in all, I think I was the fifth-greatest rock-and-roll writer of all time. Maybe the fourth. Actually, the third. The greatest non-American, anyway. And I could take on the top two Americans any day of the week.[14]

Morley shows how the 'objective' ranking can slide into subjective meanderings of social worth. These rankings and returned hits have an addictive quality. The success of Google is of such a scale that it is one of the few products and nouns that has transformed into a verb. Googling has become a verb for surfing, following a similar path to Xeroxing and Hoovering. Like these other nouns-turned-verbs, it is a standardized response to plural and complex problems. Photocopying requires an understanding of copyright law as much as where to insert paper into the Xerox machine. House cleaning requires time, rather than simply the purchasing of a Hoover.[15] These nouns-turned-verbs make us forget about process, structure and obstacles. Googling is a one-size-fits-all response

---

14 P. Morley, *Words and Music* (London: Bloomsbury, 2003), p. 118.

15 Significantly, Google is attempting to stop its name becoming a generic term for surfing the net. Alice Gould reported that, 'it is worried that its trademark is becoming generic by being used as shorthand to describe using a search engine or even searching for information on the internet. In its own words, it is seeking to avoid the "genericide" of its trademark. And there is reason to be concerned – if a brand name becomes generic it can be struck from the trademark register, as has happened in the past', from 'Stop googling that hottie!', *The Guardian*, 28 August 2006, p. 8.

to information sharing,[16] and assumes that a user has the literacy to not only utilize the search engine but the interpretative skills to handle the results.

Profitable since 2001, Google won the contract to be AOL's search engine and handles 75 per cent of searching traffic.[17] In 2003, the Expanded Academic Database, one of the most important full-text databases for education and the humanities in particular, also featured a link to Google at the top of every search page. I wish this process occurred the other way: that Google would encourage movement into more specialized databases.[18] Without the help of such software prompts, teachers and librarians must intervene to encourage the movement into refereed research, stressing that Google is the start – not the entirety – of a search. There are major consequences to our students, their future and our educational system if we are apathetic rather than proactive in the building of an information scaffold, rather than allowing a search engine to define the parameters of effective research.

The impact of Google on education, teaching and learning is assumed, but underwritten. I was given the opportunity to monitor the intervention and action research of two high school teachers in Sydney, Australia. Jacinta Squires and Lee FitzGerald, a high school teacher and teacher librarian respectively, investigated the information scaffold used by their students, and the consequences to learning outcomes. They discovered when surveying high school history students that they use Google as a first search, and mobilize the internet ahead of books. They also showed that the students hardly ever read learning outcomes, marking criteria or the library catalogue. Significantly, students also access encyclopedias for gaining information.[19] Squires and FitzGerald's action research[20] is timely and important, but has profound consequences when students enter university. Building upon their realization and research, I carry their observations to the social and political context of university.

Students commence my first year course demonstrating superficial research and comprehension skills and awkward writing modalities. They do not seek out diverse

16 Russ Singletary referred to Google as facilitating 'self-service internet research', from 'Under the bonnet', *The Australian Librarian Journal*, August 2003, p. 302.

17 L. Clyde, 'Search engines are improving – but they still can't find everything', *Teacher Librarian*, Vol. 30, No. 5, June 2003, pp. 44–5.

18 Jana Ronan captured this research strategy, stating that 'I often use Google for background information if I'm stumped, to help point me to the best proprietary database to search', *Reference & User Services Quarterly*, Vol. 43, No. 1, Fall 2003, p. 46.

19 Personal Email, 20 January 2004.

20 Pamela Lomax confirmed that action research is more than a reflection of already existing practices, but 'an intervention in practice to bring about improvement', p. 49. She stresses the importance of assessing assumptions, beliefs and values, to unpick the underlying notions of good practice. Please refer to 'Action research for professional practice [1]', *Educational Action Research*, Vol. 2, No. 2, 1995, pp. 49–57.

views to construct an argument. Rather, they presume that if something is written down, then it must be correct. Making students think, rather than assume, and read rather than cut and paste is proving a challenge. Let me reveal what was submitted in assignments to me in 2003. It provides an indication of the problems I am trying to correct, which Google is facilitating, not critiquing. To my embarrassment and horror, here is an example of a bibliography submitted for a 'research paper' in my university course.

> Reference List
> http://www.beatlesagain.com/breflib.love.html
> http://www.beatlesagain.com/breflib/teens.html
> http://ia.essortment.com/historyoftheb_rmdq.html
> http://www2.canisius.edu/~dicrenfb/his389.htm
> http://www.beatlesagain.com/breflib.teens.html

These URLs were not even referenced correctly, and were not tethered to any print-based materials. Such a list would chill any teacher, but this result was even more bizarre when revealing the context for this bibliography. At the university in which this student was enrolled, staff distribute a course reader of at least one hundred extracts from books and articles, featuring the most relevant and important material in a subject area. This student has ignored *all* this material – on popular music and fandom, for example – to write a paper on the Beatles using a Google search for 'Beatles fans'. My comments on this bibliography were, 'You must never use internet-based sources as self-standing references' and 'where are your readings from the course?'

Another example where a student wrote a paper on 'Asian gangs' reveals the problem in an even more troubling fashion. Instead of questioning how and why police place attention on Asian citizens, the student did not deploy this level of interpretation, but merely took information from highly politicized 'community' and law and order sites.

Highly racist statements splattered from this bibliography and into the essay, with assumptions expressed about 'Asians' being intrinsically violent, tribal and insular. Once more, she had inserted 'Asian Gangs' into Google and these results emerged. These bibliographies occurred even after I placed the following information in their study guides.

> In terms of research material, please remember that I reward a diversity of media in my marking. In other words, I will not be happy if a student constructs an essay on refugees or *Star Wars*, taps into Google and constructs a bibliography of sites. The web is an important, diverse database but it also has major limitations. Your effort in seeking out textual diversity will be rewarded.[21]

21 T. Brabazon, *Introduction to Cultural Studies Study Guide*, Murdoch University, 2003, p. 5.

Students ignored this warning and utilized the most simplistic of searches, not even bothering to deploy course readings that had been photocopied for them. Google standardizes searching at the time when there is a great diversity of both information and users.

In a fast food, fast data environment, the web transforms into an information drive-through. It encourages a 'type in-download-cut-paste-submit' educational culture. A 2001 study reported that 71 per cent of American students relied mostly on the internet for major assignments at school. In this same study, 24 per cent relied mostly on the library and only 4 per cent used both the internet and the library.[22] My aim in building an information scaffold is to lift that 4 per cent figure so that students are actively moving between the digital and the analogue, the unrefereed web and scholarly databases. Angela Dudfield termed this 'hybrid forms of literate behaviour'.[23] We need to teach – overtly – the meaning and purpose of refereeing. Content and context must be aligned. Further, we must ensure that these tools are actually used, rather than taught and ignored.

Google has increased the accessibility of websites, transforming the landscape of digital information into a manageable formation.[24] It also encourages sound bite solutions that are not researched or theorized.[25] In such an environment, we have to ask how to encourage intellectual rigour in an edu-tainment landscape. Google makes searching for information more democratic, but it is also demeaning of the expertise involved in well-theorized interpretation and scholarship.[26]

---

22 A. Lenhart et. al, *The Internet and Education: Findings of the Pew Internet and American Life Project*, September 2001, http://www.pewtrusts.com/pubs/pubs.item.cfm?image=img5&content_item_id=729&content_type_id=8&page=p1, accessed on 9 September 2006.

23 A. Dudfield, 'Literacy and cyberculture', 1999, http://www.readingonline.org/articles/dudfield/mail.html, accessed on 2 April 2006.

24 The use of manageable is intentional here. Frequently in the research literature, the stress is on managing information, as if the internet is an uncontrollable beast that needs to be tamed. Robert Weissberg went so far as to state that 'access to Google or Yahoo can change everything – obstacles once judged too formidable to even attempt now become manageable', from 'Technology evolution and citizen activism', *The Policy Studies Journal*, Vol. 31, No. 3, 2003, p. 387.

25 Joshua Meyrowitz has argued that after Watergate and the crisis of leadership in the American Presidency, credibility has been difficult to re-assemble because of the media environment. He realized that the perceived decline in credibility has 'surprisingly little to do with a simple lack of potentially great leaders, and much to do with a politician's ability to behave like, and therefore be perceived as, the traditional "great leader"', from *No Sense of Place* (New York: Oxford University Press, 1985), p. 269. With the public seeing too much of its politicians, the image of an untarnished great leader is difficult to create.

26 Kathy Schrock has constructed a solid checklist to assess the quality of information, including, the authority of the author, bias, citation rates, dates published, efficiency, the positioning

Being literate

The future requires no footnotes.[27]

Heather-Jane Robertson

Literacy takes many forms and is saturated with the political interests and investments of empowered voices and views. Through this plurality and complexity, the most effective way to study literacy is to consider the application of theory to practice. My concern with the scale of reading and research deployed by students opens an envelope of ideas about how literacy is shaped and changed through the digital environment. Such a concern is not technologically determinant, but places the internet in a socio-cultural context of education. The problem is not Google. The problem is that I am teaching a cohort of students many of whom are the first generation in their family to attend university, are in part-time work,[28] and do not have either the experience or expectations about the requirements of advanced and internationally aware scholarship.[29] Crucially

---

of information in context, disability access and information availability. Please refer to Schrock's 'The ABCs of Web Site Evaluation: teaching media literacy in the age of the internet', *Connected Newsletter*, 1999–2000, http://connectedteacher.classroom.com/newsletter/abcs.asp, accessed on 16 June 2002. Another significant document assessing the browsability and connectivity of web-based resources is Alastair Smith, 'Criteria for evaluation of Internet information resources', http://www.vuw.ac.nz/~agsmith/evaln/index.htm, accessed 16 June 2002.

27 H. Robertson, 'Toward a theory of negativity', *Journal of Teacher Education*, Vol. 54, No. 4, September/October 2003.

28 Convincing studies have emerged about the consequences of not only part-time work, but the high levels of part-time work, on higher education. Sue Hatt, Andrew Hannan and Arthur Baxter confirmed that 'although part-time employment was an accepted part of student life, with more than 80 per cent of the interviewees from low-income backgrounds in paid employment, students indicated that they had become concerned about working "too many hours" to the detriment of their studies. These fears were well founded … Our interviewees had reduced their hours as their studies had progressed. This was partly because they had learned by experience that paid employment could impact adversely on their studies', from 'Bursaries and student success: a study of students from low-income groups at two institutions in the South West', *Higher Education Quarterly*, Vol. 59, No. 2, April 2005, p. 122. Similarly M. Barke et al. confirmed the correlation between term-time working and lower grades. Please refer to M. Barke et al. *Students in the Labour Market; Nature, Extent and Implications of Part-time Employment Amongst University of Northumbria Undergraduates* (London: DfEE, 2000).

29 My words here must not be taken to suggest that first-generation students should not be admitted to university. My brother and I were the first in my immediate family to attend university. I remember my feelings during that first year: fear, confusion and little understanding of teachers' expectations. However, instead of ignoring the set texts, I took the opposite path, reading *everything* on course lists. This effort was triggered by fear (of failure) and uncertainty about expectations and standards.

the proliferation and popularity of the internet and the World Wide Web in education has confirmed that literacy is not an endpoint,[30] a skill to be achieved, but a process of ongoing development and change. Colin Lankshear has shown how reading and writing remain social practices that require context to gain meaning. He stated that 'literacies are inseparable from practices in which they are embedded and the effects of these practices'.[31] The ability to decode text on a screen does not always create an understanding of the process through which information becomes knowledge. In creating a 'New word order',[32] there is a need to facilitate the participation, building and transformation of information platforms to create conditions conducive to learning and teaching. Searching, reading and writing must be placed in context. New 'basics' are forming, via the movement from Fordism to (post) Fordism and the changes to capitalism and the nation state.[33] The older forms of literacy, based on encoding and decoding, must be grafted and translated to a mixed media environment. Post-Fordist theorists, by acknowledging the casualized and flexible workforce,[34] are tracking the languages and imperatives of capitalism, stressing innovation and creativity.

The notion that creativity is required to foster economic productivity and competitiveness is built on the intertwining forces of globalization and information technology.[35] For teachers, this social and economic change appears to encourage an

---

30 B. Street called this an 'autonomous' model of literacy, where literacy can be 'achieved', allowing students to move on to other tasks, rather than framing literacy as an ongoing project of skill development, *Literacy in Theory and Practice* (Cambridge: Cambridge University Press, 1984).

31 C. Lankshear, 'Frameworks and workframes: literacy policies and new orders', *Unicorn*, Vol. 24, No. 2, 1998, p. 44.

32 *Ibid.*, p. 47.

33 The increasing diversity of citizenry in the contemporary nation state also creates new challenges for adult literacy programmes, through the provision of ESL strategies. The difficulty as recognized by Jennifer Hammond, is that 'funding for adult literacy programs had recently been substantially cut' in time for the release of the Survey of Aspects of Literacy (SAL) in September 1997. Please refer to 'Literacy crises and ESL education', *The Australian Journal of Language and Literacy*, Vol. 22, No. 2, 1999, p. 120.

34 Please refer to S. Aronowitz, *How Class Works* (New Haven: Yale University Press, 2003), S. Aronowitz, *The Politics of Identity* (New York: Routledge, 1992) and A. Kroker, 'Virtual capitalism', in S. Aronowitz, B. Martinsons and M. Menser (eds), *Techno Science and Cyberculture* (New York: Routledge, 1996).

35 The theorist most associated with the celebration of creativity, information technology and economic growth is Richard Florida. Please refer to Richard Florida, *The Rise of the Creative Class* (New York: Basic Books, 2002), *The Flight of the Creative Class* (New York: Harper Collins, 2005) and *Cities and the Creative Class* (New York: Routledge, 2005). The knowledge economy is addressed in chapter six of this book.

investment in training and lifelong learning.[36] Clearly though, there is much of the old economy in the new economy. What I am seeing in my classroom is nearly half of each year's cohort placing education, research and scholarship very low on their list of important tasks. Ironically, in the midst of the knowledge economy, students are being less creative, innovative and dynamic. They are writing Fordist essays, mass-produced papers with standardized search engines. This is a disturbing realization. Supposedly, an education geared for an assembly line is inappropriate for these New Times. When Tony Blair stressed the changes to the economy in his 1997 election campaign, he concurrently stressed education (education education) as his three top priorities.[37] The reason was clear: knowledge was not only something to create or share, but to exploit.[38] Amid his emphasis, and while fighting his third election in 2005, he battled screaming headlines in *The Times*: 'Schools still cannot teach pupils to read by age of 11'.[39] Yet this critique is not the ahistorical disaster it appears. Allan Luke confirmed that literacies operate within socially-situated practices.[40] As contexts change, so must the definition and pedagogies encircling literacy. If the knowledge economy is to be more than a slogan of the Third Way political agenda, then a negotiation of critical literacies will require primary attention and scholarly priority. Reading print on paper is one goal of education. Yet understanding diverse models of encoding and decoding in a media-rich environment is also necessary.

The difficulty is that most of the debates encircling literacy focus on student 'problems' in reading and writing, and the methods used to 'correct' or 'solve' these problems. A culture of blame and guilt is established.[41] For example, the front page of

---

36 Finn Bowring confirmed that 'a focus on intellectual capital – and by extension, its container, the innovative worker – is increasingly common', from 'Post-Fordism and the end of work', *Futures*, Vol. 34, 2002, p. 90.

37 D. Coyle, 'How not to educate the information age workforce', *Critical Quarterly*, Vol. 43, No. 1, 2001, pp. 46–54.

38 Scott Bryant discussed the process of creating, sharing, exploiting and managing knowledge in 'The role of transformation and transactional leadership in creating, sharing and exploiting organizational knowledge', *The Journal of Leadership and Organizational Studies*, Vol. 9, No. 2, 2003, pp. 32–44.

39 T. Halpin, 'Schools still cannot teach pupils to read by age of 11', *The Times*, 7 April 2005, p. 1.

40 A. Luke, 'Getting over method: literacy teaching as work in "New Times"', *Language Arts*, Vol. 75, No. 4, April 1998, pp. 305–13.

41 Teachers are easy targets within the rhetoric of 'declining standards' of literacy. Bill Green, John Hodgens and Allan Luke argued that 'one of the reasons for the blaming of teachers is because everybody is an expert on literacy: parents, teachers, politicians, journalists and media experts and, of course, students themselves', from 'Debating literacy in Australia: history lessons and popular f(r)ictions', *The Australian Journal of Language and Literacy*, Vol. 20, No. 1, 1997, p. 11. This knowledge of teaching and learning is based on experience, and experiential ideology

The Australian's Higher Education Supplement squealed that 'Phonics at core of new literacy war'.[42] Using the metaphors of a battlefield – winning and losing – is inelegant and inappropriate in an environment of teaching and learning. This newspaper story investigated (again) the controversial split between a whole language approach, which encourages students to use context and visual clues to 'decode' the meaning of words, and phonics, which relies on decoding words by breaking them into syllables. This argument was also repeated in the United Kingdom. Richard Garner reported that 'One in five children leaving primary school cannot read'.[43] Support was once more offered to phonetics. Neither story suggested – rationally and logically – that different students learn in distinct ways. Too often these literacy 'tests' are seen to represent 'learning'. Invariably meta-skills – such as an awareness of what is *not* being asked in a test and why – are difficult to assess, but these abilities are important and travel from formal education into daily life. Further, there is no discussion of the political environment in which this literacy war is being waged. Luke placed this debate in context.

> This may be the story of literacy education in the late 1990s. It is not a story about the triumph of method but a story about government cutbacks and institutional downsizing, about shrinking resource and taxation bases, and about students and communities, teachers and schools, trying to cope with rapid and unprecedented economic, social and technological change.[44]

Instead of placing attention on ahistorical 'national standards',[45] with little attention to technological change or resourcing, literacy teaching and learning emerge from specific economic and political conditions. The past is not always the best indicator or model for literacy standards.[46] Demographic changes, through immigration, and political critiques, such as through feminism, have radically altered the meanings and appropriateness of teaching, learning and curricula development. Capitalism is changing: literacies morph

---

is difficult to critique. Particularly, this mode of argument is inappropriate to assess how literacy 'standards' have changed, not declined.

42 Dani Cooper, 'Phonics at the core of new literacy war', *The Australian*, 21 April 2004, p. 21.

43 R. Garner, 'One in five children leaving primary school cannot read', *The Independent*, 7 April 2005, p. 9.

44 Luke, p. 305.

45 Jurgen Habermas argued that during eras of 'crisis,' institutional structures such as education and churches become the focus of attention, with a desire to create legitimacy for power structures. Please refer to Jurgen Habermas, *Legitimation Crisis* (London: Heinemann, 1976).

46 Viv Edwards offered a clear critique of the back to basics movement and the alleged failings in reading standards. Please refer to 'Literacy or literacies?' from C. Modgil and S. Modgil (eds), *Educational Dilemma: Debate and Diversity – Vol. 4: Quality in Education* (London: Falmer Press, 2000), pp. 190–98.

in response. While debates over method are important, such discussions are shielding a more direct reassessment of the unstable relationship between literacy, employment and education.[47] An important trigger for this discussion is the recognition that 'acquiring' literacies rarely occurs solely in an educational institution, but reinforces the skills and ideologies taught in the home.[48] Therefore, formal education becomes a place to practise already existing knowledge and abilities. The different approaches to literacy development – such as whole language, phonetics, genre pedagogy and critical literacy – should not be 'tested' on isolated individual students, but used to probe a wider relationship between young people, poverty and literacy.[49] Too often encoding and decoding print is a marker of individual intelligence or achievement, rather than a testament to what students learnt in the home before entering a classroom.

In an environment where neo-conservatives and neo-liberals stress the imperatives of the market, literacy transforms into an economic engine. Without literacies in both print and digitized text, the knowledge economy cannot function. Luke termed literacy a 'social semiotic technology'.[50] This evocative phrase, which aligns the semiotic and the social, the textual and contextual, shows how institutions shape literacies. Without an understanding of the discourses encircling students, including the family, schools, universities, peer group, technology and diverse media, there remains a misalignment between learning and teaching, aims and outcomes.[51] Unsworth termed an effective convergence of this environment as 'the textual habitat',[52] recognizing that all languages require a metalanguage about the knowledge system being taught.

In such difficult times, when we are frequently teaching undergraduates who have no idea why they are at university and are ill-prepared for the rigour of international

47 Luke makes the points that literacy is not 'about' students, but requires a considered understanding of teaching and the demands on teacher's time, p. 308.

48 James Paul Gee has argued that 'mainstream middle-class children often look as if they are learning literacy (of various sorts) in school. But in fact I believe much research shows they are acquiring these literacies through experiences in the home both before and during school, as well as by the opportunities school gives them to practice what they are acquiring', from 'What is literacy?' in C. Mitchell and K Weiler (eds), *Rewriting Literacy* (New York: Bergin, 1991), p. 9.

49 B. Comber, 'Literacy, poverty and schooling', *English in Australia*, Vol. 119, No. 30, 1997, pp. 22–34.

50 A. Luke, 'The social construction of literacy in the primary school', in Len Unsworth (ed.), *Literacy Learning and Teaching Language as Social Practice in the Primary School* (Melbourne: Macmillan Education, 1993), p. 7.

51 I. Falk, for example, located 'the apparent disparity between the adults' perception of their literacy needs and the actual literacy uses to which their literacy will be put', from 'The social construction of adult literacy learners' needs: a case study', *Language and Education*, Vol. 7, No. 4, 1993, p. 225.

52 L. Unsworth, *Teaching Multiliteracies across the School Curriculum* (Melbourne: Macmillan, 2001), p. 7.

standards of scholarship, teachers can become desperate and vulnerable to the promises of technology. Student enrolment figures are increasing with the desire – initiated by Tony Blair and Gordon Brown but providing a model for elsewhere – to have half of every cohort of young people in tertiary education.[53] Standards of achievement are changing and forcing teachers – each day – to ask about the acceptable levels of research, writing and scholarship from our students. The movement to mass participation has operated concurrently with a decline in public funding for universities. By deregulating the system, university academics are encouraged to be more entrepreneurial. Internet-mediated communication seems an ideal solution to overcrowded tutorial rooms. However, research has failed to find a positive correlation between computer-mediate education and student achievement.[54]

Digitization has shaped conceptualizations of literacy and widened the meanings and flexibilities of text. Cal Durrant and Bill Green have confirmed that the fluidity of textual movement has initiated new definitions of literacy. Operational literacy – which focuses on students as code breakers – now extends beyond print to the dynamic interchange between word, sound and image. Cultural literacy, which recognizes a reader as a competent participant or user of a textual environment, also incorporates the ability to move text into other settings and genres, through cutting and pasting. Critical literacy, or the capacity to analyse text, is far more difficult to confirm or monitor in an internet-mediated environment.[55] Because 'use' of digitized information refers to the movement of text between documents, there is an awkward conflation between finding, reading and interpreting material. This seamless passage/confusion between discovering and using information is one explanation of why plagiarism is a major problem in digitized educational settings.[56]

---

53 Ulrich Teichler raised this issue in 'The future of higher education and the future of higher education research', *Tertiary Education and Management*, Vol. 9, 2003, pp. 171–85. He asked what is going to change, in terms of academic standards and teaching expectations, with the increase in student numbers.

54 Please refer to L. Cuban, *Oversold and Underused: Computers in the Classroom* (Cambridge: Harvard University Press, 2001), p. 178, and H. Robertson, 'Toward a theory of negativity', *Journal of Teacher Education*, Vol. 54, No. 4, September/October 2003, p. 280.

55 C. Durrant and B. Green, *Literacy and the New Technologies in School Education: Meeting the L(IT)eracy Challenge?*, Discussion Paper commissioned by the New South Wales Department of Education and Training, 1998.

56 For example, *The Guardian* reported that the University of Sydney, Australia's oldest academic institution, found that 73 out of the 628 students in the Veterinary Faculty were alleged to have copied material. Bernard O'Riordan reported that 'Most of the copied material had been taken from the internet and in many cases, students were caught out by anti-plagiarism software', from 'University cracks down on plagiarism', *The Guardian*, 22 March 2005, http://education.guardian.co.uk/higher/news/story/0,9830,1443049,00.html, accessed on 22 March 2005. For a wider discussion on the relationship between the online environment and plagiarism please refer to T. Brabazon, 'Herpes for

In such a context, it is necessary to focus time and attention on the building of an information scaffold, to orient students into the world of the text, so that they are able to evaluate Google searches – and websites generally – by moving outside of the digital environment and into other media. To reach this goal, Mary Macken-Horarik recommends teaching strategies that facilitate 'explicitness'.[57] The aim of this process is to give students – and citizens – the ability to move texts into diverse contexts, and observe how meanings change. Explicitness in method is required to establish an 'enacted curriculum', [58] rather than constructing (another) list of assessment criteria unread by students. The scholars cited in this chapter confirm that there will never be a single way to teach literacy. The diversity of children and adult learners means that learning is a fragile process.[59] In such an environment, finding and implementing emancipatory education is difficult. It is particularly difficult to balance the imperatives and initiatives of quality education[60] with democratic teaching and learning.[61] When adding discussions of literacy to such a project, the political debates encircling education are vitriolic and damaging. Terry Threadgold described literacy 'as a governmental technology for controlling and organizing populations'.[62] Critical literacy remains an intervention, signaling more than a decoding of text or a compliant reading of an ideologue's rantings. The aim is to create cycles of reflection. Operational literacy –

---

the information age: plagiarism and the infection of universities', *Fast Capitalism*, Vol. 2, No. 2, 2006, http://www.uta.edu/huma/agger/fastcapitalism/2_2/brabazon.htm.

57 M. Macken-Horarik, 'Exploring the requirements of critical school literacy: a view from two classrooms', from F. Christie and R. Mission (eds), *Literacy and Schooling* (London: Routledge, 1998), p. 82.

58 Claire Wyatt-Smith, Joy Cumming, Jill Ryan and Shani Doig, 'Capturing students' experiences of the enacted curriculum', *Literacy Learning: Secondary Thoughts*, Vol. 7, No. 1, 1999, pp. 29–35. These writers particularly stress the importance of recognizing the plurality of both reading and writing.

59 Mary Rohl and Judith Rivalland described the 'fragility of learning', from 'Literacy learning difficulties in Australian primary schools: who are the children identified and how do their schools and teachers support them?' *The Australian Journal of Language and Literacy*, Vol. 25, No. 3, 2002, p. 33.

60 I particularly wish to note the diverse meanings of quality in an environment of auditing and regulation. Please refer to Jouni Kekale, 'Conceptions of quality in four different disciplines', *Tertiary Education Management*, Vol. 8, 2002, pp. 65–80.

61 A fascinating analysis of emancipatory education in a quality assurance environment is Zeus Leonardo's 'Critical Social Theory and Transformative Knowledge: the functions of criticism in quality education', *Educational Researcher*, Vol. 33, No. 6, 2004, pp. 11–18.

62 T. Threadgold, 'Critical literacies and the teaching of English', from S. Muspratt, A. Luke and P. Freebody (eds), *Constructing Critical Literacies: Teaching and Learning Textual Practices* (Sydney: Allen and Unwin, 1997), p. 367.

encoding and decoding – is a cultural practice of *reproduction*. Critical literacy requires the *production* of argument, interpretation, critique and analysis.

Building an information scaffold

> One of the best disguised escapes from anxiety is the escape into information.[63]
>
> Hugh Mackay

Obviously, I had a problem to solve in my assessment structures. After surveying literacy theories for insight and assistance, I realized that there is a mismatch between my expectations of research and scholarship and what my students assume is university-level work. I presupposed that operational literacy would inevitably lead to cultural and critical literacy. Google facilitates a quick and simple 'method' for completing student assignments, inferring that they can answer complex questions about Gramscian hegemony or Stanley Aronowitz's postwork theory as easily as finding their old school friends in Facebook. I decided to state my expectations in formal course materials, facilitating 'explicitness'. The desire for an 'enacted curriculum' required that I change the assessment to overtly determine their ability to find diverse sources and interpret them. It was important that I commenced this process at first year level.

The first time I attempted to embed and assess an information scaffold in my curricula was extremely successful. At that time, my strategy was prescriptive, rather than flexible. In 2002, I wrote the curriculum for a course titled *Repetitive Beat Generation*. It was an upper-level undergraduate course, small in numbers and competitive in entry requirements. Only the best and brightest were permitted to enrol. Before writing a research essay, students were required to submit an annotated bibliography.

Annotated Bibliography – Repetitive Beat Generation

There are strict requirements on this component of the exercise. Students must include at least thirty sources. Each source is accompanied by a 20–50 word description, showing how they are to be used in the project.

Of these thirty sources,

- At least twelve must be refereed articles and books, split evenly between the two categories. Students must therefore learn how

63 H. Mackay, *Reinventing Australia* (Sydney: Angus and Robertson, 1993), p. 226.

to use databases, such as the expanded academic database. Come and see Tara – she will show you how these operate. Please note: these books and articles ***must be*** non-fiction.

- There must be at least five references from popular music.
- There must be at least one film or television programme.
- There must be at least five web sites.
- There must be at least two magazine or newspaper articles.
- There must be at least two novels or collections of short stories.

This is obviously a difficult exercise, but it is important for students to increase their research capabilities, and develop analytical skills in a wide array of media.[64]

The results from this highly regulated assessment were innovative, considered and balanced. The essays derived from this bibliographic exercise were of the highest standard I have seen. Most of the students in the group went on to honours and postgraduate work. Two students left the course and subsequently failed, unable to complete this assignment. Although I was unaware of it at the time, I created a scaffold for learning which slowed the research process, creating time for reflection and planning.

Two years later, in my upper level course, *Cultural Difference and Diversity*, I attempted this process again – not for the undergraduates, but for honours candidates. This curriculum had four modes of assessment.

ASSIGNMENT	WORTH	WORD LENGTH	DUE DATE
1. Short Analysis	30%	1,000	Tuesday, 23 March 2004
2. Essay Outline and Annotated Bibliography	10%	1,500	Monday, 19 April 2004
3. Main Essay	50%	3,000	Friday, 4 June 2004
4. Tutorial Participation	10%		Monitored throughout the semester. If more than TWO tutorials are missed, the full 10% will be deducted.
TOTAL	100%		

64 T. Brabazon, *Repetitive Beat Generation Study Guide*, Murdoch University, 2002, p. 21. This course was taught with Professor Steve Redhead, using his book – *Repetitive Beat Generation* (Edinburgh: Canongate, 2000) – as the springboard.

I made the Essay Outline and Annotated Bibliography only worth 10 per cent of this honours course, in case the assessment was not effective.

2. Essay Outline and Annotated Bibliography (10%) for Cultural Difference and Diversity

Length: 1500 words (a combined and maximum limit for the two parts)

Due date: Monday, 19 April 2004

This assessment is aimed at helping students develop their main essay. The assignment has two parts.

(A) Essay Outline

A topic for the main essay must be presented, alongside both a clearly crafted question and thesis statement. Ensure that you present the structure of the paper. Also, display what you believe will be the strengths and problems you may confront in researching this paper.

(B) Annotated Bibliography

Present at least ten references, with a short description of how these sources will contribute to your paper.

This assignment worked extremely well and the feedback from students was excellent. They found that the project crystallized their main essay and confirmed the research material available to them. The task for me was to then translate these earlier successes – in a specialist and competitive upper-level undergraduate course and an honours programme – into a first year mode of assessment.

In earlier versions of my first year curriculum for *Introduction to Cultural Studies*, there were four tasks of assessment.

Original Assessment Structure for Introduction to Cultural Studies

1. **Textual Analysis (20%)**
2. **Main Essay (40%)**
3. **Take-home Exam (30%)**
4. **Tutorial Participation (10%)**

Taking the challenge of information literacy seriously, I removed the textual analysis, which assesses students' ability to understand and apply semiotic terms such as signifier, signified, discourse and ideology, and replaced it with a project tethered to the main essay, which assisted students in building an information scaffold.

Revised Assessment Structure for Introduction to Cultural Studies

1. **Essay Justification and Annotated Bibliography** **(20%)**
2. **Main Essay** **(40%)**
3. **Take-home Exam** **(30%)**
4. **Tutorial Participation** **(10%)**

The form of this assessment, when tempered by the directives of critical literacy theory, was overt and clear, with assumptions unmasked. The following assignment reveals how I enacted and revealed my expectations to students.

1. Essay Justification and Annotated Bibliography for ICS

This assignment prepares students for writing their main essay. Students are free to choose the topic of this paper, but it must sit within the following model.

The form of the question will read –

Evaluate the relationship between text, readership and politics in ____ ______________

Students may fill in the gap with a site of their choice. Here are some options to start you thinking about your own interests.

⇒ Evaluate the relationship between text, readership and politics in David Beckham.
⇒ Evaluate the relationship between text, readership and politics in Nike footwear.
⇒ Evaluate the relationship between text, readership and politics in *Kill Bill Vol.2*.
⇒ Evaluate the relationship between text, readership and politics in Bob Marley's hair.
⇒ Evaluate the relationship between text, readership and politics in James Bond's dinner suit.

⇒ Evaluate the relationship between text, readership and politics in drum 'n' bass.

⇒ Evaluate the relationship between text, readership and politics in *Who Weekly*.

⇒ Evaluate the relationship between text, readership and politics in a football.

⇒ Evaluate the relationship between text, readership and politics in a University tutorial.

⇒ Evaluate the relationship between text, readership and politics in Microsoft Windows.

Students are only limited in choice by their own imagination. The key is to ensure that your topic is supported by material in the course reader.

Please note: It is expected that students will use between 10 and 20 sources from the course reader to write the main essay. This level of research and scholarship is non-negotiable, and must be visible in the bibliography of the submitted main essay.

This first assignment prepares you for the writing of this important main assignment. You must do the following.

STAGE ONE

Present your chosen question, justifying your choice and identifying any problems – in terms of material, interpretation or argument – that you foresee. Outline who will be the primary theorists you will use and the major argument of the essay – the point you are trying to prove. This section will be between 400 and 600 words in length

STAGE TWO

Students will use between 10 and 20 sources from the reader for the main essay. Therefore this second stage for your first assignment focuses on students finding sources OUTSIDE THE READER. Students are required to locate TEN FURTHER SOURCES and write between 20 and 40 words on each source, explaining their relevance to the project. This explanatory paragraph creates an 'annotated bibliography', rather than simply 'bibliography'.

The ten sources must be of the following type.

- Two scholarly monographs. (Please note: a monograph is a book. Ensure that the text is produced by a recognized scholarly publisher, such as a University Press)
- Two print-based refereed articles. (Refereeing is the process whereby a journal sends out an article to scholars in the field to assess if it is of international quality and rigour. Students know that articles are refereed because on the inside cover of the journals an editorial board is listed and the process of review outlined. Examples include the *Cultural Studies Review*, *The International Journal of Cultural Studies* and *Cultural Studies*)
- One web-based refereed article. (Students must ensure that the site they use – such as *M/C* or *First Monday* – is a refereed online journal)
- One website that is non-refereed (that is an online article from publications such as *Online Opinion*, a blog or fan club site).
- One magazine or newspaper article.
- One track or album of popular music.
- One advertisement (from radio, television, magazines or the online environment).
- One television programme or film.

Remember – after each source is listed – students must then write 20–40 words about the text, including why it was selected for the project.

The aim of this exercise is to teach students how to find information and assess its relevance for a project. Once completed, this material becomes the further reading for the main assignment. At that stage, students simply intertwine these sources with the set course reading. Your research for the main essay is done!

Please do not be worried about this assignment. Tara is happy to help in any way, explaining the nature of information and source material. Do not hesitate: come and see her – or email her – with any queries.

The word length for both parts of this project is a combined maximum of 1000 words

While there were problems with how I structured this assignment, it did address the concerns that have worried me in the last few years. Expectations about reading and research were revealed, and the 'unspoken assumptions' about university education were presented. Further, for those students without these knowledges about finding research material, I constructed an information scaffold so that they knew what was required, and if they did not, then they must ask.

This process aimed to make students think about the quality of information and how it is structured. It slowed their research process. The second part of this assignment enabled the development of critical literacy by asking why sources were chosen, and what they offered to the project. Attention was placed on theories of knowledge and how they were built on mechanisms of classifying, organizing and storing information. The broader lesson students learnt was that while there is an abundance of information, what is scarce is the right information in an appropriate time and place. Evaluating the quality of web and print sources requires training, time and skills.[65] Often forgotten is the rigorous refereeing process that formulates the production process for books and articles. While some material on the web is refereed, generally the pieces are short and the arguments less developed. The proliferation of homepages, where banal individual details have a potentially wide digital audience, transforms our ability to judge, rank and assess relevance and significance. This assignment attempted to (re)teach and (re)value the capacity to sift, sort and evaluate information.

Through this type of considered assessment, student users approach web searching with thought and consideration. Before entering google.com, there are a series of questions for them to ask. I know to ask these questions. Now I must – overtly and clearly – ensure that students understand *why* they must probe and frame all information and sources they discover.

1. What is the most important concept or idea in the search?
2. Identify keywords emerging from this concept or idea.
3. Find synonyms for these keywords.
4. Determine the specific strengths and weaknesses of the search engine.
5. Prepare a research plan.

65 Hilarie Davis, William Fernekes and Christine Hladky activated a study of the role and place of the online environment in complex and socially delicate research projects. They realized that 'a number of social studies teachers have considered banning or limiting the access of their students to the Internet because they feel that the Internet is a source of raw and unfiltered information that damages the integrity of their curriculum and content area', from 'Using internet resources to study Holocaust: reflections from the field', *The Social Studies*, Vol. 90, No. 1, January–February 1999, p. 34.

6. Refine and redefine the search if problems are experienced. Repeat the process if necessary, with attention to keyword selection.

Such a process is effective and efficient. Planning for searches creates electronic and intellectual expectations, and a capacity to find the right information beyond the wayward and misleading. It also commences critical thinking and interpretation before slamming into an information glut. This rational and ordered approach to information management is distinct from the random, emotive and conversational mode of searching through Google.[66] The key is not how many hits are returned from a search, but how many are relevant, current and live sites.

While web use for academic research is increasing, the quality of sources varies tremendously.[67] Teachers can build informed curricula, but we need help. Libraries and librarians are important because they punctuate the information landscape, controlling and managing enthusiasm and confusion. No search engine is an intrinsic purveyor of truth. Yet Cerise Oberman realized that,

> In today's libraries … the real problems seem to centre around what is almost an ideological commitment to the computer. Today it is not unusual to have students assert, to teacher and librarian alike, that the computer has given them all the information they need. There is something subtle at work here. The nature of the computer has convinced students that all relevant information on any topic can be retrieved solely through this medium.[68]

Students are confusing quality and quantity information. The triviality of the material found[69] means that we too often become enthused with access to information and do not ask why we needed access to information in the first place. The key skill that most of us need to learn – which is facilitated by the expertise of librarians – is how to manage and balance print and electronic resources. Unfortunately these challenges emerge in a time when libraries are struggling to maintain their collection. Tim Coates confirmed that,

---

66 An example of this process emerged through *The Independent Review* on 6 April 2005. A correspondent expressed his disquiet at contemporary music and the few current equivalents to Joy Division or Ian Curtis. Leoni Bunch, a 15-year-old, responded to this concern with 'Who the hell was Ian Curtis? The fact that I had to type his name into Google speaks for itself', p. 7.

67 Andrew Orlowski realized that 'the consequences of [hazy information] … we have barely begun to explore', from 'A thirst for knowledge', *The Guardian*, 13 April 2006, http://technology.guardian.co.uk/weekly/story/0,,1752257,00.html, accessed on 28 May 2006.

68 C. Oberman, 'Library instruction: concepts and pedagogy in the electronic environment', *RQ*, Vol. 35, No. 3, Spring 1996, full text.

69 For example, a series of sites have been developed around trivia. These include www.funtrivia.com, www.quiz-game.co.uk and www.triviacafe.com.

> Only 20 years ago the library was one of the most vibrant of civic facilities. It survived the arrival of cheap paperbacks, radio, television, VCRs and the first generation of human computers. Use was increasing. Even if libraries were slightly dull they were a family and community institution playing an essential role in lifelong learning, social cohesion and pleasurable reading. They lent 600 million books a year and provided information and study facilities that were used widely. But senior managers became enthralled by computers. They anticipated that all information could be organized in an accessible way. Not only was the electronic future technically innovative but it was also attractive to young people. Computers were introduced to libraries and book collections were allowed to fall into neglect. As a consequence, demand dwindled. Libraries found a role instead as free internet cafes.[70]

Actually, collection management of print-based sources is even more important in this internet-mediated environment than it was before digitization. Libraries are not internet cafes. They are places to not only find books, but to discover a way of ordering and organizing knowledge. Richard Sayers realized that 'our challenge is to convince the techno-faddists and economic rationalists that Google is still not yet one of the seven wonders of the modern world'.[71] It is rare for technologies or media to destroy each other. Google is a disruptive, not destructive, technology.[72] Newspapers, radio, television and the internet co-exist. Books did not die with the internet. Offices and schools are not paperless. Google will only be one stop in a long journey through research and scholarship.

The internet is not a library.[73] Google is not a library catalogue. These are dangerous metaphors. For example, Polly Curtis reported that 'Bangor University is proposing to sack eight of its 12 librarians because students can find the information they need on the internet'.[74] One of the staff facing redundancy in the era of a supposed knowledge economy was the librarian responsible for lifelong learning. The characteristic of a library – the organization of knowledge into preservable categories – has left few traces on the internet. A catalogue of accessible holdings is not a collection of numbers,

---

70 T. Coates, 'Think tank', *Society Guardian*, 7 September 2005.

71 R. Sayers, 'Managing hybrid collections for the future', *The Australian Library Journal*, November 2003, p. 410.

72 Tim Studt described these disruptive formations as 'new technologies that start off by targeting small, seemingly unprofitable market segments, but sometimes wind up taking over the entire marketplace' from T. Studt, Disruption is inevitable', *R&D Magazine*, October 2003, p. 7.

73 This is a very difficult metaphor to critique. The PEW Internet and American Life project, asked in March–May 2002 'What do you think the Internet is like?' Fifty one per cent of all Americans, 61 per cent of internet users and 36 per cent of non-users described it as a library. From Amanda Lenhart's 'The ever-shifting internet population', 16 April 2003, p. 15.

74 P. Curtis, 'Bangor librarians face internet threat', *The Guardian*, 16 February 2005, http://www.guardian.co.uk/uk_news/story/0,3604,1415830,00.html, accessed on 17 February 2005.

but a sequence of ideas. This ordering is not an archaic relic of the analogue age, but holds a social function: to allow users to search and assess information and build larger relationships to broader subjects, theories and ideas. While the web may appear to remove the physicality of information, we are yet to make this leap conceptually. The digital library is determined as much by research training, database instruction, computer support and document delivery as the availability of search engines. Information literacy integrates documents, media, form, content, literacy and learning. The expertise of librarians and teachers must – overtly rather than implicitly – support new modes of reading, writing and communicating, integrating and connecting discovery, searches, navigation and the appropriateness of diverse resources.

In my new assessment, I particularly focused on moving students between different media platforms and modes of scholarship. Each medium encourages particular methods of accessing and shaping information. Books can be flicked through just as a hypertext link can be jumped, but web-based search engines encourage a smash and grab style of reading, rather than a smoother, more reflexive engagement.[75] The World Wide Web and the innovations of hypertext change our understanding of textual composition. In arching beyond print, a new mode of digital textuality emerges. While the benefits of non-linearity and interactivity are still being evaluated, there are other concerns to be considered. In the movement to new media, are we losing literacies – the capacity to follow print and an argument in its entirety – in an exchange for accelerated 'smash and grab' scholarship?

The key for teachers and librarians is to show students the advantages of divergent modes of reading and research. By breaking an assignment into media-specific sources, such a realization is encouraged. Through databases, students can read PDFs of documents they would never find on the shelves of an under-funded library. However, students must also learn the skill of reading, chewing, spitting out and reingesting difficult writing and monographs. Such reading is difficult to accomplish on the screen. With dense historical description and high theory, the reading must be done slowly and returned to, drifting along with the sensuality of the words, so that reflexive meanings may emerge. The materiality of searching – the evocative potential of engaging with an exciting array of potential sources – is still a significant part of an intellectual journey.

---

75 It is also important to acknowledge the losses and time wasting that occurs checking dead links. Toss Gascoigne asked for examples where there was difficulty in managing governmental documents online. One correspondent stated that 'I teach a course on Youth and Society. One of the essay topics is Youth Allowance. There was a major evaluation of the program online at the beginning of the semester and I included the website reference for students. Come week 6 when they are doing the essay the link had disappeared. There is simply a generic message saying the page cannot be found', from T. Gascoigne, 'History will vanish into the ether', *The Australian Higher Education Supplement*, 11 May 2005, p. 33.

Some of the best modes of teaching do not begin with the presentation and testing of information acquisition. The difficult decision for me to make through this change in curriculum was to relinquish the 'testing' of content, via the first semiotics-based assignment. While it is important that students gain detailed knowledge about media and cultural studies, it is also now necessary that they be 'encouraged' to read more widely and read with interpretation. Teaching form rather than content allows students to be active participants in the building of an information scaffold, and more responsible for their reading, writing and intellectual choices. Yet continual intervention, checking and correction, is required to stop students creating a culture of equivalence between sources, thereby undermining higher levels of scholarship.

From: Matt
Sent: Friday, 24 March 2006 5:11 PM
To: Tara Brabazon
Subject: RE: Creative Industries HELP!

Hi Tara

Sorry to be painful but this should be my last question. Do we really need to have ten references from the readers?

It's just that by coincidence (my parents bought me a subscription to Time) I have found a couple of articles, one regarding obesity in America and one about everyday people creating wealth through the internet (with blogs, short films etc). I'd like to use these but I feel that I am getting too wound up on having ten references from the unit material,

Have a good weekend

Matt

From: Tara Brabazon
Sent: Saturday, 25 March 2006 7:40 AM
To: Matt
Subject: RE: Creative Industries HELP!

Hi Matt -

Hope you are well. Thanks for your message.

Matt – the assignments in creative industries – they have been written to use *that reading*. We do not want any further reading at all. And remember there are *many more articles* than 10 in these relevant sections of the course, so students can choose what suits them. But they must choose from the quality material that we have gathered from around the world. That is the relevant stuff. That is what we are testing is being used.

The reason that we want *these references* is to confirm that students have done the reading and are working at a level where they can interpret that material.

So *Time* magazine is not at a high enough level for University work. It's interesting and great to read, but we are asking a precise question, using a precise body of knowledge. Remember too, the quotes may be four or five words in length, that's all. But you need to confirm that you can read and use them.

Also – one of the criteria by which we're assessing your work is the use of reading. So you need to position yourself to get the marks from that part of the marking mix, O.K?

Let me know if I can do anything else...

T

It is extraordinary that a student is complaining about the use of ten references in a university-level assignment. I had collected and printed 38 separate extracts for students to use in the first six weeks of the course. Asking students to select ten from this list is neither excessive nor inflated. Obviously many more references were required for a distinction grade. But it is remarkable that by placing a (quite low) minimum level of compliance, students still have difficulty reaching this figure. Fascinatingly, Matt attempted to argue that *Time* magazine would be an adequate substitute for the carefully selected international scholarship. For this student to think that *Time* is equivalent to higher levels of research is part of the problem that needs to be corrected and addressed through curriculum and teaching and learning methods.

Our first lessons in schools and universities must teach and re-teach how to evaluate the quality of all information, including internet-based information. I encourage students to ask ten preliminary questions.

1. Who authored the information?
2. What expertise does the writer have to comment?

3. What evidence is used? Are there citations in the piece?
4. What genre is the document: journalism, academic paper, blog, polemic?
5. Is the site/document/report funded by an institution?
6. What argument is being made?
7. When was the text produced?
8. Why did this information emerge at this point in history?
9. Who is the audience for this information?
10. What is not being discussed and what are the political consequences of that absence?

Asking students to answer these questions is a way to limit the free range of searching on the internet and the unquestioning acceptance of the Google ranking. They must pause, reflect and think. These questions create a recognition that finding information is not synonymous with understanding information. Without such critical pauses, the inclusion of the internet into the school and university curriculum may ensure access to information, but it does not promote the development of high quality writing, wide reading and innovative interpretations.[76] Importantly, Google's popularity does not facilitate or encourage the discipline and structure that many of our students need. Good teaching is required, yet the credibility of the profession is low.[77] Supposedly, even former celebrities, with no apparent skills, can become teachers.

> Our hearts bleed for those ageing musicians who are unable to age gracefully and come to terms with life after room service and adoring fans waiting outside the hotel … Well it happens to the best of us. Elite athletes have to promote breakfast cereals, it's almost

76 An alternative viewpoint to the argument expressed in this chapter has been provided by Cynthia Szymanski Sunal, Coralee Smith, Dennis Sunal and Judy Britt, who stated that 'inclusion of the internet into the school curriculum will surely boost educational quality because of immediate access to information which could be readily incorporated into students' daily education', from 'Using the internet to create meaningful instruction', *The Social Studies*, Vol. 89, No. 1, January–February 1998, p. 13.

77 It is important to note, though, that teachers are often blamed for not only the results, but the behaviour of students. For example, a letter to the editor in *The Independent* by Ian Johnstone asked 'How many adults trying to become teachers have not even rudimentary child-development knowledge? How many have the skills to convert the theory of pupil behaviour management into practical classroom action? The current training of secondary teachers is woefully lacking in classroom management skills. Learning to manage pupil behaviour through teacher training courses is a priority, and any central funding spent on improving pupil behaviour should be carefully monitored', *The Independent*, Education and Careers, 7 April 2005, p. 2. Not recognized by this letter writer is that teacher training – like student education – exists in a context. The notion that 'managing pupil behaviour' should be valued ahead of curriculum expertise or advanced methods in literacy education is disturbing.

> compulsory for ex-models to design a lingerie line and former cricketers resort to advertising hair-loss products. Why not try teaching?[78]

Teaching is a profession of skill, scholarship and experience. It is not a fall-back position for those who have failed at something else or are 'passed it' in terms of their occupation. The difficulty is that information – through Google – is seen to be both abundant and cheap. Because of this, anyone can manage it – even an athlete promoting breakfast cereal. Actually, the abilities required to assess information are difficult and costly to obtain.

Teaching the surprises

Making changes in curriculum, method and assessment always creates unexpected outcomes. My sharp alteration in the first year curriculum was no exception. The integration and application of learning skills to build students' research project was a success, but my concern that their semiotic skills would be reduced without overt testing of the terminology was justified. The advantages were clear. Students struggled with the annotated bibliography. Struggle in this context was necessary and important. They recognized how little they knew about the different types of information and media, and how to dismiss, value, rank and evaluate it. This assessment was time-consuming on me as the only staff member on the course.[79] The hundreds of desperate – and quite basic – emails from students and queues in the corridor to see me made it an inefficient exercise for me, but crucial for them.

> From: Sarah
> To: t.brabazon@murdoch.edu.au
> Subject: help!?
> Date: Fri, 3 Sep 2004 17:59:44 +0800
>
> hi there.
>
> sarah here, (tartan scarf; Tuesday mornings)
>
> trying to plan my essay, but i'm not sure i 'get' exactly what the hell you're on about.

78 E. Lemon, 'Feedback', *The Weekend Australian Magazine*, 3–4 September 2005, p. 8.

79 My experience of students requiring intense attention and time was also mirrored by Lynn Kuzma, who reported that her 'project was far more complex and time consuming than I originally anticipated', from 'The world wide web and active learning in the international relations classroom', *PS: Political Science and Politics*, Vol. 31, No. 1, September 1998, fulltext article.

> no, i don't think you're raving idiot – i just don't understand what you mean by an annotated bibliography.
>
> it sounds difficult to do only 1000 words on so many sources, and even harder to do not using dot-points!
>
> sorry, it's probably really simple, but naturally, being something different, it's scary.
>
> anyway, i think i want to do either feminism or youth – that is, how we are misrepresented, and how we bring it on ourselves.
>
> oh, by the way, are we doing any stuff on feminism, coz i've been theorising with my friend about it – and managed to develope another rant! (just to add to my ever-growing repertoir)
>
> well, sorry if i sound like a loser (especially if it really is a simple concept) but if you could break down even further what an annotated bibliography is, that'd be MUCH appreciated!
>
> it's ok, you don't have write it all out on e-mail, if it's easier,
>
> i'd like to come and see you afetr the tutorial, or lecture ;)
>
> thanks again!
>
> sarah
> :)

I explained to Sarah in more detail about the annotation, and she did well in the resultant assignment. The submitted papers were uneven, but there were some important surprises. International, English as a Second Language students, who normally struggle in social sciences and humanities courses, all generated fine annotated bibliographies and presentations of their projects. This success had many causes, but the precise list of assessment demands guided their progress in incremental stages. The fascinating result – in terms of gender – was the complete surprise. While the top 20 students were evenly split between men and women, the 15 students who received the lowest grades were all young men. I had to nag and push them to finish the assignment, and most submitted the paper incomplete. At this stage, while being aware of the fascinating material emerging from Wayne Martino and others exploring men, masculinity and education,[80] there was

80 W. Martino and B. Meyenn (eds), *What about Boys?* (Milton Keynes: Open University Press, 2001), and W. Martino and M. Pallotta-Chiarolli, *Boy's Stuff* (Sydney: Allen and Unwin, 2002).

no clear or verifiable reason why an annotated bibliography and presentation of a project challenged a group of young men more than young women.

The great strength of this assignment is that – even amongst these young men – every student improved remarkably between the first and second round of grading. Their analytical capacity increased, their argument was sharper and – most importantly – their reading was wide and well referenced. Because of the expanded bibliography, the calibre of their analysis was markedly improved on earlier years. No students submitted a reference list with less than 15 sources. The guiding assignment worked. New skills were developed. Improvements were observed. Students demonstrated the ability to find and interpret information. Mindless web surfing transformed into methodical web searching.

The greatest challenge for the students was learning about the refereeing process. They had difficulties finding journal articles, having to be pushed to go to the library or taught about electronic databases while sitting next to me in my office. Online refereed articles were incredibly tough for students to find. I ended up listing a range of electronic and online journals, with their URLs, to calm them. A problem I found was they were not prepared to experiment with search engines or terms. For example, a student completing a research paper on *Buffy* – as in the Vampire Slayer – had to be strongly convinced that perhaps words and phrases like 'popular culture' and 'women', 'television' and 'femininity' could produce important research results. Slowly, her vocabulary and awareness of the intricacies of information and scholarship developed.

An early techno-celebrationist welcomed the web in education, believing that 'we can learn virtually anything from the very source of the information'.[81] Everything can be learnt from the web, except *how* to use it. What I confirmed through this assignment is that students must be taught with precision and care about finding and evaluating both analogue and digital sources. Recent innovations in Google's products are making this process easier.

The arrival of Google Scholar in 2004 was a welcome intervention that assists students completing assignments such as this, particularly as online refereed journals increase in number and their cataloguing becomes more methodical. The difficulty with Google Scholar, which is not a problem caused by the company but by the commodification of information, is that international publishers have controlled the distribution of journal articles so that university and public libraries must buy the right to access. That means Google Scholar can list these journal articles by title but the fulltext script is not available. It is a great intervention from Google to recognize that there are different types of information which require distinct modes of search engine. The challenge is to ensure that the online and electronic journals submitted to their database are from around the world and in diverse languages. In its early incarnation, publishers from the United

---

81 'Applications of learning', 2001, http://connectedteacher.classroom.com/tips/resources/communicating.htm, accessed on 16 June 2006.

States and United Kingdom dominated the ranks of refereed articles. Actually – to avoid the commercial aggregators – Google Scholar could search for the freely available refereed journals produced by academics and universities, available online and without cost. Much of this material is produced outside of the United States and the United Kingdom, bringing 'the world' back to the World Wide Web. This indexing will take expertise to validate but captures the texture and depth of the online environment.

While the quality of retrieved online information is improved through Google Scholar, the other new 'product', Google Print – that became Google Book Search – has a more archival function.

> Google's mission is to organize the world's information, but much of that information isn't yet online. Google Print aims to get it there by putting book content where you can find it most easily – right in your Google search results.[82]

The monograph content in Google Book Search is sourced from publishers and libraries. From 30 August 2006, the entirety of public domain books could be viewed, but only a few pages from copyrighted material. While the availability of research material is uneven, Google is enacting a public (and commercial) service, and the results will be impressive in the longer term.[83] Meanwhile, students continue to use Google, rather than the more complex services of Book Search and Scholar. However, a potential for growth and intervention is there. The Fordist search engine is becoming a post-Fordist sifter and sorter of text. Google has also recognized the importance of information professionals, by forming Google Librarian Centre and regular newsletters.

The lessons of my assignment change are clear for educators and education. Students require time, care, energy and good assessment to improve their digital academic research. Intervention is required. Past assumptions about levels of comprehension and desire to read widely are being warped and maligned. Teachers require professional development in library studies, internet studies and literary theory to create a worthwhile intellectual journey through this new research landscape. Most importantly, universities must value their libraries and librarians. We need to find structural ways to push our students back into libraries to discover the value of wandering up the corridors of journal stacks. Also, with library budgets declining, we need to remember and value the knowledge,

---

82 'About Google Print', Google Print Beta, http://print.google.com.au/googleprint/about.html, accessed on 27 July 2005.

83 There are important critiques emerging of this 'service'. Charles Arthur offered a convincing critique about the scale of the copyright – or at least intellectual property rights – violations. He stated, 'Google gets the book contents free, gets to sell adverts against them, and the publishers get … what? The promise that they might sell some more books. It certainly sounds like something for nothing and once again, it's Google that gets the something, and everyone else who is left scrabbling for the scraps'. *The Guardian*, 23 February 2006, p. 6.

professionalism and training of librarians. They do not provide information, but a path through information. As Cerise Oberman has argued,

> For thirty years, librarians have been responding to the electronic age: we have forecast the paperless society, ruminated about libraries without walls, and pondered the impact of an increasingly digital world.[84]

What I learnt through the change in assessment is that students do not know as much about the internet, web and Google as they think they do. Almost every student in the course review commented how difficult they found the first assignment, but how it was the most worthwhile project they conducted in their first year. They were challenged but gained confidence through the success. Most commented how the skills they discovered in my course improved their grade in others. In response I received the highest student evaluations for teaching in my career. From such a difficult course, and considering the student's struggles to complete the required work, it was a remarkable result. Cards, letters and notes flooded my office after the semester concluded.

Dear Tara,

Being a student of Intro. Cultural Studies
has far exceeded every expectation
about University that I've ever had.
The content, the dynamic approach
and the benefits are (almost)
indescribably fulfilling. Thank you.*
On top of this I have experienced
the finest example of 'teaching' I've
ever come across. You are exhilirating,
passionate, approachable and very
inspirational. My decision to follow
a dream of becoming an English/Media
Teacher has been enhanced and strongly
re-affirmed as a result of crossing
paths with you. Please know that
in me there has been deep change, growth
and vision ... you have made a difference.
In light and love I assure you that
my journey, my endeavour to do the
same begins here and now.

84 C. Oberman, 'Library instruction: concepts and pedagogy in the electronic environment', *RQ*, Vol. 35, No. 3, Spring 1996, full text.

This student gave me too much credit. Her effort, attention and respect for reading and thinking made the semester memorable and the result was created through a change in curriculum and building an information scaffold. Research training and skills are valuable. For students to attain them, they must be embedded in assessment. I wish that first year students would attend library sessions during their orientation week to gain information skills with databases, refereeing and scholarship. I also know that many spend this orientation week joining social clubs, signing up for tutorials, getting drunk and falling over. They need this transition time, and I wish them well. However, teachers of first year students must not assume that our cohort possesses skills in referencing, scholarship and knowledge management. The inference that internet-based research is convenient, less-time consuming and inexpensive[85] is invalidated by my experience. Students were unable to manage diverse types, modes and genres of web-based sources without an embedded information scaffold in their curriculum and attentive personal assistance.

The challenges of the Googlescape opened out a meaningful learning opportunity for the teacher and students that instilled effective communication. Still, there remains a gulf – a wide and expansive canyon – between principles and practice. My desire – at least for one semester – was to attempt an intervention in lazy research methods and broaden students' reading to other sources, media and platforms.[86] Providing students with tools does not mean that they are used. Hoping that students will magically read widely without building a research framework is a pedagogic relic of an earlier age. The gap between the educational and life experience of teachers and students is increasing.

My dream has always been the same: to write the perfect sentence. Words remain a joy and passion. The backlit computer screen has only intensified my love, as flickering pixels bounce around a white screen. Cut and paste allows for the endless editing and manipulation of text. The dancing, bouncing, mobile words capture the realization that we never graduate from literacy – we never 'become literate'. We only reach new stages of reading, writing and thinking. Obviously this is a politically unpopular realization. Because literacy means more than encoding and decoding – more than reading and writing – we can never assess, measure or quantify results. We must never become complacent in the level of achievement in our students or ourselves. Literacy is not a goal or an outcome. It is a process and a politics.

If this chapter has offered an intervention in literacy debates, it is the importance of techno-scepticism. The skills and techniques of well-trained teachers are required in the

---

85 An example of this early ideology of internet research is found in Cheryl Harris' *An Internet Education: A Guide to Doing Research on the Internet* (Belmont: International Thomson Publishing Company, 1996), particularly between pages 6 and 12.

86 Another curriculum strategy I have tested was discussed in T. Brabazon, 'Socrates in earpods: the ipodification of education', *Fast Capitalism*, Vol. 2, No. 1, July 2006, http://www.uta.edu/huma/agger/fastcapitalism/2_1/brabazon.htm.

information age to block students from googling their way through a degree. Students, when made aware of the plurality of sources, searches, words and ideas, again become excited by learning. The next chapter aligns this diversity of source material with the diversity of students in our universities. To make these texts and contexts – sources and researchers – align is an ongoing challenge, but a necessity. Until student testamurs read Bachelor of Arts (Google), intervention is required.

Chapter two

Digital Eloi and analogue Morlocks

> Universities bring people together. They allow for a cross-fertilization of minds on a scale and in a manner not possible anywhere else in society. Teachers can aid this process; libraries can extend it. But it is the function of teachers and university libraries that is most under threat in the information age.[1]
>
> Krishan Kumar

> Class distinctions do not die; they merely learn new ways of expressing themselves.[2]
>
> Richard Hoggart

In H.G. Wells' *The Time Machine*, the Eloi were beautiful, loquacious and elegant citizens supported by dirty, subterranean and hard-working Morlocks. Published in 1895, the novel is credited with popularizing time travel. Wells' words also confirm that even in 802701 AD, the peaceful and happy future of the Eloi is based on a ruthless class structure that causes humanity to be ruptured in two. A leisured class manages banal pleasures, while the cannibalistic and bestial Morlocks operate the machines that keep the Eloi in leisured stupor. For the socialist Wells, his dystopia was foreshadowing the inevitable result of capitalism. In the context of the information age, the Eloi populate the Googlescape, while the Morlock complete the actual work that creates the lived experience in the analogue world. Put more clearly, Lester Faigley realized that 'the revolution of the rich has been facilitated by another related revolution: the digital revolution of electronic communications technologies'.[3] The emancipatory role of education is not necessarily confluent with digital convergence. Instead, digitized wallpaper has covered over the cracks of analogue injustice.

---

1 K. Kumar, 'The need for place', from A. Smith and F. Webster (eds), *The Postmodern University? Contested Visions of Higher Education in Society* (Buckingham: Open University Press, 1997), p. 29.

2 R. Hoggart, 'Introduction', to George Orwell's *The Road to Wigan Pier* (London: Penguin, 2001: 1937), p. vii. Hoggart wrote this introduction in 1987, at the height of Thatcherism. His words were retained in the 2001 reprint.

3 L. Faigley, 'Literacy after the revolution', from T. Taylor and I. Ward (ed.), *Literacy Theory in the Age of the Internet* (New York: Columbia University Press, 1998), p. 7.

Representations of social difference produce evocative literature and outstanding journalism. One of the other great portrayals of cultural divisions is George Orwell's *The Road to Wigan Pier.* Travelling to Barnsley, Sheffield and Wigan, he found filth, decay and dense inequality. In 1937, Orwell reminded his readers that class-based inequality still punctuated contemporary England. His argument is at its most profound when analysing the home economics of working class households. He argues that these families 'don't necessarily lower their standards by cutting out luxuries and concentrating on necessities; more often it is the other way about … in a decade of unparalleled depression, the consumption of all cheap luxuries has increased'.[4] To make his case, he analysed the shopping list of the unemployed, with particular attention to food. His interpretation, 70 years after this landmark text was published, still has accuracy and poignancy in these *Supersize Me* times.

> The miner's family spend only tenpence a week on green vegetables and tenpence halfpenny on milk … and nothing on fruit; but they spend one and nine on sugar (about eight pounds of sugar, that is) and a shilling on tea … The basis of their diet, therefore, is white bread and margarine, corned beef, sugared tea and potatoes – an appalling diet. Would it not be better if they spent more money on wholesome things like oranges and wholemeal bread? … Yes, it would, but the point is that no ordinary human being is ever going to do such a thing … The peculiar evil is this, that the less money you have, the less inclined you feel to spend it on wholesome food … When you are unemployed, which is to say when you are underfed, harassed, bored and miserable, you don't want to eat dull wholesome food.[5]

Orwell's observation explains the explosion of fast food restaurants, soft drink, cheesecake shops and pizza during a time of unstable, 'flexible' work with no guarantees. There is not enough job security to manage a mortgage, but sufficient cash for a mobile phone with an ever-changing ring tone. A credit card blurs the division between rich and poor. With no money in the bank, easy credit can put clothes on your back.

Technology does not erase class differences. It merely creates new mechanisms through which they are expressed. While all technology is immersed in social practices, the more empowered the citizen, the greater the array of 'innovations' available to deploy in daily life. While packet switching was meant to move data around the network without fear of redundancy, Wood and Graham showed how economic injustices and inequalities are restructuring, reordering and hierarchizing information.

> Internet Routers are now being programmed with software that actually prioritize packets of information differently, based on real-time, corporate judgments of the real or potential profitability of the person sending the traffic. This means that the 'premium' users seen to be

4 G. Orwell, *The Road to Wigan Pier* (London: Penguin, 2001: 1937), p. 81.

5 *Ibid.*, p. 88.

> more commercially attractive may, over the same infrastructure, be able to access web sites in times of Internet congestion whilst other, less attractive users experience 'web site not available' signs. As a result, corporate internet firms now routinely prioritize the traffic from the 'premium,' selected users that they think will bring the best revenues and exposure to their brands, their services, and their corporate tie-ins … Importantly, neither the privileged, or the marginalized users in this case are likely to even know that this process has shaped their experience of the network.[6]

Cisco, a manufacturer of internet routers, advertised their 'service' to corporate media and internet firms. They confirm their 'absolute control, down to the packet, in your hands. You can identify each traffic type – Web, e-mail, voice, video … [and] isolate … the type of application, even down to *specific brands*, by the *interface* used, by the *user type and individual user identification or by the site address*.'[7] The internet was originally configured to grant each packet of data equal value. There was a democracy to packet switching: it was not packet sorting. Now, functions and users are being splintered and ranked for economic benefit.[8] The Morlocks are unaware of this process.

Remembering Orwell's point, the sacrifices of working class citizens for 'luxuries' – for a computer, internet access or a mobile telephone – have consequences in the rest of their lives. They may have dial up access to the internet and Google, but the costs to their health, family and financial future are more difficult to evaluate. The costs emerge in the long term through a lack of savings or superannuation. This chapter builds on the movements of literacy and curriculum introduced in the first section, focusing on the morbid dance between technology and inequality. These two strands of analysis – on literacy and social in/justice – frame the remainder of the arguments in this book. The aim is to enmesh an information system into a social system. In summoning Orwell's

---

6 D. Wood and S. Graham, 'Permeable boundaries in the software-sorted society: surveillance and the differentiation of mobility', Paper for the *Alternative Mobility Futures*, Lancaster University, 9–11 January 2004, p. 6.

7 Cisco, cited in D. Winsbeck, 'Netscapes of power: convergence, network design, walled gardens, and other strategies of control in the information age', in D. Lyon (ed.), *Surveillance as Social Sorting: Privacy, Risk and Automated Discrimination* (London: Routledge, 2003), p. 183.

8 Nick Booth reported that 'computer systems are being used to snub you more effectively, depending on your value to the company you're calling. This is how it works. In the customer record is a field that rates your importance based on your spending power. If you have deep pockets, you may merit a "1", marking you as first-class customer whose calls should be answered pronto by a senior customer service agent. The same field, in the record of a poor customer, might contain a "3", which tells the system to treat you like a third-class customer (or pond life, as one IT executive described non-priority customers). The system will put you to the back of the queue. If you eventually get through, your call will be routed to the cheapest call centre … this is the new power of databases: a subtle means of reinforcing a financially-based class system', from N. Booth, 'Press 1 if you're poor, 2 if you're loaded …', *The Guardian*, 2 March 2006, p. 3.

Wigan and Wells' Morlocks, a pattern of exclusion is revealed. To make teaching and learning better and greater, these metaphors of segregation transform into warnings and models of difference. As Zeus Leonardo has affirmed, 'quality education begins with a language of critique, at the heart of which is a process that exposes the contradictions of social life'.[9] The goal is to find a way to instigate a dialogue between objective and subjective renderings of oppression.

We all hope our teaching transforms social structures and individual lives. The success of this aspiration is highly questionable. Cannadine offers a reminder of the gulf between our hopes and the expectations of those who remain outside our universities.

> There was also the more fundamental division: between those who had a university degree and those who did not, or between those who were 'educated' and those who were not, or between those who were literate and those who were not and however education was envisaged in social structural terms, it was more concerned with teaching people their place than with giving them opportunities to advance.[10]

Much of education teaches students that they are not good enough, that they do not belong and that they are not important. Marking and assessment pinpoint and emphasize weaknesses, problems and failures.[11] Such judgments have enormous effects on how an identity is created. Cannadine is correct: when we learn, we learn our place. In urban environments, the gap between the affluent and poor is increased through technological change.[12] While education facilitates social mobility, it also perpetuates disadvantage. Jessamyn West, editor of Librarian.net, has monitored this difference.

> The people who can afford to buy computers and Internet services often stay home to read and do their research, which means that libraries are increasingly becoming places where poor

---

9 Z. Leonardo, 'Critical social theory and transformative knowledge: the functions of criticism in quality education', *Educational Researcher*, Vol. 33, No. 6, August/September 2004, p. 12.

10 D. Cannadine, *The Rise and Fall of Class in Britain* (New York: Columbia University Press, 1999), p. 49.

11 Ironically juxtaposed against the demand for results, outcomes and standards, Polly Curtis and Rebecca Smithers reported that Edexcel, one of the three main exam boards in England, employed secretarial and administrative staff to mark religious education GCSE papers. This decision was justified because of the pressure to deliver timely results. Please refer to 'GCSE papers marked by admin staff', *The Guardian*, 22 August 2006, http://education.guardian.co.uk/gcses/story/0,16086,1553841,00.hmtl, accessed on 22 August 2006.

12 Please refer to June Gordon's 'A shoelace left untied: teachers negotiate class and ethnicity in a city of Northern England', *The Urban Review*, Vol. 35, No. 3, September 2003, p. 194.

> people go to use public services. Meanwhile, communities all over the country have to make tough decisions about what should receive funding.[13]

When money is diverted from libraries, it impacts most on those who cannot afford computers and online facilities in the home. While libraries and librarians cannot solve injustices, they can manage and moderate them. With funding cut from the sector, the social cost will not only be vast, but immeasurable in its long-term consequences.

As Universities have expanded in their number of students and campuses, it could be assumed that the distribution of capital and opportunities between classes has also changed so that more Morlocks are able to inhabit the sandstone buildings and mock-Gothic architecture. If that was the case, then this current chapter would focus on the most effective delivery of platforms and literacies to the Morlocks. However it is clear that another story juts out of this narrative of digital distribution. Geoff Maslen reported that,

> Despite efforts down the years by universities to increase the proportion of students from disadvantaged backgrounds they remain underrepresented, just as they have for 150 years. Research consistently shows that students from higher socio-economic status backgrounds dominate the student body in a majority of universities but especially in the research-intensive institutions.[14]

In 2003, researchers at the Centre for the Study of Higher Education (CSHE) at Melbourne University in Australia, a 'research-intensive institution,' demonstrated that despite the platitudes and policies to encourage students from a lower socio-economic background, diverse races, those with a disability, and women in non-traditional areas, the talk has not created results. Instead, the language of objectives, generic competencies, measurements and targets has blocked any clear-headed recognition of how and why students from disadvantaged backgrounds decide (not) to attend university. Without thinking through the diverse understandings of words like choice, motivation and opportunity, equity policies will fail.[15] There is also little possible modeling or mentoring of disempowered and disconnected students by a diverse faculty. Lucile Vargas revealed that, in the United States, the tenure rate for white male and females was 73 per cent. It was 66 per cent for men of colour and 56 per cent for women of colour.[16] For young women of colour, there are few role models to crystallize their aspirations. At his most

13 J. West, 'Will the internet put public libraries out of business?', *Wired*, August 2005, p. 030.

14 G. Maslen, 'Poverty remains a major barrier to tertiary education', *Campus Review*, March 30, 2005, p. 3.

15 *Ibid.*

16 L. Vargas, 'When the "Other" is the teacher: implications of teacher diversity in higher education', *The Urban Review*, Vol. 31, No. 4, 1999, p. 359.

honest and blistering, John Halliday asserted that the purpose of formal education is to 'provide many thousands of jobs for generally middle class people supposedly training working class people for jobs for which training as an activity distinct from the job itself, is not really required'.[17] In such an argument, university education not only encourages competency, but compliance.

For Marx and Engels, the experience of inequalities through factory conditions in the industrial revolution built a consciousness of injustice and a desire for change. Yet many theories of class are of historical interest at best, and nostalgic at worst. Some representations are evocative literary journalism like George Orwell's *The Road to Wigan Pier*, or fictional, like Alan Sillitoe's *Saturday Night and Sunday Morning* and Irvine Welsh's *Trainspotting*. Television has replayed and recirculated these classed images through *EastEnders*' Queen Vic pub and *Coronation Street*, capturing a local community with intertwined social lives. These working class representations are sourced from the mid-nineteenth century, sketching the conditions of the labouring classes through the popular memory of Charles Dickens and Poor Law inspectors. What makes *East Enders* significant and different in its classed representations is that Afro-Caribbean, Asian and Turkish households are presented along with inter-racial marriages. The complex and intricate configurations of black, white and Asian families in class-based terms requires sustained analytical attention. When assessing the classes and colours of our students and staff, popular culture is currently leading the policy.

The mechanism through which educators manage technological inequality and how it is mapped over social injustice is probably the primary issue for the first quarter of the twenty-first century. Focusing on web-literate citizens and scholars creates ideological blind spots that are difficult to remove. As Morgan Lang recognized,

> It is obvious that the WWW is in some ways an ideal research tool in that it allows people residing in countries with well-developed communications networks to express their thoughts in coherent, tidy, and easily obtainable texts. It is also obvious that people who communicate via the WWW tend to be educated, middle-class white people, people who hardly constitute a representative sample of any cultural affiliation other than that of a global association of individuals whose commonality originates in their ability to obtain and wield telecommunications technology.[18]

Just like the Eloi, and similar to Orwell's comfortably middle class reading audience, there is a community of Googlers who are searching for interesting, web-literate and curious people like themselves. There is little awareness that in the mines, or even deeper below

17 J. Halliday, 'Lifelong learning and the world of work', Paper presented at the European Conference on Educational Research, Lahti, Finland, 22–25 September 1999.

18 M.Lang, 'Futuresound: techno music and mediation', http://www.music.hyperreal.org/library/fewerchur.txt, accessed on 30 March 2001.

the metaphoric surface of the cyber-planet, are people who cook, clean, build and work without the benefits of digi-leisure.[19] When times are truly bad, we are drawn to the light, the frivolous and the stupid. This phenomenon – which could be called the Paris Hilton effect – is facilitated by Google, where bored surfers fill their cursors and minds with irrelevancies. We lose the capacity to sift, discard and judge. Google is white bread for the mind; creating pleasant, tasty searches with little nutritional content. Information is no longer for social good, but for sale. For example, when the Domesday Book was digitized, it was not available as a free public service from the National Archives to the online community. Instead, each downloaded page cost £3.50, charged to a credit card.[20] This financial filtering of information presents a fee. A decade before the release of the digitized Doomsday Book, Herbert Schiller expressed his concerns about the declining capacity for interpretation and comprehension amongst his fellow citizens.

> The ability to understand, much less overcome, increasingly critical national problems is thwarted, either by a growing flood of mind-numbing trivia and sensationalist material or by an absence of basic, contextualized social information.[21]

Such an absence is not the fault of technology. Burning or blaming the machines – although understandable – is a political cop-out. Under the crush of progressivist narratives, Luddite resistance must fail. Instead, critique and questioning is required of those invested in text over context and software over society. Instead of raising these concerns, the history of computing has constructed a narrative of great men developing hardware and programming. Miniaturization and the arrival of solid-state electronics reduced the costs of technology. Yet hardware does not trigger social change. It was software that created a market. Word processing and spreadsheet applications made computers – the hardware – not only understandable but useable. Google has value-added to the computer, making technology seem simple, banal, functional and an enabler of lifestyle.

When technology becomes ubiquitous, it disappears. The oven, a washing machine and a toaster are all technologies. My mother still remembers the morning rituals of lighting the copper to wash clothes. Yet we rarely look on the washing machine as technology. It is an appliance and a convenience. The internet has not yet disappeared into our social lives, which is why all the troubles and inequalities in the culture, with regard to class, gender, age, race and the global distribution of wealth, are all either

19 To monitor 'the new poverty', please refer to P. Toynbee, *Nickel and Dimed* (London: Granta, 2002), F. Abrams, *Below the Breadline* (London: Profile, 2002) and P. Toynbee, *Hard Work* (London: Bloomsbury, 2005).

20 Stephen Moss wrote a fascinating review of his experience downloading the Domesday Book in 'Domesday Books goes digital', *The Guardian*, 5 August 2006, p. 11.

21 H. Schiller, *Information Inequality* (New York: Routledge, 1996), p. xi.

blamed on the internet or seen as an outcome of it. The difficulty is that social groups benefit and lose from technological change in different ways. The Luddites were handloom weavers who lost their expertise, skills and stature in their community because of the mechanized loom. They decided to blame the machines and destroy them. Yet the mechanized loom did not alter the status of the weavers. The ruthless capitalism of a fast-industrializing Britain, with little capacity to validate or understand working class men and their skills so as to change-manage their employment opportunities, is what did the damage. Blaming a system requires consciousness, agency and power. Blaming the machines is easier and more targeted.

Technology will not make our societies more socially just. It merely overlays new methods to reinforce already existing inequalities and exclusions. Universities, while filled with scholars who believe in fairness, respect and equity, are not a panacea for the working class. The Morlocks rarely peep into the halls of scholarship. At best, the wannabe Eloi fill the classrooms. Colin MacCabe confirmed:

> It is the middle classes who predominantly use the universities, a use generously subsidized by the taxes of the lower paid. There is probably no state benefit as important to the middle classes. The government which told parents who have already laid out more than £100,000 on private schooling, or have moved heaven and earth to get their child into a good state school, to prepare for a massive whack in the wallet could expect comprehensive punishment at the polls ... a state built on middle-class privilege cannot be expected to deliver social justice. The increase in intake from comprehensives merely continues the unfair benefits of the system to the middle classes. It hardly touches the inner-city poor.[22]

MacCabe's solution to such a dilemma is to open universities to privatization and the market, reduce the number of institutions and limit the number of graduates. Such outcomes would supposedly create a 'world-class university system',[23] transforming the state-based university sector into corporatized entities of excellence. What of the Morlocks who – while currently excluded – would surely suffer more through the imposition of high level private fees? His answer is to summon religion, the other easy answer to difficult questions. While the market would solve the problems of the rich, MacCabe states that 'those who wish to see education play a role in the development of a more equal society must pray for a decent secondary school education for every child in the country'.[24] Whether the answer is prayer or technology, education is not building social justice or economic mobility. Yet increasing the barriers to university entry cannot assist those already struggling or excluded. Strategic intervention is required.

---

22 C. MacCabe, 'Set our universities free', *The Observer*, Sunday 1 March 2004, http://observer.guardian.co.uk/comment/story/0,690,146503,00.html, accessed 14 March 2005.

23 *Ibid.*

24 *Ibid.*

Phil Agre succinctly recognized that 'there's a big difference between forwarding e-mail and building a political movement around your values'.[25] Google is a metaphor, just as Microsoft Windows was a metaphor, of accessibility, efficiency, usefulness, speed, openness and community. Google searches occupy time, filling our blinking gaze with the daily drudgery of bloggers[26] or the petty successes of finding our names returned on web searches. I Google, therefore I am. There is no care or awareness of those who are not Google-citizens or who do not share the desire to search for information (about ourselves). Instead, we fill in time to stop us thinking about those for whom the blinking cursor is not a siren's call. As David Massey has argued,

> These are the groups who are really in charge of time-space compression, who can really use it and turn it to their advantage, whose power and influence it very definitely increases. On its more prosaic fringes this group probably includes a fair number of Western academics – those who in other words, write most about it.[27]

Massey has mapped a dangerous intellectual cycle: googling ourselves and writing about googling ourselves. Such a cyclical and insular process means that education – the outward search for knowledge and challenge – becomes even more important. Instead of celebrating the speed of research, the building of coalitions and digital movements around the globe, those citizens who are locked outside of this time-space compression need to be heard, not 'given' a voice or spoken 'on the behalf of' by those deaf to the necessities to redistribute (cultural) capital.

Critical consciousness and social mobility are possible through education, but they are extremely difficult to achieve, requiring motivated teachers, a proactive family and

---

25 P. Agre, 'Ralph Reed on the Skills of Democracy', *The Network Observer*, Vol. 2, No. 19, September 1995, http://dlis.gscis.ucla.edu/people/pagre/no/september-1995.html#who, accessed on 24 August 2002.

26 In classic *Wired* fashion, Kevin Kelly unproblematically celebrated blogging. In his article 'We are the Web', *Wired*, August 2005, he stated that 'No Web phenomenon is more confounding than blogging. Everything media experts knew about audiences – and they knew a lot – confirmed the focus group belief that audiences would never get off their butt and start making their own entertainment. Everyone knew writing and reading were dead; music was too much trouble to make when you could sit back and listen; video production was simply out of reach of amateurs. Blogs and other participant media would never happen, or if they happened they would not draw an audience, or if they drew an audience they would not matter. What a shock, then, to witness the near-instantaneous rise of 50 million blogs, with a new one appearing every two seconds … These user-created channels make no sense economically. Where are the time, energy and resources coming from? The audience', p. 099. Obviously the concern with such a celebration is the assumption that it is democratic, that blogs – intrinsically – are available to all.

27 D. Massey, 'Time/Space Compression', in J. Beynon and D. Dunkerley (eds), *Globalization: The Reader* (London: Athlone Press, 2000), p. 59.

peer group, well-funded educational institutions and good policy. The best of teaching and learning creates relationships, while developing student skills in analysis, oral and written communication, effective research and literacy skills. But these meta-skills are displaced or undermined. Instead, the Ultraversity, the distance learning subsidiary of Anglia Ruskin University, allows students to complete their entire degree online. Luck justified this mode of study with an unsettling rationalization.

> I'm training to become a graphic designer and I wanted a vocational degree that allows me to develop other avenues such as product photography. I'd thought about a conventional university but I get uncomfortable sitting in a classroom where everyone's working at the same pace.[28]

This is an astounding statement. A graphic designer, in the midst of a creative economy, must learn to work in a team and maintain a tight production schedule. That a student is validated for not sitting in a classroom and not collaborating is the unfortunate byproduct of the digitized 'revolution' of education. Another disadvantage of this 'university' is that motivation for teaching and learning is not addressed, which is why there is a 40 per cent drop out rate from courses.[29]

Such values and ideologies must have meaning and a context. As Zygmunt Bauman has confirmed, 'the culture of consumer society is mostly about forgetting, not learning'.[30] Google's blinking cursor requires a focus on simple and conversational keywords, displacing the complexity and depth of expansive research and forgetting those unable or unwilling to make the transition from analogue to digital literacy.

The aim of a socially just education is to grant a chance for the silenced to speak and to be heard and valued, not ignored. Those of us immersed in the structures of scholarship must ask if it is valid resistance to walk away from the classroom, to ignore education that is perceived of no benefit. My concern in the last few years has been that students have not recognized the value – beyond economic worth – of learning. Too many schools and universities fed into the easy ideologies of high-paying employment being the only goal of a university qualification. When the corporate prize did not materialize, with flexible, casual work the end point of many degrees, students rightly questioned the purpose of their vocational course structure. When education is reduced to economics, its wide-ranging value and power is reduced. Education is not

28 Luck, in Stephen Hoare, 'The university where everyone's a stranger', *The Guardian Higher Education*, 20 June 2006, p. 11.

29 *Ibid.*, p. 1.

30 Z. Bauman, *Globalization: The Human Consequences* (New York: Columbia University Press, 1998), p. 8.

simply a branch of the economy, but builds social capital.[31] Concurrently the public accountability of student 'success' at schools and university is being measured and ranked.[32] The impact of this competitiveness in the long term cannot be foreseen.[33] Actually, we require new tools, policies and achievement. Citizens also require more public discussion in how we define and determine the value of education, reading, writing and thinking.

Education is a struggle. The massification of higher education has reshaped what is expected of graduates. To affirm the importance of excellence, quality and international standards, rather than commercial investment and generic competencies, can be framed as elitist. It is too convenient to argue – at the very point that working class citizens, women, people of colour furtively walk into universities – that standards are falling. What has happened in our universities is that more students are being taught in under-

---

31 Robert Putnam's development of social capital theory must be acknowledged here. What is interesting about his landmark text *Bowling Alone* (New York: Simon Schuster, 2000) is the lack of direct attention to education. Much of the book assumes the value of schools and universities, with only one chapter – 17 – focusing on 'Education and Children's Welfare', pp. 296–318. The difficulty with the term 'social capital' and indeed 'social connectivity' is that they are ambiguous. Causality is always difficult to prove in social science. But the number of variables Putnam addresses in his work makes definitive interpretations impossible. There are also unexpected results of such ambiguity for formal education. He states, for example, 'the level of informal social capital in the state is a stronger predictor of student achievement than is the level of formal institutionalized social capital. In other words, levels of social trust in a state and the frequency with which people connected informally with one another (in card games, visiting with friends, and the like) were even more closely correlated with educational performance than was the amount of time state residents devoted to club meetings, church attendance, and community projects. This is not to say that formal activities were unimportant. Rather, what this admittedly crude evidence is saying is that there is something about communities where people connect with one another – over and above how rich or poor they are materially, how well educated the adults themselves are, what race or religion they are – that positively affects the education of children. Conversely, even communities with many material and cultural advantages do a poor job of educating their kids if the adults in those communities don't connect with one another', pp. 300–301. The difficulty with his argument is that he is stressing the value of informal communication networks, rather than addressing the decline in infrastructural development and policy for educational institutions. It is important to note that Putnam acknowledges the importance of family and parental involvement in education, rather than 'blaming' teachers for a decline in teaching and learning.

32 For a discussion of this public accountability, please refer to Gary Pike and Joseph Saupe, 'Does high school matter? An analysis of three methods of predicting first year grades', *Research in Higher Education*, Vol. 43, No. 2, April 2002, pp. 187–207.

33 Ingo Liefner explores some of these consequences and problems in 'Funding, resource allocation, and performance in higher education systems', *Higher Education*, Vol. 48, 2003, pp. 469–89.

funded institutions. Supposedly, this environment of mass education has become a positive basis of advertising and policy. Under the headline 'Now is a good time to be a student', Catherine Armitage affirmed that,

> It's a great time to be a university student. That's often overlooked amid the focus on negatives such as the long-term decline in university funding and the loss of student facilities on campus as a consequence of voluntary student unionism. For prospective students, however, top of the list among the good things is that it's easier to get into university than probably at any time in the past.[34]

Not mentioned in this article is the consequence on these prospective students, the university curriculum, marking standards and teachers' professional development when 'entry' into the institution becomes the topic of interest and importance, rather than what happens to these students through their courses. Failure rates – in both on and offline subjects – is the great unmentionable of this new 'age' of higher education. Indeed, on page two of the higher education supplement featuring Armitage's article was the headline: 'Log on for all you need to know'.[35] The message is obvious. It is a breeze to gain university admission and the web provides 'all you need to know' when the student arrives on campus.

Without staff increasing their work rate, efficiency and goodwill, our universities would have tumbled into incompetence years ago. Andrew Vandenberg realized that 'the staff who teach students are now less likely to be tenured teacher-researcher and more likely to be comparatively cheap, casually employed post-graduate students, especially in faculties of commerce and informational technology'.[36] In other words, at the point that students require more subtle, precise and targeted attention from staff because of their diverse intellectual, social and economic backgrounds, less experienced junior scholars are 'administering' their curriculum. The too easy embrace of professionalism, competency and education has presented a bill. The 'old style' intellectual – like Edward Said and E.P. Thompson – cannot be supported by our current system. Finding a new style of intellectual for these difficult times is the challenge. As Russell Jacoby has recognized,

---

34 C. Armitage, 'Now is a good time to be a student', *The Weekend Australian: Your Degree*, 8–9 July 2006, p. 1.

35 N. Barnard, 'Log on for all you need to know', *The Weekend Australian: Your Degree*, 8–9 July 2006, p. 2.

36 A. Vandenberg, 'Learning how to engage students online in hard times', *Education and Information Technologies*, Vol. 10, No. 1/2, 2005, p. 32.

> Fat salaries and secure positions hardly preclude original and subversive work; nor do paltry wages and insecure positions guarantee revolutionary and critical thought. This cannot be stated forcefully enough.[37]

Different modes of education are dueling for ascendancy. Either learning outcomes service the workplace *or* they disturb and question the truths of the market economy. Our challenge as educators is to see if the 'or' in the last sentence can be replaced with an 'and'. For such a project to emerge, the meaning of the compound noun of Higher Education needs to be unpicked. The difficulty in creating a responsible scholarly environment for critique and debate means that questions of accountability are further embedded with determinations of social justice and diversity. In a (post) information society, strategies are required for responding to multiple modes of communication. The view presented in the digital world is frequently closed and self satisfied. Images and experiences prioritize the world view of people from European backgrounds, the financially secure, the heterosexual and the masculine. These circulated images of normality construct communities that implicitly exclude difference. In such an environment of exclusion, communication is not an innocent process. The digital divide is locked into other injustices, of age, race, class and level of education.[38] Powerful groups impose their readings of the world through social space.

Through digitization, cultural literacies – or the literacies of others – can be repressed, ignored and forgotten. An aim of Tony Blair's third term in government was 'changing the middle-class character of the web',[39] to ensure that all families with children had computer access by 2008. While such a goal was election-time politicking, at least there was recognition that handing out computers or broadband will not create digital literacies. Access is not enough. Michael Cross reported that,

> When aiming at the socially excluded, content is the key, not connection. The success of digital television and mobile phones shows that people will go digital when there is something in it for them.[40]

Actually, content is not the key. Context is the imperative. Only when technology has a social purpose and appropriate context is it useful. It must be embedded in social practices and daily life so that it 'disappears'. Internet-literacy is not inevitable, triggered by the availability of hardware, software or content. Questions of motivation and

37 R. Jacoby, 'Intellectuals: inside and outside the university', from Smith and Webster, p. 66.

38 Thomas Novak and Donna Hoffman studied the relationship between racial identification, income and educational level and internet use. Please refer to 'Bridging the racial divide on the Internet', *Science*, Vol. 280, No. 5362, 17 April 1998.

39 M. Cross, 'Class consciousness', *The Guardian*, 7 April 2005, p. 15.

40 Cross, *ibid.*

context, rather than access and content, are necessary. As educators, it is our first job to teach students why education is important, and why learning must be respected.

> From: eoin
> Sent: Wednesday, 27 July 2005 9:24 AM
> To: Tara Brabazon
> Subject: COM102
>
> Hi, I enrolled in COM102 but I wasn't able to make it to the first lecture.
>
> I was just wondering how I should go about signing up for a tutorial or anything else important I missed.
>
> Thanks
>
> Eoin

Before Eoin sent this email, he had three months' holiday between semesters. The tutorial lists were outside my door for the month preceding the first lecture. They were still there when this young man sent his email. The 'anything else important I missed' clearly did not include the lecture itself. Access was not Eoin's problem. Motivation was the key to his behaviour. Until this issue is explored, broadband, interactive discussion fora and i-lectures are pointless.

I have an even more disastrous example of how the systematic disregard and disrespect of education, reading, writing and thinking has facilitated disrespectful behaviour from students.

> From: Bernie
> Sent: Friday, 12 May 2006 3:34 AM
> To: Tara Brabazon
> Subject: MCC106
>
> My name is Bernie and I am enrolled in MCC106. You would not know me, as even though I am enrolled I have not been coming to uni at all this semester. I have not submitted any work that has been due as honestly I had lost interest in university after some events that

> transpired in recent times in my life made it seem irrelevant. However, I now realise this has been a big mistake and I really want to complete this unit and therefore my course at the end of this year. I am very interested in completing this unit even though it is for credit points towards graduation. Is there any way that something can be worked out so I do not fail this unit?
>
> I am eager to come in and see you at any time to discuss this [I am unavailable tomorrow Friday 12th due to work], which I think is the best thing to do. I just hope I have not left it too late.
>
> Can you please get back to me and advise me of anything that can be done?
>
> Regards,
>
> Bernie

The best internet-mediated delivery, the most interactive of web sites, cannot forge the connection and passion that is necessary to create and facilitate expansive and exciting education. Compare Eoin's and Bernie's statements with those of Joseph.

> From: Joseph
> Sent: Thursday, 23 December 2004 11:00 AM
> To: Tara Brabazon
> Subject: merry christmas
>
> Dear tara
>
> thank you so much for an interesting and memorable semester.
>
> my other two second semester units were a little dry and boring, so i was very fortunate to have had you in com102. your passion, enthusiasm and commitment to the unit was fascinating and a huge pleasure for me to be a part of. your time and care for your students was also admirable.

> i must say, most tutors and lecturers i've had in these last few years all lack these attributes – probably because of a variety reasons (remuneration standards maybe) – and kind of dont give a stuff about the people they're teaching, they just go to uni and go home. but you, you're completely the opposite.
>
> at the start, i never thought i would get a good mark in this unit, probably because of my perceived lack of critical thinking, but you expanded my scope and horizons immensely so i could take things i saw in society and life and think about them more deeply. thank you so much for this. you've given me more depth in my thinking capabilities and changed the way i look at certain things within cultures and sub-cultures (or society in general)!
>
> i hope my major essay didn't let you down greatly and that it met your expectations. i was so keen on finishing the year on a high that i really wanted the essay to be of a high standard.
>
> i was just wondering, when is the best time for me to collect it?
>
> take care tara and all the best
>
> Joseph

Joseph was thinking about difference, and thinking differently. He focused his research on sport through the semester, particularly Italian football. We applied media and cultural studies theories to this topic. He was motivated to learn. He was challenged and often tentative, but was successful. It was teaching, learning and curriculum that changed his world view, not software, hardware or applications. Joseph used digital resources well, but they did not make him a conscious and successful student. Instead, he was motivated, and he did not miss sessions of teaching. His decisions were not based on access to content, but motivation in the context.

There has never been a more important time to create an informed political culture.[41] Such an objective requires considered political attention addressing the differential access

41 The function of the university in building democracy and citizenship has been discussed by Tomas Englund, 'Higher education, democracy and citizenship – the democratic potential of the university', *Studies in Philosophy and Education*, Vol. 21, 2000, pp. 281–87 and Sven-Eric Liedman's 'Democracy, knowledge, and imagination', *Studies in Philosophy and Education*, Vol. 23, 2002, pp. 353–59.

to educational environments and the social, intellectual and physical tools required to create a scholarly journey of achievement. The results gained from increasing access to the digital environment cannot be guaranteed in advance. It is the start of learning, not the end. As Neil Postman has argued,

> Poverty is a great educator. Having no boundaries and refusing to be ignored, it mostly teaches hopelessness. But not always. Politics is also a great educator. Mostly it teaches, I am afraid, cynicism. But not always. Television is a great educator as well. Mostly it teaches consumerism. But not always.[42]

Postman's confirmation of education without guarantees is important. Digitization means that we too often think in binarized terms: yes/no, on/off, literate/illiterate. Networks of (analogue) subtlety are required. Consumerism is tethered to technology innovation, change and use. The endless desire for 'the new' devalues the relevance and importance of 'the old'. Attention should be placed to power, representation and identity before issues of access are addressed.

Ronald Simpson, in reviewing his professional life in universities, believed that his experience has taught him an important lesson. He believed that there are four ways to understand the events in life.

Important and urgent
Important and non urgent
Not important and urgent
Not important and not urgent[43]

Most of us spend far too much time worrying about the urgent, but not important. The week before I wrote these words, I spent two days trying to track down a box of photocopying at my university that I had marked 'Tara to pick up'. For some reason, the administrators did not understand the meaning of 'Tara to pick up' and proceeded to place $3,000 of books and irreplaceable conference papers in internal mail that took two days to work their way through university departments. It made me crazy. I spent two hours in yoga returning evil thoughts to my third eye about what I would like to do with this administrator.

Such thoughts are not the point of universities. If we have a skill to teach our students, it is to be able to differentiate between the urgent and important to ensure that every event and expression has a place and time. In our contemporary workplaces we are so frantically consumed and distracted by crisis management that we miss the

42 N. Postman, *The End of Education* (New York: Vintage Books, 1996), p. ix.

43 R. Simpson, 'Reflections on an academic career', *Innovative Higher Education*, Vol. 26, No. 3, Spring 2002, p. 156–7.

causes of the initial problem. Vocationalism and competency act as a diversion from asking difficult questions, like who is not enrolled in our universities? Does computer-mediated education reinforce or undermine social justice? Stuart Hall expressed how the enthusiasm for cultural studies was implicated in such denials and distractions.

> The need for that analytical, theoretical and imaginative leap into experiences which are different from ours is one which I think cultural studies has lost the impetus to make. In the early stages, perhaps we spoke too much about the working class, about subcultures. Now nobody talks about that at all. They talk about myself, my mother, my father, my friends, and that is, of course, a very selective experience, especially in relation to class.[44]

Just as Orwell's miners preferred sweet, expensive food – just as the Eloi were unable to fix the machines built by earlier generations – we are drawn to the beautiful and easy, and repulsed by the ugly but important. Googling ourselves, our friends and family lets us forget about those who transcend ourselves and our narrow world. It is much easier – and safer – to watch digital Dorian Grays rather than searching for the grotesque portrait in the analogue attic.

---

44 S. Hall, 'Cultural studies and the politics of internationalization: an interview with Stuart Hall by Kuan-Hsing Chen', from D. Morley and K. Chen (eds), *Stuart Hall: Critical Dialogues in Cultural Studies* (London: Routledge, 1996), p. 402.

Section Two
Culture

Chapter three

Stretching flexible learning

Let me tell you about my mornings. I wake at 3am, work on my weekly lectures until 5:15am, and then attend an early morning aerobics class from 6am. By 7:20am, I am in my University office, desperately trying to answer emails faster than they are arriving. I fail. At any particular time, I am between 100 and 300 emails behind where I should be. Unaware of the collective angst being caused, students appreciate the ability to contact their teachers anytime, with any query. While this desire is understandable, it wreaks havoc on an academic's life. I no longer 'do work' at work. I treat my office as a consulting room. The amount of time I am in my office and not seeing students or addressing emails is counted in the minutes, not the hours. Administration and research is done in the morning, evening and weekends. Intense hours of writing, reading and thinking are poached when I could be doing something else, like talking to my family, cleaning the house or – even – relaxing. As the demands of university life have increased over the last decade, my house has got messier. Piles of paper punctuate the carpet. I am always between 30 and 50 hours behind in house cleaning. The gap between putting washing on the line and taking it down is unpredictable and has nothing to do with the dryness of the clothes. In the last intense five years in the academy, I have noticed that, at the 'end' of a working day, it is necessary to push on for one more hour, one more task, when every fibre in my body and brain is screaming exhaustion. This is how it feels being an academic in the contemporary university system. Few talk about it.

The emotional demands of this new extended working day are extraordinary. Let me tell another untellable story. In October 2004, I was in the intense period of 'the week before the essay is due' session with my first year students. There were desperate souls camped outside my office when I arrived at 7:20am, and they were hovering outside my office all day, hoping for a five-minute conversation between postgraduate meetings. Finally, at 5:25pm, the office appeared to clear. It had been a long day. I was beyond exhaustion, reaching the point where my own bones do not have the strength to carry the body weight home. I quietly packed my briefcase.

At 5:29pm, a young woman staggered around my door frame, obviously drunk and clearly upset. She was close to hysterical. She had been 'cutting' herself, slicing and stabbing at her arm with a razor, and told me that she was going home to do it some more. By 7pm, I had managed to calm her, called her father and stopped the tears. I was now much more than exhausted, but disturbed, disoriented and confused about what – precisely – we are meant to be doing in our universities.

Such availability to students – to be their battering ram, dock, iPod and family – is apparently no longer sufficient. Universities are demanding that staff embrace 'flexible learning', which is reified to internet-mediated communication rather than the many potential media and modalities that this phrase could incorporate. This is a particular sort of flexibility. At the moment that our students are at their most alienated, detached and confused, educational administrators[1] believe that they also want the capacity to time-shift their studies and become consumers in our system. In my experience – as someone who teaches rather than someone talking about other people teaching – students want what we all desire: to feel connected to something and someone beyond ourselves, hopefully a person or idea to give us meaning and context.

We are seeing students with incredible emotional challenges in our classrooms. Assuming that 'flexibility' can solve their problems is not only naïve, but dangerous. Most courses include at least one student with personal troubles – who cuts themselves, discovers drugs for the first time or has a complex past that they bring into our classrooms. New university students are not new people. For example, a 'challenging' student enrolled in one of my first year courses. Her attendance was irregular and she appeared to disconnect from teaching staff and her classmates. Her first assignment, which was meant to be a 1,000-word evaluative paper of Charles Leadbeater's *Living on Thin Air*, was 'submitted' to be marked by being pinned to my office door. It was just under 200 words, printed on a second-hand piece of paper without a name or course code. She did not write about Leadbeater. Instead, she presented three atrociously written paragraphs about her life, using metaphors of floating through clouds. This paper was – to put it bluntly – strange. I was concerned, and sent the following email to try and create some positivity and connection with her.

1 Stanley Aronowitz offers a remarkable reading of educational administrators in the current university sector in his book *The Knowledge Factory* (Boston: Beacon Press, 2000). He argued that 'over the past 30 years, administration has become a separate career in academic life', p. 164. He asks 'what are the consequences of administration as a career? First and perhaps foremost, career administrators tend to lose touch with the educational enterprise. Their allegiances and self-conception becomes increasingly corporate as they gradually surrender any pretense of doing consistent writing and teaching', p. 165.

From: Tara Brabazon
To: Jackie
Subject: Hi Jackie
Date: Sun, 16 Apr 2006 07:39:53 +0800

Hi Jackie,

I hope you are well. I'm just checking up on you. Bec just told me that the paper that was pinned to my office door was yours. No problem, we've got it. But all the other students in the course put it in the assignment box – where all the assignments go – for the School of Media, Communication and Culture. I was so worried, because it wasn't stapled, had no assignment sheet attached to the front, and it could have been stolen while I was at my meeting.

I'm just so happy that we've got it and we've worked out what's going on.

Jackie, my suggestion is that I see you weekly until the next assignment is due. Before each lecture and on an overhead, I always put up the hours each week that I can see students, and unfortunately I didn't see you for this assignment. I'm always happy to help in any way.

But can we make sure that I see you to discuss the course once a week, to make sure that all is well? I'm happy to see you at 10:30am every Tuesday through the rest of the semester. I'll make sure that this is your time and no one interrupts our session. Also, Rebecca is in the office for her consultancy times straight after the lecture, and has been all semester. I know she would love to see you.

So please let me know what you would like us to do, to ensure that we can help you get a strong result this semester.

Be well

Tara.

The reply sent a few days later was simply one of the oddest responses from a student I have ever received.

From: Jackie
Sent: Thursday, 20 April 2006 10:16 PM
To: Tara Brabazon
Subject: Hi Tara

Hi Tara,

Thankyou for trying to help but i am not actually retarded or academically challenged, despite what my essay might suggest, i just gave up on that paper and upon realising that no amount of hours sitting in front of my computer were gonna make it any better, decided to just stop wasting my time and hand it in. And as much as it tears at my very soul to receive the lowest mark possible, i would rather that than cause myself unnecessary hours of stress and anxiety, something to which i have been all too familiar with in the last couple of years.

So please don't think that all my assignments are going to be as morbidly degenerate as that one. It was just my first assignment and i had two more which i had also forgotten about which were due the same week. I decided rather than wuss out and ask for an extension i would just accept my responsibilities and get used to it.

By the way sorry for just pinning it on your door, i was in a great hurry to get it in on time and i was still not entirely sure how to hand things in. It will not happen again now that I am clear.

Cheers.

ps. No, this email was <u>not</u> plagiarised.

pps. I'm sorry if this email offends you, I'm sure I'll regret it later. I know you're just trying to help and i do appreciate it alot, but i just didn't want you to expect that i need special treatment. Something else that i am very familiar with. I know it is hard for you to understand my attitude without knowing me at all and I apologise for my forward manner and aggressive defensiveness. I have a lot of trouble accepting help and generally being a nice, decent person. I will try to stop by your office soon though, if you're not totally disgusted at me.

Was this an example of a mistaken or drunken email? How was I meant to respond? What could any of the teaching staff do to help this young woman? What is clear is that if a 1,000-word essay creates 'unnecessary hours of stress and anxiety' then the rest of her university career will be untenable. While the teaching staff did work with this student and she did improve through the semester, it was an incredibly difficult experience. But it was important for Jackie to build social connections before academic analysis could even be attempted.

So here I am placed: in an office with students cutting themselves or complaining about special treatment, an in-box filled with messages promising penis enlargement, and administrators wanting me to be more flexible. As I force myself to leave work, with a bag bulging with forms to complete that were not invented five years ago, I have gained enormously from attending yoga on Saturday and Sunday afternoons. As I lay in corpse pose feeling like death, I realized that educational administrators preaching flexible learning and teaching could learn much from the discipline and rigidity of yoga masters.[2] The disparity between these practices – of building a flexible body and building a flexible classroom – leave me bemused and fascinated. In yoga, a flexible body is created through intense concentration, discipline and motivation. Improvements are measured in years, not hours. In education, a flexible classroom is based on compliance, conforming and competence. This chapter explores the ideological application of 'flexibility' in education, but deploying the metaphoric lessons and structures that yoga – rather than the market economy – provide. If McDonalds, Google, Walmart and Amazon.com can provide a model for business practice in contemporary universities, then there is no reason why alternative models cannot be offered from even more diverse sources. If flexibility is the aim and ideology, then let theorists look at a model for corporeal flexibility that requires no investment in technology, but builds on centuries of knowledge, practice and reflection.

The structure of the chapter mimics the three elements of yoga: pranayama, asanas and savasana. The first stage prepares the body and mind by reflexively considering its position in space and time. The second component – the asanas – activates the hard work required to position and manage our new university students from diverse backgrounds and with diverse needs. As in a yoga class, each body exhibits different strengths and weaknesses in attempting the same postures. Distinct methods are then used to assist the development of an individual's flexibility. The final part, the savasana, peels back the levels of relaxation and contemplation to explore the reasoning for the journey from flexible learning to virtual education, and why internet-based teaching has become the simple solution to profound social and educational problems.

2 There are five paths to yoga discipline. The first is Hatha yoga, moving into Karma yoga, Bakti yoga, Gyana yoga and Raj yoga. I am using Hatha yoga as the basis of my metaphor and model.

Such an exercise is not the joke that it may appear. A study commissioned by Hewlett Packard and conducted by Glenn Wilson, a psychologist at the University of London, confirmed that endless typing at a phone or computer keypad – along with the clearly obsessional checking for text messages – temporarily removes ten points of a user's IQ. Sometimes described as infomaniacs, these digital ditherers are so addicted to checking their in-box and message bank that they are continually distracted and concurrently lacking concentration. Not surprisingly for those of us on the other side of the gender divide, the problem is greatest amongst adult male workers. The hypothesized cause for this drop in IQ is that the constant distraction of messaging and emails prevents concentration on important tasks. Rapid reaction replaces thoughtful reflection. As Wilson confirmed,

> This is a very real and widespread phenomenon ... We have found that infomania, if unchecked, will damage a worker's performance by reducing their mental sharpness.[3]

Concentration is not an innate skill. It is like cardiovascular fitness, strength training and muscular flexibility: it must be developed in incremental stages. Therefore, with educational and work patterns punctuated by the cyclical pattern of incoming messages, precise focus on significant tasks is continually disrupted. The many methods and modes of yoga teach the benefits of quiet, the gift of simplicity and the belief that we have our entire lives to grow, improve and change. Yoga does not separate one part of life from other purposes and goals, but creates a holistic approach to the physical, mental, spiritual and emotional. May our universities accomplish the same synergy by ending the confusion of distraction with productivity.

Prepare your body. Calm your mind. Check your alignment. There is much to do. The mantra is simple: flexibility is built on discipline, concentration and commitment. Work within your limitations.

Pranayama

Breathing, like learning, is a process and behaviour that we naturalize. By unsettling and destabilizing the natural, we relearn what we think we know. Pranayama is a focused breathing through the nostrils, feeding oxygen to the brain rather than the stomach. It encourages the regeneration of the internal organs and a calming of the nervous system by reducing clavicular breathing and activating the diaphragm. It also encourages the repair of a body that has been neglected through shallow breathing. Mental clarity is developed and bodily awareness emerges. Breathing is a basic and assumed practice. Yet most people are supremely inefficient when doing it. Similarly, learning is framed

3 G. Wilson in M. Horsnell, 'Low IQ 2day, m8? It's the technology, stupid', *The Weekend Australian*, 23–24 April 2005, p. 17.

as a straightforward practice, easily malleable and shaped through the ideologies and expectations of the day. Flexibility begins with the breath. Learning begins with assumptions. This component of the chapter unravels the suppositions pouring from the fount of flexibility.

'Flexible' learning is becoming important for undergraduates in an era when postgraduate education is increasingly regulated and timetabled. This means that the least experienced students are neglected through the imperative for flexibility, while the most experienced and successful students – our doctoral candidates – gain consistent and regulated attention. The necessity for multiple supervisors, review panels, progress reports, annual reports and reviewed programs of study are increasing the surveillance and reducing the freedom of postgraduates to develop intellectual mobility and self-sufficiency. Concurrently, undergraduates have the option of fully online study, streamed lectures and no need to attend class at all. Germaine Greer even welcomed such innovations, writing that 'in 2006, it would make more sense to issue the lectures on DVD, and spend the hour in the lecture room dealing with student's questions'.[4] Those of us who actually teach – and have taught through the changes of the last decade – know that such a scheme is not only impractical, but offensive. With students not reading materials and rarely committing to any of the rigours and discipline of scholarship, they do not actually possess the framework or intellectual background to formulate questions on the set topic. Greater debate is required not only on educational leadership but on the mentoring and modeling of scholarly behaviour. Although it is unpopular to admit, student-centred learning is an excuse for cheap learning.[5] The 'convenience' to the student – which appeals to those who want an easy ride through their education – is cheating them of an authentic, passionate, confusing, challenging, complicated but precious learning encounter. All students deserve teacher's time, patience, expertise and curricula skill. As shown in the first section of this book, the expansion of literacy demands and the increasing availability of information requires more discipline, more effort, more imagination, more commitment and more scaffolding from teachers and

4 G. Greer, 'Another hard day in the library', *The Guardian*, 1 February 2006, p. 6.

5 In their interviews with university staff, Tania Lewis, Simon Marginson and Ilana Snyder confirmed that 'in all of the universities we studied, managers and academics alike talked of the need to move towards a model of flexible learning, emphasizing in particular a student rather than teacher-centred approach to education. In the case of management, the rhetoric of student-centred learning tended to be seen as going hand in hand with a market-driven, enterprise model of the university … In addition, many managers see the notion of a democratized, student-centred learning model as breaking down the boundaries between university learning and learning in so-called "real world" settings', from 'The networked university? Technology, culture and organizational complexity in contemporary higher education', *Higher Education Quarterly*, Vol. 59, No. 1, January 2005, p. 66.

librarians.[6] It is easy to place materials online. It is much harder to teach and learn how to manage, interpret and analyze digital text, sound and images. To improve teaching and learning – to create a flexibility *of mind* rather than a flexibility *in time* – requires a statement of clear goals and outcomes. Once these are established, the approach and method can be determined. Competence summons different strategies to excellence. Convenience enacts a different agenda to disciplined commitment.

Flexibility has replaced a series of important initiatives that was used in the analogue age to increase the social range and diversity of people who attend university. The running of twilight lectures, increasing the opening hours of libraries and telephone-based tutorials, sometimes termed teleconferences, were all ways to assist students who juggled the demands of family, work and study. However, it is often the case that mature-aged students, those with the most burdens on their time, are also the most committed to undergraduate courses. Throughout my teaching career, it has been the mature-aged students who have attended all the lectures and tutorials, and then mobilized all the other opportunities and facilities that flexible learning provides. Then there are other students who are playing (with) the system, using a busy life(style) as an excuse to mess with their education, demanding flexibility because they have made poor choices.

Date: Fri, 3 Sep 2004 15:07:51 +1000 (EST)
From:
Subject: TUTES
To: t.brabazon@murdoch.edu.au

Dear Tara,

I am enroled to attend you Cultural Studies Tute on Tuesday morning at 8am. Unfortunately I work night fill and have been unable to make it as yet, I was wondering if it would be at all possible to change my tute time to the one diectally after the lecture on Monday mornings. Hopefully this is a feasable option and does not disrupt your Tute layout at all.

Regards

6 Elliot Soloway and Raven Wallace argued that 'unless teachers and students (and parents and administrators) are willing to invest healthy doses of time, effort, and good humor, searching the Web may well not be an educationally productive activity, from 'Does the Internet support student inquiry? Don't ask', *Communications of the ACM*, Vol. 40, No. 5, May 1997.

This email was sent to me at the end of week five in a thirteen-week course. One month before the semester started, I placed the tutorial times on a noticeboard for students to pick an appropriate session for their timetables. There were six tutorials offered. The student signed *herself* into the 8am tutorial, along with 25 other students. The other tutorials – including the one after the lecture – were all (over)full. I did allow the student to attend a later class on Tuesday, horrified at the idea of her missing any more of the course.

Many questions jut from this young woman's email. Why had she chosen night fill as a part-time job? Why – if her timetable was so circumscribed – did she not sign up for a tutorial of choice before semester commenced? If she has difficulty balancing work and university, why did she not enrol in the distance education mode of the course?[7] The greatest flexibility in our pedagogical spectrum is through distance education. These print-based materials are geared for those who are without the ability to come onto campus, perhaps through physical mobility or economic limitations. The curriculum specifically addresses these needs. Print on paper is flexible: it can move through time and space. Any student with a postbox and a space to read can complete a course. This is flexible learning. Courses requiring broadband downloading capabilities will never have the accessibility and mobility of print on paper. But this student chose to study on campus, and yet was unable to attend classes.

For weeks after receiving this email, I was shocked and concerned. When unpicking my emotions and calming myself (pranayama-style), I think I was most angry, not that she missed the tutorials, but that she had decided to place greater attention and emphasis on part-time work rather than a university education. With so many students desperate for a chance to gain an education, the idea that this opportunity would be treated so flippantly, without any regard for how others may judge her actions, is remarkable. When this young woman attended the later tutorial on Tuesday, the group – which was bonded at this stage of the semester – did not appreciate her commentary as it lacked any understanding of the first month of the course. She was blithely unaware of their displeasure and continued to speak without a detailed awareness of semiotic subtleties or intricate theories of media audiences. She approached the tutorial with an open mouth, not an open mind.

This student would gain from flexible learning, the ability to time-shift university classes or listen to sessions through online streaming and not be reliant on a fixed time and place for education. The question is, should this ill-disciplined and unscholarly behaviour be validated? Should laziness at worst, or an inability to evaluate and prioritize social

7 Lynnette Porter has instigated an outstanding presentation of the many modes and methods of distance education in her book *Creating the Virtual Classroom: Distance Learning with the Internet* (New York: John Wiley and Sons, 1997). She states that 'distance learning is not a panacea for all educational or training ills, but it does offer additional possibilities for educating and training more people than can be easily and efficiently accommodated in more traditional settings', p. 1.

responsibilities at best, be endorsed by university structures? In her case, I moved her into the later tutorial. She only managed to attend two of these later sessions through the semester. She completed all the written work but included few references, demonstrating little course reading was completed. Not surprisingly, when she chose a topic for her main essay, her focus was Paris Hilton. No course reading, terms or concepts were used. There is something appropriate in the fact that a woman on night-fill, with no self-discipline or awareness of why she was at university, would select a 'successful' celebrity as her 'research' focus, a person famous for being famous.

Such university student expectations of teachers are founded and based on the expectations of education at high school. A customer-service culture creates an environment of complaint and grievance.

> The potential risk of complaint by parents and students is high, and perhaps dangerously high in relation to 'stressed-out' Year 12 students [those in their final year of high school] whom teachers report are the greatest (and most demanding) users of teacher-student e-mail communication at this time. Already, teachers report receiving e-mails from year 12 students at all times of the day and night, including weekends and holidays. They expect to be answered … now! What will happen when the teacher is out, away, or just plain tired and fails to respond? What if the student feels their major assessment mark has suffered due to the lack of response by the teacher? Accusations of professional negligence? These are the areas of threat to job security, especially in independent schools where some students/parents have unrealistic expectations and/or undue influence.[8]

Flexible learning – when simplified and reduced to internet-mediated education – must be introduced carefully and critically. It involves a major and troubling shift in educational expectations and twists attention away from student motivation. Consider this definition from Macquarie University in Australia:

> Flexible learning aims to meet individual needs by providing choices that allow students to meet their own educational requirements in ways suiting their individual circumstances.[9]

Such an ideology is more relevant to shoe shopping than education. Similarly, Lawrence Beard and Cynthia Harper value internet-based instruction as allowing students 'to complete course work at their convenience in the privacy of their own home'.[10]

8 S. White, 'How would you like it? E-mail use is becoming a problem for teachers', *Online Opinion*, 29 January 2003, http://www.onlineopinion.com.au/print.asp?article=963, accessed on 30 January 2003.

9 'Flexible learning, what is it?', Macquarie University, http://www.cfl.mq.edu.au/html/flex1.htm, accessed 31 August 2004.

10 L. Beard and C. Harper, 'Student perceptions of online versus on campus instruction', *Education*, Vol. 122, No. 4, 2002, p. 658.

The language choice is crucial here. The emphasis is on individuals and choice, not communities and context. The role and function of groups and collectives – sharing a time and place – discussing the issues of the day is no longer a priority. Students become consumers, selecting generic competencies for their shopping trolley, dodging around the issues and ideas that might require more than a passing glance. Yet this truth is masked as flexibility, becomes confused with access.

As shown in the last chapter, access and social responsibility in education is a crucial concern. The importance of recognizing multiple entry points into degrees, prior learning and cross-crediting of units and programmes is pivotal to contemporary universities, particularly in nations with large migrant populations. It is important to recognize the learning conducted in other countries as being relevant and equivalent to contemporary educational initiatives. However, there are three (official) definitions of flexible learning that have nothing to do with entry requirements, support of diverse equity groups or validating and enlarging literacies:

> Less reliance on face-to-face teaching and more emphasis on guided independent learning; teachers become facilitators of the learning process directing students to appropriate resources, tasks and learning outcomes.
> Greater reliance on high quality learning resources using a range of technologies.
> Greater opportunities to communicate outside traditional teaching times.[11]

The assumptions behind these statements are what will, over time, lead to declining standards in universities. The notion that students must be taught – with discipline, clarity and precision – about standards of international scholarship is outside of the brief of flexible learning. As someone who has taught first year university students every year of my professional life, it is clear that there is a sizeable group of students – anywhere between 20 and 50 per cent – who have great difficulty with reading and writing skills and require time-consuming but crucial remedial attention to these abilities before higher level interpretations can be explored. This is not a problem isolated to the 2000s and triggered by Google. Actually, Graham Gibbs reported in the late 1970s,

> As an assignment my students were asked to show me their notes from a chapter in a 'How to Study' book concerned with note-taking. About half the students had copied out, word for word, a statement from the text advising them to always write their notes in their own words![12]

---

11 'Flexible learning, what is it?', *op. cit.*

12 G. Gibbs, 'Can students be taught how to study?' in D. Billing (ed.), *Course Design and Student Learning* (Guildford: University of Surrey, 1978), p. 76.

We cannot assume that students intrinsically know how to write notes, read scholarly monographs or formulate a thesis, antithesis and synthesis. We cannot assume that they can manage their time.

> From: Katherine
> Sent: Wednesday, 12 April 2006 10:43 AM
> To: Tara Brabazon
> Subject: assignment
>
> Hey Tara
>
> I know this is last- minute but unfortunately i'm a last minute girl. I need help with my assignment. I'm getting confused with the topic and I can't seem to find good references, or enough references for the topic.
>
> When are your consulting hours? Because I desperately need help.
>
> Love Kate

Yes, this email was sent not only on the day an assignment was due, but five hours before the deadline. Every student was provided with an already photocopied collection of readings, but Kate could not find 'good references'. Flexibility will not help Kate. Time management will. Although the first paper she submitted to this course was poor, I intervened in her 'last minute girl' reputation in the month before the major assignment. Before she could be taught about creative industries, she needed to be taught about the demands, discipline and rigours of university-level scholarship. At its most basic, students need to be taught dependently before they can explore independence. Perhaps the most dangerous situation is when teachers make assumptions that students can complete a task that they do not understand, and do not have the language to express their miscomprehension.

The second assumption of flexible learning is that 'new' technologies intrinsically create a productive learning environment. The convergence of high quality learning resources and technology is not only neophiliacal but denies the history of education. Technological platforms require care in their introduction. Only the applications that assist student learning should be mobilized, and this requires clear learning rationales to be determined. Technology does not create high quality learning resources: teachers and librarians do. Their expertise then evaluates the mode and type of applications and programmes to be used. Technology does not create learning. Teachers do not create learning. Students do not create learning. Instead, the space between students and teachers summons the transformative dialogue of an educational encounter. In that space may be an internet connection or a PowerPoint presentation, but just as likely it could be a soccer ball or a guitar. The best of teachers are able to deploy diverse sources to tease open these spaces between teachers, students and learning outcomes. They are not being valued in a 'flexible' age.

From: jo
Sent: Thursday, 23 June 2005 11:06 AM
To: Tara Brabazon
Subject: Thank you for Digital Hemlock!

Hi Tara

My name's Jo, I'm 36 (argh) and am a relatively new fulltime TAFE teacher of media and marketing in Sydney (finishing my 2nd semester). I left the corporate world (was an IT Journalist and PR specialist), completed my undergrad degree by Distance Ed (more successfully than I'd imagined), and am now on 'scholarship' to do my Grad Dip VET while teaching fulltime.

I discovered your book while collecting materials for my final uni essay on teaching strategies. What a breath of fresh air your material is already! I am surrounded by teachers who swear by the powerpoint and overhead. I even had a prac assessor tell me I might want to improve my teaching by having overheads!

It has got to the point where modules are being developed with teacher guides including overheads as the resource material. Nobody wants to entertain the notion of going outside the boundaries – I find it incredibly frustrating. That said, there are two other teachers in my section who have asked me to put together a booklet of alternative methods of teaching. My challenge will be to create an alternative one week in three, every time you teach a course.

I am the only teacher who students ask at the end of the semester what courses I'll be taking the following semester so they can choose them.

I hate overheads. I pretty much hate powerpoint. Instead of an exam in my TVET class which was focused on news media research (year 12 students) I had a treasure hunt where all the students had one hour within college grounds to complete their research. With some basic ground rules the students were assessed and I am confident their ability is really knowledge and not a memory dump.

I do provide my students with my email address, and encourage them to use it with a promise I will respond within 24 hours. This is because I am not on campus very much to receive messages. I have recently decided against putting class notes online because I feel students should be coming to class. If a student misses a class and has initiative enough to contact me for the notes within a reasonable period, then I am happy to email them – however, due to the nature of our work, these notes are typically limited and don't reflect the full amount of learning that happens in a session. For example, my notes might say 'Discussion: Corby media coverage/public response'. I also of course have lots of video/audio materials which can't be disseminated this way.

My students rarely miss a class. I figure if I'm tired at the end of the day, so are they. I find it interesting, however, that I am grappling with the appropriateness of my methods. Teachers in my institution seem to like to hold power over students. The students who manipulate the inconsistencies in the system have encouraged this response. I have been concerned that I might become too personable with students by continuing to seem to be 'on call' via email, for example, and during our discussion of media where I relate instances from my past experience as a journalist.

Your book has reassured me that being personable does not mean unprofessional. I seek to become an inspirational teacher, and as such I won't settle for less.

Jo is a remarkable teacher. She is the embodiment of a reflective, considerate educator who recognizes that the 'delivery' of courses does not equal teaching. Pivotally, she is undertaking professional development and thinking about media in its diversity and complexity, rather than only utilizing those components that can be slotted into a PowerPoint presentation. Jo also highlights the greatest challenge in implementing flexible learning.

This final assumption about flexible learning, which also troubled Jo, is with regard to time. Through the last ten years, staff have continued to add tasks to an already filled teaching and research day. The clutch of arriving emails takes between two and three hours each day to answer. Sent by students 'outside traditional teaching times', they must be answered in a scholar's (lengthening) working day. The advantage of lectures and tutorials is that they are highly efficient – Fordist – modes of education. The cost of a post-Fordist education that fits into a student's 'lifestyle' is the efficiency of university academic work. There is never 'off' time. There is little space to – cleanly and without interruption – research and develop new ideas. The cost of student flexibility is staff productivity.

Concurrently, the reliance on online streamed lectures as the basis for 'flexible learning' raises major concerns for those students who do not have regular use of an internet connection. Yet a discussion of this problem is displaced, quickly and ruthlessly, onto individual staff members.

> Multimodal units will require iLecture ... Ensure instructions are included in your Unit Information and Learning Guide for off-campus students who are unable to access the iLecture system and need a copy made of the recordings.[13]

This institutional sleight of hand is subtle and disturbing. Not only must staff change how they deliver lectures for the requirements of i-lectures,[14] but they are then responsible for reproducing an analogue tape of these sessions, so that individuals have 'choice' and 'flexibility'.[15] These off-campus students have had purpose-built study guides and materials developed for them, using the most flexible of media: print on paper. Now that such a medium is discredited because it does not involve a screen, staff must enact the time-consuming – and actually pointless – task of individually copying their own lectures onto analogue tape or compact disc.

Policies of flexible learning are triggered by the changing function of universities in society.[16] We are now servicing the workforce, not knowledge, scholarship, citizenship

---

13 'Updating units to the flexible model', Murdoch University, http://www.murdoch.edu.au/admin/cttees/flic/convert.html, accessed 31 July 2004.

14 The i-lecture platform is addressed in the next chapter.

15 Stephen Brookfield has also monitored this strategy. He realized that 'the concept of vocation serves the interests of those who want to run colleges efficiently and profitably while spending the least amount of money and employing the smallest number of staff that they can get away with', from *Becoming a Critically Reflective Teacher* (San Francisco: Jossey-Bass Books, 1995), p. 16.

16 Tania Lewis, Simon Marginson and Ilana Snyder described this change as 'a period of rapid transformation that has seen notions of academic collaboration, knowledge sharing and community engagement jostling for ideological airspace with discourses of managerialism, entrepreneurialism and marketization. Added to this complex and often volatile mix is the more

or social justice. In meeting students' *needs* and granting them a *choice* in course delivery, academic time is spent keeping this new student-customer satisfied. The displacement of retraining costs of a business's staff onto Universities has been concurrent with reductions in funding by government to the educational sector and the permeation of information technology. Together these changes confirm that more students can be taught more cheaply and may not even have to attend the campus. Not well documented is the fact that students must copy and print their own materials from the internet, shifting the costs from the university to the individual.[17] The cost of m-learning – mobile learning – allows spatial flexibility but does not acknowledge that discipline and motivation is often linked and locked into a routine with clearly specified expectations and outcomes. The cost of transforming universities into commercial enterprises, with students as clients and consumers, will only be revealed in the long term. Scholarship is not training. The quest for knowledge is often not equivalent to – or aligned with – the quest for profit. What is required, particularly in the first few years of university education, is structure and discipline not flexible modes and time-shifting. It is unpopular to assert, but flexibility must be earned. Such a statement works against the administrative and political truths of our era of training, skill and competencies, but it does have some support at least at the level of teacher education. Lorraine Ling, Eva Burman and Maxine Cooper recognized that,

> Teachers and student teachers require a structure which will provide them with the ability to reflect upon the teaching in values in education and with models against which they may confront their own value system and attempts to equate it with one based upon a recognized theoretical framework.[18]

If such an imperative is necessary for teachers and student teachers, then why must undergraduate education be punctuated by flexibility and time-shifting, rather than structures, models and systems?

More students are attending our universities now than at any point in history. Courses and classrooms are overflowing. Resources are scarce, academic staff have less time to

---

recent push towards reconceptualizing universities as informational and network organizations', from 'The network university? Technology, culture and organizational complexity in contemporary higher education', *Higher Education Quarterly*, Vol. 59, No. 1, January 2005, p. 58.

17 Rob Phillips realized the consequences of web-based learning when he stated that 'the online approach also saves on printing costs to the department, but only by disadvantaging students, by shifting print costs to them', from 'What research says about learning on the Internet', http://cleo.murdoch.edu.au/aset/confs/edtech98/pubs/articles//phillips.html, accessed on 5 May 1999.

18 L. Ling, E. Burman and M. Cooper, 'The Australian Study', from J. Stephenson, L. Ling, E. Burman and M. Cooper (eds), *Values in Education* (London: Routledge, 1998), p. 59.

conduct professional development to render their teaching more efficient. Every new technological innovation – internet-mediated asynchronous communication, internet-mediated digital synchronous communication, i-lectures and podcasting – is seen to solve the 'problem' of lectures. David Hearnshaw, in his dystopically titled article 'Will podcasting finally kill the lecture?' offers a glimpse of this future.

> The dream of swapping the weekly lecture with a podcast may be as attractive to the lecturer as it is to the time-strapped student keen to replace attendance at lectures with work or social obligations. Podcasting, where students download the latest lecture to listen to on their MP3 player in their own time, seems to have all the right credentials. Proponents infer that students will achieve more through this style of delivery – self-paced, flexible and convenient. These qualities are undeniable, but can podcasting really deliver?[19]

Once more, a technological change in learning is justified through flexibility and convenience, so that it does not disrupt students' 'social obligations'. Hearnshaw argues that 'an effective replacement for lectures can be based around an audio presentation if, ironically, it mimics a lecture'.[20] So, the podcast is more effective if it is 'like' a lecture. The logical next question would be, why not simply utilize a lecture?

If inexperienced students are expected to be independent learners, responsible for their own time and scholarship, then there will be consequences. Failure rates will be high.[21] Because of 'student-centred learning', the blame for this failure is the individual, not the institution. If flexibility is the trigger for this agenda, then blame will be the mechanism through which failure will be justified, not the marketized education system or the ideology on which it feeds. Stephen Alessi and Stanley Trollip realized that 'students will make errors and frequently be unaware that they have remade them'.[22] An error is only an error if it is recognized. Without disciplined attention from teachers to these vulnerable students, errors, mistakes, inaccuracies and mis-interpretations will be perpetuated. They will fail, and they will not know why.

The issue of teaching absentee students means that the World Wide Web becomes an easy way to reduce the pressure on facilities, ignore the training issues of staff,

---

19 D. Hearnshaw, 'Will podcasting finally kill the lecture?', *The Guardian*, 19 September 2006.

20 *Ibid.*

21 In 2004, Middlesex University staff faced questions from senior managers if more than 15 per cent of students failed a module. Staff were required to write a report to their academic group chair to explain the failure rate. Please refer to 'Middlesex staff "pressured not to fail students"', *The Guardian*, 13 August 2004, http://education.guardian.co.uk/administration/story/0,9860,1281913,00.html, accessed on 13 August 2004.

22 S. Alessi and S. Trollip, *Computer-based Instruction: Methods and Developments* (New Jersey: Prentice Hall, 1991), p. 7.

and – instead of addressing motivational issues – removing students from the campus altogether to create a virtual university. Promoting generic attributes and group work is a way to 'manage' staff time, so that a single mark for the group is sufficient. It is odd and sad, but the most strained and stressful meetings that occur in our workplaces are not focused on the threats of neo-liberalism and 'flexibility,' or the impact of the market on tertiary education. Always the worst meeting each year involves the allocation of workload. Times are tough. A full-time staff load in one of my former departments was 800 points for a year, where a two-hour lecture equates to two points. It takes many lectures to gain a full load. Invariably, some paradigms and disciplines fill their load easily. Others do not. At one meeting, a senior staff member was attempting to fill up her load with (any) tutorials. She stated that 'I can teach any first year course, as long as I stay a couple of weeks ahead of the students'. I had to close my mouth from the amazement and shock. Universities are the embodiment of the best, most difficult and challenging knowledge, taught by experts, to the brightest of the generation. That is our project. Staff with expertise gained over decades not days are needed to teach these great students. They deserve no less.

Tough decisions must be made. From 2002 to 2004, I had to address how the funding reductions were also reducing the options for students. There was no part-time teaching budget available to me in these years. I not only lectured to hundreds of students, but tutored them and marked their papers. I have no problem with this level of commitment, except the question of time. Even in these conditions, the undergraduate students did extremely well, but I had to make serious choices. Although having taught in and with effectively designed web-based courses since 1997, I decided to remove the bulk of this material and the interactive discussion fora. The rationale for my decision was time and quality control. I realized that I did not have an extra hour each day to teach and monitor the discussion list for the course. I could not commit to this space and guarantee its standards, so I removed it. While universities around the world were increasing their online component, I disabled mine because of budgeting cuts. I assembled priorities around face to face teaching and embedded this directive in curricula decisions. Adding one more hour to a 14 hour day – every day of the semester – was not possible.

Instead of discussing flexibility, with all its attendant ideologies of consumerism and choice, I placed attention on student motivation. A motivated student will do anything – overcome any obstacle – to gain an education. I have taught students from the poorest of backgrounds who have overcome incredible challenges. My favourite example is a student who wrote a first class honours dissertation on her family's kitchen table and on a park bench between casual shifts at McDonalds. She never missed a meeting with me, and went on to complete a doctorate, having attained a scholarship. She was not successful because she was flexible. She was successful because of discipline and hard work. Teaching and learning strategies commence with such motivation. Listening to a streamed online lecture does not facilitate the wonder and energy of learning. Completing computer-based drills does not activate enthusiasm and energy at the passion and challenge of knowledge.

Student-centred learning must not – implicitly or overtly – discredit the expertise of scholars. As Brookfield realized, 'students know teachers have particular expertise, experience, skill, and knowledge. To pretend otherwise is to insult students' intelligence and to create a tone of mistrust from the outset'.[23] Educational cultures, particularly at universities, are not environments of equivalence. University education is built on a hierarchy. Power imbalances are the grammar of universities. Denying the expertise and scholarship that has created academic excellence in the name of student-centred learning or flexibility is to lie to our students. The proletarianization of teaching work, facilitated through a technocratic consciousness, has transformed education into a discussion about the distribution of resources, not the activation of social change. To create what Aronowitz and Giroux described as 'a language of possibility'[24] requires an authentic recognition of the inequalities and injustices that confront students as they move through the university system. This meta-knowledge of meaning systems places information and disciplines in a socio-cultural context.

Greater attention is required on professional development, and less on the intrinsic and assumed value of technological innovations. Internet-based education, being sold on the basis of flexibility, is facilitating poor behaviour from students. When asked in a university survey, 'What have you gained from studying units with internet-based learning that you have not gained from more traditional approaches?', their replies were chilling.

> I have gained more practical knowledge of computers and how to use them in the workforce.
>
> Flexibility – can work from home; can fill in breaks; effectively can overload on units.
>
> More freedom to do other things. It doesn't seem as time consuming.[25]

These statements are not great testaments to flexible education. While the first point is an interesting one, and internet-based education does increase digital literacies, the rationale for this expertise is workplace needs. The other two comments are damaging and disturbing. The flexibility encouraged through online units facilitates bad behaviour,

---

23 S. Brookfield, *Becoming a Critically Reflective Teacher* (San Francisco: Jossey-Bass Books, 1995), p. 6.

24 S. Aronowitz and H. Giroux, *Education Under Siege* (Massauchusetts: Bergin and Garvey Publishers, 1985), p. x.

25 'Student IBL Survey Report', http://www.curtin.edu.au/home/Allen/we3/igt/tool21.html, accessed on 9 July 2002.

permitting overloading of units and the ability to make education slot into a lifestyle. This lifestyle university may fit into post-Fordism, but higher learning requires effort, commitment and focus.

At its most effective, Pranayama re-energizes the body, creating both corporeal health and mental acuity. Flexible educators need to learn this lesson and bring the body back to teaching and learning. Sherry Shapiro, summoning her expertise as a teacher and a dancer, realized that the goal is 'a pedagogy where the body/subject as a lived medium becomes part of the curriculum'.[26] As we reach the end of our focused breathing session, amazed at the assumptions that are circulating through education, there is a realization that flexible learning, as it is currently framed, is focused on time-shifting studies and displacing students from campus. Far less attention is placed on *what* is learnt through flexible methods. Not asked is *who* is learning and *why*. That is the task of the next part of this chapter.

Asanas

Asanas are the yoga exercises that stretch and flex each part of the body. The goal is slow, but lifelong, improvement. It is a system of postures that are moved through in a methodical and precise order, with the aim of becoming aware of the function of each muscle in the body. The goal is to make the muscles and the mind conscious of their positioning in space. Comparison with others in the class is not the purpose of the asanas. Competitive yoga is a paradox, not a tautology. The aim is to practise, improve and feel better about the self in the world. While it is possible to practise asanas individually, the best way is to have a teacher who carefully and precisely guides the students through the movements and their meaning. The subtlety of yoga, adjusting the positioning of an arm, hip or knee, requires direct and experienced guidance. Asanas twist the body in a different way than that existing in our daily lives. The aim of these postures is not to create rapid change, but to carefully extend the potentials of the body.

My rule of teaching has always been to begin where the students are, rather than where I want them to be. Asanas work from a similar principle. Each person has different flexibilities: start from a comfortable stretch, breathe and extend further. It is a gradual, evocative process, with tangible rewards. This metaphor for flexibility, inspired through the intense work and concentration of the asanas, offers a powerful model to understand the effort required to make our university system malleable for the diverse students entering our campuses.

Yoga leads the body through postures never normally considered, defamiliarizing the relationship between 'normal' movements and behaviours. Similarly, there is a default

26 S. Shapiro, *Pedagogy and the Politics of the Body: A Critical Praxis* (New York: Garland Publishing, 1999), p. 9.

position rarely discussed that universities train middle class students for middle class jobs. Our structures, assessments, curriculum and language are embedded in middle class practices, beliefs and ideas. The need to move from this position of comfort – to stretch – and expand our visions and postures is necessary if educators are to embrace flexibility as a social agenda, not only as an excuse for the introduction of new technology and applications to reinforce the values of those already in power.

The tradition of undergraduate university education from the United Kingdom continues to punctuate the wider global system. Most degrees were awarded to members of the middle and upper classes, who entered universities at 18 and 19 after completing an established curriculum at secondary education. They would take an honours degree in three years and enter the labour market into a relatively high paying white-collar job and commence or continue the path to social mobility. This narrative explains why universities, and particularly books about universities, are nostalgic formations. Even when John Henry Newman published *The Idea of the University* in 1852, he was writing about the Oxbridge system from the 1830s. He was arguing against the professionalism, credentialing and specialization that he believed was infiltrating the university system.

> Now this is what some great men are very slow to allow; they insist that Education should be confined to some particular and narrow end, and should issue in some definite work, which can be weighed and measured. They argue as if everything, as well as every person, had its price; and that where there has been a great outlay, they have a right to expect a return in kind. This they call making Education and Instruction 'useful,' and 'Utility' becomes their watchword. With a fundamental principle of this nature, they very naturally go on to ask, what there is to show for the expense of a University.[27]

The debate about the level and role of vocationalism in universities has existed for centuries. What is liberating about Newman's words is that he continually stressed the connections between knowledges and disciplines, and the imperative to teach this link to undergraduates.

Education history offers unique challenges. To study earlier modes and rationales for higher education is not only productive, but politically revelatory. The current system, dogged by the languages of neo-liberalism, managerialism and profit, is distanced from the humanist – but nostalgic – model offered by Cardinal Newman. By the end of the nineteenth century, the purpose of universities became obvious: to reinforce the grip of those holding power, and to simplify the teaching and learning experience to 'imparting' knowledge, rather than the reflexive interpretation of material. John Henry Newman affirmed the importance of a liberal education, as it created an environment where an interest in scholarship and learning would be sustained through life. By creating

27 J. Newman, *The Idea of the University* (Washington: Regnery Publishing, 1999), p. 139.

an 'inward endowment',[28] rather than immediate gratification and use, universities affirmed a commitment to knowledge. While Newman's work has famous passages that are regularly quoted, it is important to grasp the complex context of his argument. His words are trapped between the traditions of the Victorian era and the challenges of the industrial revolution. The need for universities to (either) make gentlemen or advance science shadows the book's theses. For Newman, a liberal education trained the mind, just as physical education honed the body.

> A habit of mind is formed which lasts through life, of which the attributes are, freedom, equitableness, calmness, moderation, and wisdom … This then I would assign as the special fruit of the education furnished at a University, as contrasted with other places of teaching or modes of teaching. This is the main purpose of a University in its treatment of its students.[29]

This vision of education was already disappearing as Newman wrote about it. What makes his work interesting is that there is no sense that university education was aimed beyond the elite. The assumed body of important knowledge was rarely specified, but consensually acknowledged and agreed by the educated. These unspoken assumptions have resonance within the contemporary higher education system, with the institution betraying these historical origins.

Most surprising in the review of the historical education material from the nineteenth and early twentieth century is the easy suppositions made about students. Abraham Flexner, writing in 1930, had witnessed the arrival of increasing numbers of students who seemed less able to manage the rigours of university life.

> In our efforts to satisfy the varied and changeable tastes and needs of the many, we have for the time being to a considerable degree lost sight of the importance of solid and coherent – though not inflexible – training of the able.[30]

Disciplined – though not inflexible – education of the able/elite is restated as the goal of teaching, with the massification of education leading to the loss of this imperative. Flexner, in an early rendering of the 'dumbing down' mantra, believed that universities were spending time teaching skills that should have been taught within a secondary school. The 'democratization' of education was therefore not a welcomed or celebrated initiative.

---

28 *Ibid.*, p. 103.

29 *Ibid.*, p. 93.

30 A. Flexner, *Universities: American, English, German* (London: Oxford University Press, 1930), p. 31.

The university system has been unstable – stretching beyond its comfort zone – throughout much of its history. The greatest difficulty facing the sector is always a crisis of purpose. The embedded question in most of our managerial, research and teacherly functions is how to adapt and translate an elite model into a popular system. The pivotal question is not only how many students are necessary to service 'national' goals, but what these students should learn, and how they could be instructed. Peter Scott, at the end of the 1980s and having suffered a decade of Thatcherite intervention in the sector, discovered not only a 'bias in favour of the vocational', but a reduction in the breadth of the undergraduate education, creating 'short-termism'.[31] His realization has confirmed a clash of purpose between staff and students. These purposes are increasingly adversarial through the arrival of more students before this conflict could be resolved.

Because the difference between education and training was not determined when universities were teaching smaller numbers from a more affluent background, when the system expanded, the contradiction festered and warped curriculum and pedagogical methods, and ruptured the important dialogue between teaching and research.[32] The presentation and negotiation of inequalities and social mobilities are overtly revealed through documents from the United Kingdom. The Blair Government specified the function of class on the educational discourse within the 'New Labour' agenda.

> The main motivating factor, which encourages potential students from lower social class backgrounds to enter HE, is a belief that a higher qualification will bring improved job and career prospects, and also improved earnings and job security.[33]

There is a notion that working class students do not have the rights, desire or capacity to complete education like the middle class. They are only to be trained in work-related skills, so that another generation of young people can service the needs of the middle classes who are themselves educated at higher scholastic and critical levels. Speaking on behalf of the working class in this way means that they are excluded from all but a few vocational courses, because job-related training serves the interests of the empowered.

---

31 P. Scott, 'The power of ideas', from C. Ball and H. Eggins (eds), *Higher Education into the 1990s* (Milton Keynes: Open University Press, 1989), p. 15.

32 The profound tragedy of schemes to 'assess' and 'monitor' research quality is that – too often – educational managers make institutional decisions to become either a teaching 'factory' or a 'research-intensive' institution. In Australia, Dorothy Illing described this process as 'federal government policies force universities to focus on either teaching or research', from 'Top unis split over research funding', *The Australian*, 18 August 2005, p. 6.

33 H. Connor and S. Dewson, with C. Tyers, J. Eccles, J. Regan, J. Aston, 'Social class and higher education: issues affecting decisions on participation by lower social class groups', Research Brief No. 267, Institute for Employment Studies, Department for Education and Employment, United Kingdom, March 2001.

Actually, the interests of the middle class are perpetuated by reducing the choices and critical thinking of the weak, the poor and the underprivileged. Improving the job prospects of the working class merely 'value-adds' the workplace, and grants them neither ambition nor an intellectual trajectory. Imagine if such statements were made about indigenous students, the black community or women: the notion that women's educational prospects should be limited to childcare, or that Aboriginal students should work in the health sector because that addresses a pressing need of 'their' community. To suggest that the working class want a quick, skill-based degree which will get them a job little better than their parents because of degree inflation is class-based prejudice at its most ruthless.

When reviewing the 'massification' of the sector, working class children, adults and parents often obtain less information about education than middle class groups. Henry, Knight, Lingard and Taylor realized that 'the school assumes middle-class culture, attitudes and values in all its pupils'.[34] There is a gulf between the vocabulary, language and grammar spoken in working class homes, and that spoken and written in the educational discourse.[35] Cultural or linguistic differences, determined via class or race in particular, are difficult to track because middle class values quietly frame educational institutions, expectations and experiences. The dominant group holds a bank of resources, influential peer groups and family connections. This matrix of ideologies ensures that middle class citizens are able to suture appropriate behaviour into a context. Every classroom encases diverse literacies. Unfortunately, too many universities operate as if all students have access to the dominant motifs and motives within a society. The imperative for flexibility is one such word. Flexibility is a privilege. The capacity to have choice and opportunity is the right of the few, not the many. Success in education is not a question of being gifted, bright or exceptional. It is a matter of possessing cultural capital and mobilizing it in the ways marked and graded by the dominant order.

Obviously the hidden curriculum – maintaining the power of the powerful – is still integral to the university system. While education is a way to gain social mobility, the means of selection, reinforced through entrance examinations, university fees and familial support, are used to continue the authority of those who already hold these social advantages. While we rarely hear about the need to educate only the best and the brightest in our system, the sector is still dominated by those groups because our understanding of culture and value has not changed sufficiently to allow more diverse populations and literacies onto the campus. Access and flexibility are not adequate words or initiatives because the myth of meritocracy is placing the blame on students

---

34 M. Henry, J. Knight, R. Lingard and S. Taylor, *Understanding Schooling: An Introductory Sociology of Australian Education* (London: Routledge, 1988), p. 142.

35 Such problems are obviously exacerbated when a language distinct from the national language is spoken in the home.

who are unable to succeed in the system.[36] Working class citizens have the right to the same disciplined, focused and compassionate teaching and learning techniques and curricula that have assisted middle class students throughout much of the (post) industrial history of universities. Ivan Illich's *Alternatives to Schooling*, which was so radically energized by the progressive education movements in the 1960s, believed that institutions blinker people's thinking, so that citizens are unable to think of better ways of organizing society.[37] Carl Bereiter built on this argument, believing that 'lower-class black kids remain lower-class black kids, only they become literate'.[38] The argument in *The University of Google* is different. Ignoring Google is not an option. Excluding the disempowered – the lower class, the black, the physically or mentally challenged – from the digital environment will perpetuate and increase the inequalities of the analogue world. It is damaging to assume that those emerging from homes without books, computers, broadband or family members with advanced educational qualifications have models for educational achievement. The interventionary aim must be to present and discuss the assumptions of power and knowledge present in universities and improve the curriculum so that standards can be maintained but with more socially attuned methods.[39]

In a society with aspirations for social democracy and a functional knowledge economy, high quality education must be available to all on the basis of ability, not

---

36 I am arguing here that the time, effort, resources and attention that have been granted to training the elite deserve to be mobilized to teach those from diverse backgrounds. I do recognize Eric Robinson's late 1960s critique of this goal. He stated in *The New Polytechnics* (Harmondsworth: Penguin, 1968) that 'the function of the public school and university system has been to train a ruling elite. To model a system of mass education on this is obviously nonsense. But many British educationists, particularly those on the political left, have seemed to be attempting this because they have interpreted the upper class tradition not as a training for leadership but as more personal liberation and cultivation which should be extended to the working class', p. 151.

37 I. Illich, *Alternatives to Schooling* (Melbourne: Australian Union of Students, 1972).

38 C. Bereiter, *Must we Educate?* (New Jersey: Prentice-Hall, 1973), p. vi.

39 To clarify my point here: I am arguing strongly in favour of staff improving their methods and understandings of teaching and learning, with interdisciplinary attention to many of the ideas and theories emerging from library studies. Such a goal ensures that – even though students are derived from diverse backgrounds and may be 'underprepared' by the (perhaps nostalgic) standards of the past, our improved methods and attention will ensure their survival, success and achievement in this system. Such an initiative was confirmed by Geoff Pugh, Gwen Coates and Nick Adnett, 'Performance indicators and widening participation in UK higher education', *Higher Education Quarterly*, Vol. 59, No. 1, January 2005, pp. 19–39. The argued that 'students from under-represented groups may require more extensive support or more radical changes in teaching and learning strategies if they are to approach completion rate norms … a priority should be to find ways of ensuring more students succeed in completing their course and qualification rather than intensifying the marketing effort to expand recruitment', p. 33.

background. Flexibility is not the solution to a lack of resources, teacher education or student motivation. Flexible learning is a way to deny these problems, displacing questions of method, scholarly apparatus or economic inequality onto mobilities in time. For example, Jerome Young presents his way of addressing the e-learning environment.

> I no longer pass out syllabi on the first day of class for my smaller … classes. Instead, I give students a single sheet of instructions on how to acquire an account on the university computer, how to find the course syllabus, and how to print it.[40]

The notion that students from diverse backgrounds may require more information in managing diverse media and web literacies than a single page of printed instructions which details how to enter the online learning environment assumes that students have a level of internet competency and funding to print out materials that should be available free of charge to those enrolled on a course.

The greater the time gap between leaving school and arriving at university, the greater the diversity of learning styles.[41] Course design and presentation must change and move to accommodate this changing cohort. Academics often assume that if problems emerge, that mature-aged students have the life experience to ask questions and make connections.[42] Instead, the aim for teachers of these students is to reconcile the gulf between lived experience and scholarship. The literacies in new technologies of this group are difficult to track. Darren Holloway, in his survey of social injustice, found that 'older persons, the unemployed and households on low income in Western Sydney, Australia are less likely to have Internet access'.[43] Obviously systematic, structural and historical class inequality and an expanding underclass is an unmentionable in teaching theory. The desire for aspirational classes and social mobility, ideas integral to the Third Way agenda, requires a democratic and meritocratic education system, but the precise methods for teaching working class students in middle class universities are more difficult to establish. R.W. Connell has taken this topic as one of the focuses of his distinguished academic career. Indeed, his book *Teachers' Work* 'is about working-class

---

40 J. Young, 'Computers and teaching: evolution of a cyberclass', *PS: Political Science and Politics*, Vol. 31, No. 3, September 1998.

41 This crucial realization was affirmed by Sue Knights and Ron McDonald in 'The needs of special groups of students: adult learners in University courses', in D. Billing (ed.), *Course Design and Student Learning* (Guildford: University of Surrey, 1978).

42 For a discussion of mature-aged students, please refer to J. Currie, G. Bossinga, C. Baldock, D. Mulligan, 'Now opportunities for women? Tertiary graduates and the labour market with special emphasis on the experiences of mature age women', Report No. 4, *Studies in the Sociology of Work*, School of Education and Social Inquiry, Murdoch University, June 1986, p. 2.

43 D. Holloway, 'Disparities in internet access: a case study of the digital divide in Western Sydney', *Australian Journal of Social Issues*, Vol. 37, No. 1, February 2002, p. 59.

children turning into middle-class citizens'.[44] Part of this process requires a valuation of the ideology of individuality over the importance of collective good and community.[45]

These conservative pressure points of education – flexibility, choice and individuality – feed the aura of a literacy crisis. Whenever this 'crisis' is summoned, it signals a crisis of a system that extends beyond middle class expectations. To develop flexibility of mind and intellect requires discipline, focus and attention. To become deflected by language of crisis is to undermine concentration and flit around in panicked confusion, not rational and logical problem solving. Flexibility is a way to deny working class students the educational experience and attention they require. When they fail a course with i-lectures and emails, databases and PowerPoint, it is their fault. The availability of software is supposedly enough. If they did not use them, through a lack of literacy, equipment or expertise, then the student is to blame in such an environment. Actually, curricula expertise is required to tell the truth to students about a system of inequality, hierarchy and suppositions.

Savasana

In yoga, the body is the instrument of improvement and focus. Equipment is not required. The aim is to move and manipulate muscles and joints used in daily life, but in new ways. At the end of the vitalization of muscles, joints and internal organs through breathing, twisting, and forward and backward folds of the body, relaxation is the final stage of yoga. The aim is to quieten the mind and pass through the levels of relaxation. Focus is returned to the important and the present rather than the trivialities of the past. While the body and mind are resting, they are also recharging.

This savasana stage of the chapter explores the consequences of embracing the clutter of technology, rather than the subtle and instrumental improvements in learning. Through the development of digital media, there has been a focus on technical skills rather than a recognition of how existing competencies can be deployed in new ways. The extent of student involvement in and with these 'flexible' materials is highly questionable. David Newlands and Melanie Ward reported that

> Students in our experience accessed the Web materials at various times, of day and night. The vast majority felt that the quality of the Web materials was at least as good as their own notes from traditional lectures. These results would seem to confirm the benefits of using

---

44 R.W. Connell, *Teachers' Work* (North Sydney: Allen and Unwin, 1990), p. 15.

45 James Comer has argued that 'at the core of our culture stands the belief that a life outcome is determined by the individual alone. The fact that this belief is so widely held speaks to the power of the pioneer ethos. But it is a myth … The individual is one key. The opportunity structure that the society provides is the second', from *Waiting for a Miracle: Why Schools Can't Solve Our Problems – and How We Can* (New York: Penguin, 1998), p. 77.

> the Web in allowing students to work at their own pace and in providing richer learning materials. Closer analysis of student behaviour however yields some less positive results. Forty per cent of the students printed out notes without reading them and only one quarter used the hypertext links provided or went in search of additional information for themselves ... It appeared that the students were reluctant to explore the Web and take charge of their own learning and were instead more concerned with producing a paper copy of the Web materials.[46]

Information and communication technologies are meant to increase students' control of their learning management. Actually, flexibility in the presentation of materials has created an inflexibility of mind. Little self-sufficiency is generated. Instead, there is a greater reliance on staff materials. The questions encircling computer-based materials and applications need to change. In shifting questions – from 'what do they do?' to 'why are they here?' – the momentum for change can be slowed to start assessing the quality and purpose of online teaching and learning.

Teachers have always used technology. The key is to ponder and justify in academic – rather than economic – terms the integration of ideas and tools. To develop a socially just and socially aware matrix of integrated curricula materials requires time and reflection, not crisis and agitation. To gain flexibility of time, the cost is educational standards, disciplined thought and dense personal challenges. The best of education, teaching and learning is inconvenient, not sandwiched between part-time jobs and text messaging. Teachers are working with a diverse group of students, but it is assumed that the same basic tools, methods and literacies can apply to all. Instead of producing online lectures, downloadable PowerPoint slides and generalized generic skills, there is a far more complex series of questions to ask: 'What do students need to know? What do students want to know? What do students already know?'[47] By stressing the process of teaching and learning, not the product, it becomes clear that technology may be changing, but pedagogy needs to change more rapidly. Herbert Schiller reminded us that 'there are underpaid and, consequently, undereducated teachers'.[48] Flexible learning is appropriate for a deskilled jobs sector. It is easier to blame students for their failures, rather than our methods.

Comfortable students are not good scholars. Comfortable students are consumers of learning. Flexible education that fits into a student's lifestyle merely continues the

---

46 D. Newlands and M. Ward, 'Using the Web and E-mail as substitutes for traditional university teaching methods: student and staff experiences', Unpublished paper, Department of Economics, University of Aberdeen.

47 S. Greenwood, 'Contracting revisited: lessons learned in literacy differentiation', *Journal of Adolescent and Adult Literacy*, Vol. 46, No. 4, December 2002/January 2003, p. 345.

48 H. Schiller, *Information Inequality: The Deepening Social Crisis in America* (New York: Routledge, 1996), p. 29.

trends in education for the last 20 years, which James O'Donnell termed 'dehumanizing and distancing'.[49] Downloading information is a distinct experience from being challenged, critiqued, unsettled and probed. Technological tools are confused with learning goals.[50] The asynchronous capacity of email and discussion fora does permit increased dialogue between students and staff. There is a flexibility of time, but the quality of the interactions is more debatable. The point of education is to encourage effective communication and promote meaningful learning opportunities. Questions of access must be tempered by motivation. Information must be given and received, diverse literacies developed and online socialization initiated. Yet instead of these more complex concerns, the role of the education has been simplified. For example, Gilly Salmon, when describing the role of the teacher, listed the first two functions as 'flexibility' and 'adaptability to audience'.[51] Responsibility to maintain international standards of scholarship was not mentioned. The quality of information and social support do matter. Without focusing on lifting international standards for education, there will be a deep and insidious corruption of universities. Monitor Lynnette Porter's argument about web-based education.

> Learners who want to 'attend' a school whose name is instantly recognized as a prestigious institution now can take at least some courses without having to relocate near the institution. For example, learners who want to take a course from Harvard University may be able to participate through courses offered on the World Wide Web. Although the experience may never compensate for being a part of the student body on the Harvard campus and learners are not guaranteed a degree from Harvard by participating in distance learning courses, nevertheless, they can benefit from their association with a high-quality institution noted for its academic excellence.[52]

Such a strategy has to do with corporate branding and marketing, not teaching and learning. While access can be guaranteed, quality and accountability cannot. The 'benefit' Porter discusses is not academic.

---

49 J. O'Donnell, *Avatars of the World: From Papyrus to Cyberspace* (Cambridge: Harvard University Press, 1998), p. 155.

50 David Pottruck and Terry Pearce have stated that 'e-mail and voice-mail have, of course, exacerbated the problem in the last ten years. Unfortunately, for all their convenience, these innovations have made it much easier to believe we are communicating when we are merely informing', *Clicks and Mortar: Passion Driven Growth in an Internet Driven World* (San Francisco: Jossey-Bass, 2000), p. 11.

51 G. Salmon, 'Reclaiming the territory for the natives', *Online Learning: Exploiting Technology for Training*, London, 23 and 24 November 1999, http://www.emoderators.com/moderators/gilly/london99.html, accessed on 13 July 2002.

52 L. Porter, *Creating the Virtual Classroom: Distance Learning with the Internet* (New York: John Wiley and Sons, 1997), p. 14.

The assumption that any technology, let alone any application, intrinsically improves the quality of learning must be discredited. It is a sad realization that, at the very time that the teaching and learning is bladed of funding and credibility, assumptions exist that technology will solve all manner of educational problems. Through virtual learning, virtual universities, i-lectures and e-ducation, the basic question remains how teaching is 'done' and the methods activated to ensure a productive, passionate site of scholarship and challenge. There is an ideology that learning mediated through computers improves social access to education because of the resultant flexibility. Actually, disconnecting students from the university, assuming that technological applications will intrinsically provide the platform for learning, discredits libraries and librarians. We need to remember the spark and value of real learning in real time and how it can translate and activate the spark of education from those often excluded from scholarship.

From: Jan
To: <T.Brabazon@murdoch.edu.au>
Subject: THANK YOU
Date: Mon, 20 Sep 2004 23:14:52 +0800

TARA THANK YOU SO MUCH FOR MAKING US ALL FEEL SO SPECIAL. I BEING ONLY ONE OF MANY ENJOY YOUR LECTURES BUT THE TUTORIALS ARE EXTREME. (MEANING I ENJOY THEM GREATLY) I LOVE THE INTELLIGENT THOUGHT YOU BRING OUT IN CLASS.

THE KIDS(I MEAN NO INSULT) MAKE ME PROUD TO BE AROUND THEM IT MAKES THE DIFFICULTIES OF MY AGE AND EDUCATION BACKGROUND BEARABLE AND BEATABLE I HAVE FELT NOTHING BUT ENCOURAGEMENT FROM ALL OF THE YOUNG PEOPLE THAT I HAVE ENCOUNTERED THEY MAKE ME VERY PROUD OF THE YOUNG OF OUR WORLD. THE ENCOURAGEMENT I HAVE FOUND FROM THE YOUNG AT SCHOOL HAS GIVEN ME GREAT HOPE FOR THE FUTURE OF MANKIND. I HAVE GONE OFF ON A BIT OF A TANGENT BUT I JUST WANTED YOU TO KNOW HOW MUCH I ENJOY YOUR CLASS AND I RECOMMEND IT TO EVERYONE I SPEAK TO.

(I THOUGH I HAD BETTER WRITE THIS LETTER BEFORE I HAND IN MY ASSIGNMENT IN CASE MY JUDGMENT CHANGES) HA HA YOURS

This student enjoyed the diversity and dialogue in a classroom. As a mature-aged student, she confronted challenges through her learning, but was supported through the process. With direct encouragement from classmates, her difficulties were 'bearable and beatable'. Regardless of background, all the students join to share a moment in space and time.

Access to education is different from flexible learning. The internet has become the bandage linking these two ideas. Actually, when students from non-traditional backgrounds attend university, they require *more* teaching, *greater* contact and *more* discussion of how information becomes knowledge. Teaching and learning is a negotiation of meaning, opening students to opportunities for interaction and reflection. The best of scholarship requires a flexibility of the mind, built on a disciplined mobilization of academic protocols, scholarship and verifiable interpretation. It may be sacrilege in societies saturated with markets, branding and neo-liberalism, but perhaps education is not meant to be cost-effective. Money has been removed from all levels of the educational sector. Lectures and tutorials are bursting with larger numbers. Investing in technology is not the answer to the decline in teaching and learning. Investing in people – both teachers and students – will produce the required response. The most important question to ask at this time is what we will do for our students in the postindustrial information age, and ponder the choices and the commitments that actually matter. Our lives are shaped – and actively transformed – by small events and few people. Yet these moments of intervention are revelatory and transcendent. A kind phrase, the smile of reinforcement and a nod of understanding cannot only make a student's day, but give them the confidence to do better and be better.

With yoga, the slower the posture and movement the better. The aim is control, not speed. Disciplined stages through poses are required to gain flexibility. Internet-mediated education enhances fast information delivery, access and retrieval. It makes education convenient, not better. Flexible learning, with time-shifted materials available online, only increases the apathy and disconnection of students from their campus. Yoga is a metaphoric reminder to all educators about the connections between mind and body, along with the importance of being patient and moving at a particular pace, while recognizing individual differences within a group.

Flexibility, as a word and agenda, is not the basis or foundation for education. To reconstruct our universities requires methods to sort out and manage priorities. Neo-liberal labour markets are meant to be flexible. Educational systems are meant to be rigorous. The best of education – like the best of yoga – stretches the mind and creates a new view of the taken for granted. The assumption that students can regulate their own learning is just that, an assumption. Flexibility and freedom must be earned and is based on years of training to ensure that external discipline is embedded internally. The question is why – at this historical moment – flexibility of time is valued over all other flexibilities.

To study teaching is different from other social practices. Recognizing the deep grafts between education and the rest of our lives also requires acknowledging that other behaviours and modes of knowledge have value. My yoga teacher has taught me much about education and flexibility. He has also taught me about commitment and discipline. For example, a decision was made at my gym that all instructors would only be paid for a one-hour class. Yoga – through the three stages outlined in this chapter – generally takes 90 minutes and sometimes longer. Other instructors abided by this managerial imperative, shortening or removing the mediation and restricting the warm-up period. My instructor made a decision that he would continue teaching for 90 minutes, even though he was paid for an hour. His professionalism and dedication to students and the practice of yoga demanded inflexibility and discipline. Managerialism and cries for efficiency did not move him. There is a lesson here.

Chapter four

An i-diots guide to i-lectures

Sound is a medium of communication that shadows the truths of our era. Its message is difficult to determine with precision, but facilitates the passion of the best popular music or the intense reflection and concentration of riveting public speeches. Sound slows our interpretation of words and ideas, heightens the awareness of our environment and encourages quiet interiority. Listening to music, for example, taps into our personal stories of loss, love and hope. Hearing waves crash onto a beach is simultaneously rhythmic, soothing and gothic. Laying in bed, just about to cross over into the twilight of sleep, we hear our breath and the complex silence of a darkened house.

Follow me on this journey. At the conclusion of this paragraph, close your eyes. Wherever you are – in the easy chair at home, in a library or sipping a long black in a coffee shop, I want you to eliminate your visual engagement with the world – just temporarily – and become aware of the sonic layering in the environment. For one minute, be conscious of the sounds of undulating breath, and how it punctuates the soundscape. Listen to the sonic layers around you. Close your eyes now.

Upon reopening access to the visual realm, there is a realization of the intricate complexity of sound about which we are frequently unaware. As the starkness of light and printed words are darkened, the pools of sound become more deep and resonant. The layering of sonic media, punctuated by our breath, encourages an alternative interpretation of the world. Breathing is more intensely physical and ears arch out into space to position the body in distinct and new ways. Hearing sound – and processing that experience – activates intricate aural literacies.

Sound punctuates buildings, workplaces, leisure complexes and family life. It bleeds through the media – from film soundtracks to streamed university lectures. To map and mobilize sound requires concise interpretation of the critical approaches that allow us to understand its role in creating space, place and identity. It is challenging work, as the visual bias of Western culture is unraveled and we start to hear sounds ignored or assumed. As Paul Duncum has confirmed, 'there are no exclusively visual sites'.[1] While popular music is an important part of this aural landscape, there are many contexts and modes of sound. Education rarely manages to work with this complexity. Handling print and text is easy. Monitoring and moderating the layering of aurality adds art and

1 P. Duncum, 'Visual culture isn't just visual: multiliteracy, multimodality and meaning', *Studies in Art Education*, Vol. 45, No. 3, Spring 2004, p. 252.

craft to education. Too often, we as teachers cheapen the soundscape with monotone verbal deliveries in lectures, interjected with stammering and confusion, and do not open our ears to the myriad other rhythms, melodies and textures in the sonic palette. Not surprisingly, digitization has only increased this tendency. This chapter demonstrates the strength, importance and benefits of sound to education, sweeping through the range of sonic media and the significance of sonic literacies. As a case study, I focus on i-lectures, the audio streaming of lectures through the web. The ineptitude through which the i-lecture platform was introduced into universities crushed and cheapened the revelatory potential of sound in education. My (printed) words in this chapter ask educators and readers to think more productively and proactively about voice, rhythm and sound. In building on the discussion of flexibility in the last chapter, there is a demonstration of how the fetishization of a technological platform – i-lectures – has bled complexity, plurality and diversity from sonic education.

Lectures have taken a battering in the last few years. One of the oldest modes of teaching, lecturing is criticized because, as Peter Stearns suggested, 'it establishes a hierarchy of authority between the lecturer and students and because it enjoins a rather passive learning mode on the audience'.[2] However, there are more positive interpretations of lecturing, particularly as it establishes a model for intellectual leadership. Lectures are multi-modal formations, using sound, vision, gestures, and often scent and touch. As a space where a group of people gather to think about big ideas, the lecture has pivotal symbolic importance. Also, the 'passivity' of lectures is debatable.

Bad lecturers generate bad lectures. The best of lectures require research, intense preparation, mobilization of diverse media and rehearsal. We have all seen bad scholars write a few headings on the back of a cigarette packet. They should not be allowed to teach, as they bring our universities into disrepute. The best of lectures are informative, entertaining, persuasive and stimulating. Generally, each lecture I write takes about three weeks to gather the materials. Then they take three days to write from these notes, and another five days to prepare the media and presentation. The research required for a good one hour lecture is immense. Skills are developed by students to understand and interpret orality and evaluate the hierarchy of important information. Complex mixed media literacies are activated. In recognizing this layering of ideas and media, lecturing is too important to deny, undermine or cheapen.

Digi-space

Teaching requires the creation of a learning space with boundaries and rules. To be an effective teacher requires more than a body and a voice, but necessitates the creation of

2 P. Stearns, 'Teaching and learning in lectures', from A. Booth and P. Hyland (eds), *History in Higher Education* (Oxford: Blackwell Publishers, 1996), p. 97.

a conducive environment which forms a context suitable for students, their goals and feelings. Further, there is a necessity to provide options, opportunities and pathways for the myriad methods in which students learn. Digital platforms challenge and change electronic storage and the distribution system for data. Therefore, there is a shift in the relationship between teachers and learners when digitization enters the discourse. When budgets are sunk into hardware and software – rather than paper in the photocopier, equipment in lecture theatres, books, libraries or more places for students – an ideology is configured which values digiware over peopleware.

Technologies in education have three general functions: to present learning materials, to permit an interaction between learner and text, or to facilitate communication between learners and teachers. Precise and different educational strategies are required to enable each of these functions. These choices must be related to the aims of teaching and learning, not the limits of the technology. In this way, very precise criteria are established for determining the effectiveness of a particular platform. It also provides a way to assess if change in educational practices and infrastructure is motivated by cost savings or a commitment to improved quality learning for students. There are distinctions between technologies for teaching and for operational purposes.

From: Rita
Sent: Tuesday, 2 August 2005 3:57 PM
To: Tara Brabazon
Subject: iLecture for COM102?

Hello Tara,

my name is Rita ***** and im currently enrolled in COM102. however i have a timetable clash between this lecture and another and i am only able to alternate which lecture i go to everyweek.

I was just wondering if the notes of the COM102 lecture will be available on WebCT or the lecture on iLecture?

im trying to figure out if i am able to stay in both units. :)

Thanks for your time,

Rita

In this case, the point of i-lectures is for convenience. It is not linked with Rita's teaching and learning experience. The timetable clash would be easily solved if she enrolled in the distance or correspondence version of either of these 'clashing' units. Then, carefully developed print-based materials would allow her to fit both classes into her life. Students have always had timetable clashes. They have not always had i-lectures.

For an institution, computers increase efficiency. Simply because email improves – or at least speeds up – the distribution of minutes from a meeting does not mean that it facilitates educational communication between the scholar and student. The language of instruction is different from the language of administration. Technologies for teaching must be determined by and through the student's home environment and be low cost.[3] The audio-visual media are remarkably important to teaching and learning moments and need to be judiciously chosen. No technology – even a convergent one – intrinsically makes learning student-centred. There are many methods to enact interaction between staff and students. For example, I teach sport and grant it a week of focus in survey courses for cultural and media studies. Mixed media presentation makes it profoundly successful. Analogue video was used in the lecture and tutorial. A song commenced the lecture – from the digital platform of a compact disc – but what I (and students) remembered from the week was the balls. Throughout the lecture and tutorials, several soccer balls moved their way around the room. It added a physicality and corporeality to the educational experience. Particularly for a group of young men and women in the course, they enjoyed the physical movement of the experience. The digital streaming of the audio of this lecture could not capture the bodies and their physicality through the teaching sessions of this week. Similarly, the fabrics used to teach fashion, the scents and smells deployed to explore semiotics and the dancing integral to the understanding of popular music are completely inappropriate to the digital compliance and standardization of web-mediated lectures.

One guide for online learning asks that the web-based instruction transcend the diversity of approaches in the traditional classroom.

> The ideal online learning environment is one that goes beyond the replication of learning events that have traditionally occurred in the classroom and are now made available through the Internet. It provides for different ways of learning and the construction of a potentially richer environment that provides for fresh approaches to learning, caters for different learning styles, as well as allowing for greater diversification and access to learning.[4]

---

3 A.W. Bates raises these arguments in an important early chapter. Please refer to 'Technology for distance education: a 10-year perspective', in A. Tait (ed.), *Key Issues in Open Learning – A Reader* (Harlow: Longman, 1993), pp. 241–265.

4 'Guide to enhance quality in online learning', online_quality_guide, University of Western Australia, accessed 8 August 2004.

This online learning guide from the University of Western Australia displays how to create digital resources that fulfil student learning goals. The document stresses that the internet activates and actualizes different ways of learning from conventional face-to-face delivery. The aim is not to replicate 'traditional' or corporeal teaching. Instead, there is a 'construction' of a 'richer environment' and 'fresh approaches'. Not mentioned in this document is the economic and political environment in which budgets for tenured staff have been under scrutiny. Putting 'materials' online has been part of a strategy to cut costs, not to 'freshen' teaching and learning. It also encourages bad – or at least strange – behaviour.

From: Yuanetta
Sent: Thursday, 4 August 2005 6:04 PM
To: Tara Brabazon
Subject: Re: lecture notes

Hi Tara, just wanted to know if you post any notes on line from the lectures? I assumed you would so I made no attempt to write anything down from the previous lectures, so I'm having a bit of a panic, now that I can't find anything on the web.

If you don't, could I have access to the overheads you used so that I could make some notes, please? I'll come to your office at a time that's convenient for you.

Thank you

Yuanetta

I was wondering in the first two lectures why some students were sitting in the lecture theatre with no paper, pen or bag, and staring at me. Why would first year students 'assume' *anything* about teaching and learning, particularly in the first few weeks of a university course? The notion that she *expected* notes would be available online means that technology has become a crutch and a replacement for learning. I wondered why students had simply not read the required readings, and why this particular year and course was distinct from previous cohorts. The answer is that web-based learning was triggering poor decision making in students. The 'reading' they determine to be sufficient is off PowerPoint slides, derived from a lecture. Attendance is not required because the audio delivery of the session is available, to which they may or may not listen. Such assumptions are corrosive of effective learning and reading.

In response to students making bad choices, some universities are striking back. What is surprising is the mechanism through which the popular press is 'analysing' this demand for students to fufil their scholarly functions.

> Thousands of undergraduate students are being forced to sign good behaviour contracts with their universities and warned they could be expelled if they breach regulations … The contracts put the onus on students to attend lectures and tutorials, but have been condemned by the National Union of Students. The NUS claims that contracts are 'one-sided,' and do not spell out what standard of teaching students should expect to get for the £3,000-a-year top-up tuition fees they are being charged … It will oppose any arrangements not agreed with students and is calling for a debate over the obligations on all sides in an era where most undergraduates in England must use loans to fund their fees.[5]

There is no comment by any contributors that explain the context for these contracts, or why there should be any debate that students attend lectures and tutorials for a course in which they are enrolled and – indeed – as the NUS specified, for which they have paid. If it takes a contract to specify the necessary expectations and processes of teaching and learning, then the student's signature is useful. Discussions of teaching quality are a ruse in such an argument. Students are not consumers and they are not buying an education. I am one of many teachers who spends more – much more – than £3,000 a year on teaching materials distributed to students, before unpaid labour even enters the equation. Education is not a business, and teachers do not serve or service students. That is a cul de sac of a case.[6] There needs to be a focused and considered discussion of why students are not attending classes for courses they selected. That is the problem. Concerns with teaching quality, learning strategies and professional development come after the recognition that attendance in class is crucial to the creation of an intellectual matrix of knowledge and models of learning.

There is a reason why students have a network of teaching and learning resources, including lectures, tutorials and required readings. Together, they summon a matrix of scholarship. Students must complete the course reading before the week's teaching. That is their responsibility. The lecture offers an interpretation of the reading, and the tutorial allows students to independently dialogue with their peers, connecting their research to the lecturer's interpretation and the others in the group. It is a matrix of scholarship. Overheads and PowerPoint slides are not 'required reading'. They are a

---

5 J. Meikle, 'Students told: turn up or face expulsion', *The Guardian,* 11 September 2006, p. 1.

6 It is also odd that this story about student contracts was featured on the first page of *The Guardian* on the fifth anniversary of the 9/11 bombings. Not only was it an inappropriate interpretation, but an inappropriate story selection and placement.

medium of interpretation, a skeleton of a lecture. Students like Yuanetta need to calm themselves and reassess their priorities. Ponder this whining and published diatribe from Tania Murphy, a student who – for some reason – believes she has been forced to complete a university degree.

> The lifestyle of a full-time student who also works is possibly the most stressful and unhealthy lifestyle in existence and yet it is most strongly inflected upon the young and inexperienced, which is possibly why we get so many first-year uni drop-outs. Personally, I believe that all students especially those not living with their parents, who manage to keep their grades above a C without become anorexic or developing a strong affection for drugs whilst juggling study, work and a social life should be given a trophy, a trip to Vanuatu, an iPod shuffle and 50 million dollars spending money for themselves and 23 friends. Instead they get a piece of paper saying, 'Congratulations, you are quite stupid, but not as stupid as 78 per cent of other students in the state, so you're now eligible to attend university for a further four years of study! Horray!' Only when changes are made to the education system to allow students the eight hours recreation and eight hours rest they deserve, can we really say we support human rights.[7]

In all honesty, undertaking a university education is much easier than working full-time in a workplace. At university, people actually care if students attend and enjoy their learning experiences. Bosses will never attend to their employees like academics support students. If university is the worst experience in the lives of these young scholars, then the full-time workforce – where 60 hour weeks (before housework) are increasingly common – will be untenable. Education is not a burden, and if this student believes that it is then she needs to go full time into the paid workforce and, if she is displeased, return to the campus. With this attitude, education and this opportunity is wasted. Significantly, she believed that the 'education system', not her attitude, family or employers, should change to make her life easier.

Thinking about this relationship between teachers, students and curriculum is complex and intricate. Inserting technology into that equation adds even greater intensity. There are consequences for making education location independent, a digi-space of i-lectures and PowerPoint slides. Whitehead argued that in 'teaching you will come to grief as soon as you forget that your students have bodies'.[8] These words were written in 1932. While much has changed in the subsequent seventy five years, the creation of teaching moments, learning outcomes and social change requires a dense, incisive and humble tether to this past. It is sound, voice, rhythm, melody and harmony that have been the great casualties of education.

---

7 T. Murphy, 'The school of hard knocks', *X Press*, No. 964, 5 August 2005, p. 6.

8 N. Whitehead, *The Aims of Education and Other Essays* (London; Williams and Norgate, 1942: 1932), p. 78.

Hearing the difference

In a lecture theatre and tutorial room, we write our words to be punctuated by the body and gestures, appended by a diversity of sources including overhead transparencies or PowerPoint slides, moving and still images, objects, scents and fabrics. At its best, teaching spaces activate all the senses. To remove this sensory complexity and focus on only sound and aural literacies necessitates a high level of pedagogic expertise and experience in sonic media. Norquay described this process, acknowledging that 'writing for talk is different from the writing you do for print'.[9] Greater attention is placed on signposting the structure of the presentation, providing overt indicators that allow the listener to follow the development of an argument.

In my adolescence and early adulthood, I had the great fortune to participate in training for radio. This was in the 1980s when women were rarely heard on this medium. However, I was identified quite early as not only a competent public speaker, but in possession of a low speaking voice. With the gift of a drag queen growl, I had the opportunity to learn about speaking on radio during a time when women's voices were inappropriate or uncomfortable to the patriarchal spaces around the masculine ear. These lessons were important. It is a skill in learning how to make words spark off the page and appear as if they are not being read. A range of verbal techniques are necessary to compensate for a lack of body language.[10] The aim is to encourage vocal variety and dynamism through rate, pace, volume, pitch, inflection and pause. Further, the use of short sentences for aural delivery, to forge a direct link between subject and predicate, is an imperative. These competencies are different from the characteristics of the archetypical bad lecturer, with a few headings prompted by PowerPoint slides. This mode of 'preparation' encourages rambling ideas and sentences that do not end. Actually, good audio-only presentations are highly scripted, with each word crafted and selected.[11] Vocal training is also extremely important. A recorded voice is distinct from

---

9 M. Norquay, 'Writing for the ear', in L. Burge, M. Norquay and J. Roberts (eds), *Listening to Learn* (Ontario: The Instructional Resources development – Ontario Institute for Studies in Education, 1987), p. 1.

10 These strategies were effectively discussed by Earle Topping, 'Voicing for the ear', in L. Burge, M. Norquay and J. Roberts (eds), *Listening to Learn* (Ontario: The Instructional Resources Development, 1987).

11 I am particularly reminded here of the outstanding training instigated by the Royal National Institute for the Blind in the United Kingdom. They instigate courses and training in 'audio description'. There is an Audio Description Association which runs nationally recognized courses through the Open College Network. The RNIB and Vocaleyes have also developed guidelines for the description of museums, galleries and heritage sites. Please refer to 'Audio Description Training', RNIB, http://www.rnib.org.uk/xpedio/groups/public/documents/PublicWebsite/public_leisure, accessed on 30 April 2005. It is important to note, considering

the voice that we hear in daily life. Emotion and energy must be injected into the sound, to compensate for the lack of body language and props.

A great advantage of digitization and the proliferation of web-based sources is that historically significant sonic media can gain a wider audience and activate new educational opportunities. Currently 12,000 items of sound recordings from the British Library archives are being digitized. The materials include one of the earliest sound recordings, of Florence Nightingale speaking, and also classical and popular music, broadcast radio, traditional music and oral histories. Lynne Bindley, chief executive of the British Library, stated that,

> Sound recordings represent a massively untapped resource in the field of education. They are relevant to all subjects and we are delighted that this programme will bring wide access to rare, historic and hugely valuable sound resources.[12]

This sonic database will be incredibly important to web-mediated education. It will take time, money and high levels of interpretation and information management to craft these sounds for education. The value though, will be extraordinary. Meanwhile bad lecturers and speakers are uploading mediocre scholarship and sounds, while this quality database remains untapped.

There is a justification for this low grade sonic scholarship. Lecturing is extremely difficult. It is not a performance. It is a very precise form of public speaking. The intensity of concentration is different from any other activity in life. No other event requires that level of preparation and focus. It is not an efficient use of time, but it is an important deployment of expertise. The mixed mode delivery – moving between print to vision, music to scents, fabric to a soccer ball – is incredibly stressful. After an hour, my clothes are saturated, and much to my embarrassment, I continue to sweat through the following two-hour tutorial. While I focus on pulling my voice down to a masculine register and slowing the delivery, there are thousands of other teaching variables I also have to remember while watching student faces for mis/comprehension. Therefore, the delivery of teaching materials for the voice and ear alone requires a different sort of focus to the mixed modal lecture venue. The point is clear: time must be spent developing media resources for sonic media. Streaming a lecture – cutting the voice away from the body – is not only semiotically painful and inappropriate but creates poor

---

the scale of these initiatives, that aural webcasting of university course material offers incredible opportunities for students with disabilities, alongside increasing the literacies of other scholars. However, training and professional development, such as that offered by the RNIB, is required for the most effective mobilization of aural media.

12 D. MacLeod, 'British Library puts sound archive online', *The Guardian*, 16 April 2004, http://education.guardian.co.uk/higher/artsandhumanities/story/0,12241,1193478,00.html, accessed on 19 April 2004.

quality educational resources. Good lecturers have different skills to good broadcasters. Through professional development and training, teachers may develop sonic awareness and pedagogically appropriate delivery. Good materials for the ear will not emerge from a lecture theatre. Lecturing is a different process from producing audio-only programming.

Part of the ease with which lectures have been procured for audio streaming on the World Wide Web is a result of a misunderstanding of the specificity of the lecture as a venue for education. Jonathan Ross and Robert Schultz, for example, attacked the lecture medium as a way to celebrate the 'revolutionary' and 'transformational' nature of the internet.

> Unfortunately, however, the lecture format – a technique of covering content that is preferred by students with sequential, auditory processing abilities only – continues to dominate as a preferred form of teaching in many college classrooms.[13]

There are flaws in this argument. Firstly, the most provisional lesson in semiotics teaches that meaning is determined via the relationship between form and content, signifier and signified. There is no such entity as 'content' that exists without being shaped by form or media. Secondly, and most importantly, very few lecturers use only aurality. In fact if they are present in the auditorium in and through their body, then there must be a visual component.

Putting lectures online or on audio cassette was and is not an effective use of these platforms. There is a better way to actualize the potential of sound: write specific material that works for the ear, have professional training in the potential of the voice, and record the material with precision. This carefully prepared material opens out effective learning through the senses. Such time-consuming – but important – strategies create a media-rich environment. Instead, the focus is allowing students who miss lectures to further disrespect the educational process and 'make up' for their poor attendance. It is also changing students' expectations of higher education. For example, the Ipswich campus of the University of Queensland was set up with the goal of flexible, wireless delivery of content. The consequences were enormous.

> While there is obvious preference for on-line learning at the Ipswich campus, the initial promotion of 'flexibility' led many – perhaps most – students to expect that they would not have to attend classes. Students became disgruntled with the notion of class attendance, and great efforts were made to accommodate them: in 2000, for example, night classes with

---

13 J. Ross and R. Schultz, 'Using the World Wide Web to accommodate diverse learning styles', *College Teaching*, Vol. 47, No. 4, 1999, p. 123.

just two or three students were run in various courses. Since 2001 a different view has been taken.[14]

Inexperienced students will behave rashly, make poor judgments and cut corners if such options are made available. Instead they must be reminded how much their words and ideas matter, and how – with effort, care and respect for knowledge – they can make a difference. Similarly to the experience in Queensland, Australia, a sophomore at Duke University, Ryan Sparrow, justified the use of his iPod.

> Sparrow explained one way he prepared for his presentation. "I downloaded the lectures from the [class website] and I put them on my iPod", he said. "One of them I listened to while I was at work at the Provost's office. I was upstairs in the attic doing some filing and I got to just listen to the lecture and take some notes". (The recording from Belkina's first lecture was particularly helpful for Sparrow, who had missed that class after staying up late to complete an engineering project.)[15]

Sonic materials can be written specifically for the iPod in the memo function. They can incorporate questions, diverse sounds and material written specifically for the ear. The iPod has great potential for teachers and students. But to simply record lectures, with or without copyright approval from the lecturer, is not a strong deployment of sonic media platforms.

There are other ways to use the slimline white case with wheel menu. The last few years has seen the iPod enter popular culture. The gleaming white platform for digital compression files is not either intrinsically helpful or damaging for education. However, with good curriculum, it can be an avenue and place for the presentation of teaching and learning materials. The iPod has the potential to create a higher quality webcast of audio content than the i-lecture, written and recorded specifically for that purpose. No lecture rooms need to be wired. Copyright concerns are discussed and explored more overtly. Staff can – through the iPod's microphone attachment – record material that is high quality, appropriate for the web and the cohort of students, and is a polished presentation written for that purpose. But such a scheme would require investment in staff training, not technology.

Ryan Sparrow was part of Duke University's scheme in August 2003 to give 20 gigabyte iPods to first year students. They were preloaded with orientation materials in spoken and text form, along with information about Duke's academic environment, student life and activities. While the primary way the iPod was used by students was

---

14 Contemporary Studies programme, *Submission to Review*, University of Queensland, Queensland, May 2003, p. 25.

15 'iPods help carry on class discussions', http://cit.duke.edu/ideas/newprofiles/lucic.do, accessed on 20 March 2005.

to download music, it was also being deployed for course work, recording lectures and interviews, organizing image and text files, and also became a portable hard drive. While these are expected functions, it is the potential of sonic, mobile education that is most riveting and extraordinary. Audio books, including language dictionaries, allow the development of sonic literacies and broaden the experience of education into diverse sites of life.

The desire to digitize, categorize and codify analogue, mixed media lectures into an inappropriate, audio format not only discredits the complexity of sound, but the resistive and plural energy of a lecture space. Sounds require precise mapping and shaping of differences. It is not an 'enhancement' to internet education.[16] It must be used carefully because sonic media have some disadvantages. The speed of listening is slower than reading. While this reflexive pace is effective in pondering abstract ideas, the overall structure of material is more difficult to track. Long monologues and dense factual material from lectures are difficult to capture through sonic media. Meacham and Butler described sound as a 'means of personalizing material, providing variety and interest, and presenting information whilst the eyes are occupied elsewhere, or merely resting'.[17] The most effective use of aural sources occurs when they are integrated with other media to motivate students and personalize the delivery of the instructor. The (only) reason why audio analogue cassettes were useful for distributing lectures is that they were practical and cheap. The best use of audio emerges when objectives are clearly stated and the form and content are related to the learning outcomes of the course.

A.W. Bates, in reviewing the successes of the Open University, has presented one of the most significant historical investigations of sound in teaching.[18] He explored the significance of media selection in distance education, capturing the history of audio cassettes for Open University courses. He stated that,

> Audio cassettes are low cost; all students already have facilities at home; they are easy for academics to produce, and cheap and simple to distribute; students find them convenient to use; and, when designed properly, they encourage student activity. (UK OU audio-cassettes are rarely lectures.)[19]

---

16 Barrie Barrell discussed visual and sound 'enhancements' in this way, rather than investigating the specificity of each media. However, he did ask the question whether – through the impact of new media on education – we are losing literacies. Please refer to 'Literacy theory in the age of the internet', *Interchange*, Vol. 31, No. 4, 2000, pp. 447–56.

17 E. D. Meacham and B. A. Butler, *Audio Tapes for Distance Education* (Riverina-Murray Institute of Higher Education: Division of External Studies, 1988).

18 A. W. Bates, 'Technology for distance education: A 10-year perspective', in A. Tait (ed.) *Key Issues in Open Learning – A Reader: An Anthology from the Journal 'Open Learning' 1986–1992* (Harlow: Longman, 1993), pp. 241–65.

19 *Ibid.*, p. 242.

There are lessons to be drawn from the Open University's use of audio cassettes. They were chosen because they were low cost, accessible, able to be produced by academics without intervention from others, and convenient to use. Significantly, in terms of educational design, lectures were inappropriate in developing effective sound-based OU educational strategies. While institutional use of technology aims to improve efficiency and productivity, teaching technologies must be influenced by other directives such as the student's home environment. Audio cassettes were cheap. Broadband and computers are not. There is also a consideration of media appropriateness for different levels of educational courses and student cohorts. Bates established a checklist of six criteria through which to assess educational technology:

Assessment of Educational Technology
Cost
Learning effectiveness
Availability to students
User friendliness
Place in the organizational environment
Recognition of international technological inequalities

Source: A. W. Bates, 'Technology for Distance Education: A 10-year Perspective', in A. Tait (ed.) *Key Issues in Open Learning – A Reader: An anthology from the Journal 'Open Learning' 1986–1992* (Harlow: Longman, 1993), p. 243.

Instead of deploying such modes of assessment, funding is cut from 'conventional' teaching budgets to promote web-based resources, thereby reducing the options of staff in maintaining the current palette of mixed media. The illegality of webcasting (copyrighted) sound means that audio and visual materials from film and popular music are removed from conventional – corporeal – lectures. The plurality and density of 'old' media such as film, photographs and television, and their attendant literacies, is lost in the desire to render lectures uniform and legally downloadable.

The i-lecture – a platform developed by the University of Western Australia and being sold around the world – is an archetype of how and why web-based streaming of lectures is being deployed. I-lecture software digitally records a lecture and, through streaming, allows it to be heard via the World Wide Web. The system is automated, so that staff are not involved in – and implicitly cannot 'ruin' – the recording process. They simply switch on a microphone and recording commences, ceasing 50 minutes later. The media file is then transferred over the network from the lecture theatre via the file transfer protocol (ftp). The recordings are compressed, uploaded and streamed to servers distributed over the network. Students then access these recordings. The assumption of this application is that – after a decade of web-based literacy and proliferation of hardware, software and wetware – staff have not developed 'the content' (or literacy) necessary to run a 'virtual' university. At least with i-lectures, 'content' is made available,[20] without staff input or – more troubling – without training and professional development of academics.

Through this discussion of content management, there is a seemingly unspeakable issue to consider. Before a student records a lecture onto an iPod or a lecturer switches on the microphone for an i-lecture, intellectual property concerns must be addressed. Alan Albright, specialist in intellectual property litigation in the United States, asked of students, 'Do they have permission from the person who wrote the lecture? That would be a copyright concern'.[21] Yet the copyright and intellectual property rights of staff have been ignored and perhaps violated. Such transgressions without notice or respect are symbolic of an institution created around technological change, not teaching expertise.

i-Staff

> Criticism of university culture paints a picture of an elitist academy of self-proclaimed scholars with little interest in teaching or community service.[22]
>
> Mary Mundt

University academics wear many roles beneath their scholarly robes. While the nutty professor, ivory tower writer, evil genius or lazy womanizer are all images of the professoriate,[23] these motifs are largely redundant. I do not know a single academic who works less than a sixty hour week. Their health suffers, family life suffers – and the emails keep popping into the inbox. It may be politically unfashionable to state, but still extremely necessary, that teachers at all levels of the system are not coping well at the moment. Overwork and over management have sliced through the profession of teaching. There is an assumption that administration is facilitating teaching. Actually, the inverse is the case. Ambition, promotion and predictable career advancement are

---

20 For example, on one Murdoch University i-lecture web page, it stated 'iLectures are made available from within online units or if there are no other online resources, from the Unit Welcome Page', from 'i-Lecture – how to use iLecture', Murdoch University, http://www.murdoch.edu.au/teach/ilecture/usage.html, 2003, accessed on 31 July 2004. In other words, staff that have not learnt how to use the hardware or software – or choose not to make their course materials available – have their 'content' uploaded and released to students.

21 J. Shreeve, 'iListen and iLearn', *The Independent*, 22 June 2005, p. 44.

22 M. Mundt, 'The urban university: an opportunity for renewal in higher education', *Innovative Higher Education*, Vol. 22, No. 3, Spring 1998, p. 251.

23 Thomas Dyer wrote an outstanding short pieces about the 'Images of the professoriate', *Innovative Higher Education*, Vol. 23, No. 2, Winter 1998, pp. 83–4.

shredded. Mechanisms for coping, rather than innovation, are the imperative. For example, a 50-year-old teacher – Jackie – admitted to researchers:

> I think I've had so much of the stuffing knocked out of me, I just haven't got enough energy left. I just don't want to be bothered. So although it might have made me more capable of resisting bullying or pressure, it dampened down any ambition; it's just dampened it down completely.[24]

It has been fascinating in the last few years watching university administrators trying to force academics to 'get materials online' without cutting their workload or encouraging professional development. Compliance has been enforced through top-down policies, yet resistance emerges at the grassroots. Experienced staff are retiring, switching to part-time or leaving the system. They are managing change by relocating to another job. Further, staff are starting to ignore the rigid timetables of compliance, being prepared to opt out of promotion structures and face censure in the annual performance development reviews. They are silently ignoring the directives of administrators who run universities but could not run a tutorial. The long-term costs to the systematic and structural degradation of the institution are enormous.

Even more seriously, universities – when managing the i-lecture project – have either ignored or confused the issues of intellectual property rights and copyright.[25] Teaching, and in particular lecturing, has not been configured as a scholarly act that creates and builds knowledge.[26] While being guided by the same national law, different universities have assembled distinct rules and interpretations. For example, Macquarie University in Australia made the following claim on their website:

> The University owns, produces and licenses various types and amounts of intellectual property (IP) for the purposes of instructing our students … Your use of Macquarie University's iLecture system requires you to be aware of the different types of IP that are being used in your lectures by yourself or your students … a recorded lecture may contain; Macquarie owned IP, such as your spoken course content, notes, or recitation of notes or lectures by any other Macquarie staff or fellow … A recorded lecture therefore may not make use of

24 Jackie from G. Troman and P. Woods, 'Careers under stress: teacher adaptation at a time of intensive reform', *Journal of Educational Change*, Vol. 1, 2000, pp. 253–75.

25 Lawrence Beard and Cynthia Harper referred to 'the unresolved problems in ownership and copyright of instructor's online courses', from 'Student perceptions of online versus on campus instruction', *Education*, Vol. 122, No. 4, 2002, p. 49.

26 Ronald Simpson expressed this concern in his article 'Teaching as a scholarly activity', *Innovative Higher Education*, Vol. 22, No. 3, Spring 1998, pp. 153–55. He considers how academic curricula vitae are assembled, and the amount of space granted to teaching rather than research in promotional policies. He also asks how to encourage a commitment to further learning when teaching is treated in this way.

> music CDs, or play hired or purchased DVDs, tapes of movies, TV shows, etc. For a lecture that makes use of this material, it is suggested that you pause the recording by switching off the microphone.[27]

Macquarie has – without question or debate – claimed the intellectual property rights of academics over their own lectures. Simultaneously, they have also noted the copyright held by others in music and videos. They also confirm that 'copyright is a type of personal property right that is founded on a person's creative work'.[28] Therefore by definition, lectures are neither personal property nor creative work for Macquarie. Neither Murdoch University in Western Australia nor the University of New South Wales overtly mention the copyright of a staff's lecturing form or content. Both institutional websites focus on the staff gaining the copyright of audio-visual materials.[29] This absence is significant. The University of Western Australia, which developed the system, completely contradicts Macquarie's determination. Michael Neville and Michael Fardon cite Australian employment law, that the works generated by an employee usually reside with the employer. They also recognize that academic employment contracts differ from this determination.

> When the iLecture project was first undertaken at UWA, academic staff had all rights to their IP with the exception of digital works (e.g.: software) that remained with the university. A recent revision of regulations has seen the rights to recordings and papers being retained by the Academic with the University having a right to reuse the Intellectual Property. To address some teaching staff concerns that they would be made redundant by the recording process, the UWA iLectures team worked with teaching unit coordinators to get their view if recordings should be retained from year to year. To date this has been successful in keeping teaching staff involved in the process. Clear IP policies acceptable to teaching staff are critical to garnering their support for the lecture recording process.[30]

Significantly, the Law School at Melbourne University has not enforced the institution's intellectual property rights over i-lectures. Instead, the School confirms that 'it is essential

---

27 'Macquarie University Copyright Unit', Macquarie University, http://www.copyright.mq.edu.au/lecture/, accessed on 31 July 2004.

28 'Copyright for staff', Macquarie University, http://www.copyright.mq.edu.au/faq.html, accessed on 31 July 2001.

29 'i-lecture – copyright', Murdoch University, 2003, http://www.murdoch.edu.au/teach/ilecture/copyright.html, accessed 24 July 2004 and 'i-lectures FAQ', http://ilecture.unsw.edu.au/FREQUENTLY%20ASKED %20QUESTIONS.CFM?DC=5, accessed on 7 July 2004.

30 M. Neville and M. Fardon, 'Case study: stages in establishing a large scale streaming media implementation – an institutional perspective', Paper for the Arts Multimedia Centre, University of Western Australia, http://ilectures.uwa.edu.au/misc/NevilleFardon_Educause_N48.pdf, accessed 1 August 2004.

to note that iLecture is an opt-in capability. Only if an academic staff member chooses to have their class included, will it be recorded and made available on the web'.[31] Such a strategy smoothly detours a discussion of a lecturer's intellectual property rights and copyright being violated. In comparison to Melbourne, Murdoch University disregards the high level of ambivalence in academic employment contracts. Murdoch ensures compliance by making all units pass through a School Development Process, and five steps for the implementation of i-lectures as part of 'flexible' learning.[32] Ownership is not the issue. Administrative compliance is the focus.

Intellectual property for academics will be the major debate for the next decade. Academic freedom necessitates that creative intellectual productions are individually developed and owned. Teaching materials are – ambivalently at times – claimed as part of this definition. The only caveat to that statement is the development of software. If the arguments of Macquarie and Murdoch are followed through to a logical conclusion, then these universities could also make a claim to the profits made by academics on their scholarly monographs or professional writing and speaking activities. All products of an academic's mind are supposedly owned by the university, in exchange for a salary.

In stark contrast, Robert Schrag, Professor in a Department of Communication, notified his students in September 2006 that each of his lectures could be purchased online for US$2.50. He argues that the tuition fee at the university buys access to the lectures in the classroom. If other copies were required, then they must be purchased. Schrag confirms that 'the university agrees that each professor owns the words that he or she speaks in the classroom and can do whatever they wish with them – put them in a textbook, on a CD, sell them as MP3s – whatever'.[33] It is digitization that raises these intellectual property rights issues because it is extremely easy to reproduce and distribute sounds and images. Such an ease in uploading, downloading, streaming and saving is not well managed within copyright law, which is based on the concept of a single identifiable author. In the United States, there is a tradition that the faculty own their own creative written works, with the exception of patents and inventions. With the commercialization of intellectual property online, this right may be challenged. The debate resonates provocatively with the copyright issues involved in the ownership of online course material. Without a clear and unambiguous contract, monitoring

---

31 'Information systems & services', http://www.law.unimelb.edu.au/iss/informationsystems/services/ilecture/, accessed 31 July 2004.

32 'Updating units to the flexible model', Murdoch University, http://www.murdoch.edu.au/admin/cttees/flic/convert.html, accessed 31 July 2004.

33 R. Schrag, in K. Brackett, 'Professor gives students the option of purchasing his lectures online', *Technician Online*, 13 September 2006, http://www.technicianonline.com/home/index.cfm?event=displayArticlePrinterFriendly, accessed on 19 September 2006.

intellectual property rights remains a difficulty.[34] By the Australian Copy Act of 1968, copyright material may be used without the owner's permission only if it is by 'fair dealing'.[35] The ambiguity of this phrase does not assist university administrators and academics in the process of knowledge ownership. In the United States, however, intellectual property rights have assisted academics in asserting their ownership of teaching materials.[36]

Organizational conflict is a major and understated problem in our universities. It is not a question of personalities, but a series of challenging and stressful business conditions that allow such disagreements to emerge. Conflicts over processes and tasks – or teaching loads – are symptoms of an organizational culture in disarray or discord.[37] Particular tasks such as enforcing specific modes of teaching can trigger organizational agitation, rage and resistance. Without overt modes of communication between academics and administrators being deployed so as to reveal agendas and assumptions, knowledge will not move into social systems. Further, by continually stressing the new and the innovative, the intellectual capital that staff have built through years of experience is discredited. Validating technological change through economic savings or – frequently unsubstantiated – student interest will not encourage already overworked staff to work harder, particularly when their experience has been denied in the past.[38]

What makes i-lectures successful, or any other software application that facilitates the web-based audio streaming of lectures, is how it is justified, managed and valued in universities. Academic knowledge and teaching are not respected while issues of intellectual property rights and copyright law are either ignored or handled differently

34 Georgina Holmes et al., 'Who owns course materials prepared by a teacher or professor? The application of copyright law to teaching materials in the internet age', *BYU Education & Law Journal*, No. 165, 2000.

35 'Fair dealing', Information Sheet G79, Australian Copyright Council, New South Wales, August 2003.

36 B. Pietrykowski, 'Information technology and commercialization of knowledge: corporate universities and class dynamics in an era of technological restructuring', *Journal of Economic Issues*, Vol. 35, No. 2, June 2001, p. 303.

37 A fascinating analysis of academic departments and their disagreements was assembled by James Hearn and Melissa Anderson in 'Conflict in academic departments: an analysis of disputes over faculty promotion and tenure', *Research in Higher Education*, Vol. 43, No. 5, October 2002, pp. 509–29.

38 John Robertson has provided a fascinating study of why the resistance to information and communication technology has been so great. His 'Stepping out of the box: rethinking the failure of ICT to transform schools', *Journal of Educational Change*, Vol. 4, 2003, pp. 323–44, has focused on the relationship between the computer and its user, with attention to social, cultural and educational relationships.

by distinct universities.[39] In actuality, copyright law applies to all recorded materials. Stunningly, Australian universities have assumed that academic staff will obtain – and pay for – the clearance of copyrighted materials, but that they will not be compensated for their own intellectual property being moved and traded through digital platforms. That is, staff pay for the right to use materials from which the university gains profit through the uploading of i-lectures.

> You are responsible for obtaining appropriate permission for all material delivered by the iLecture Recording System. This includes copyright clearance and/or payments for any material that you have requested to be recorded.[40]

This remarkable situation has not been challenged by staff or their unions. For academics working in media-related fields, this is an expensive disaster. Why should individual staff be responsible for funding material to improve the institutional quality of university teaching?

While universities remain focused on staff paying for copyrighted materials, there has been a blind and bland disregard of universities paying staff for their intellectual property rights and copyright. Copyright law is based on a single identifiable author. A lecturer is clearly the author of the material they deliver. In UK law – through the Copyright Designs and Patents Act 1988 – a low level of originality is required.[41] A lecture would easily fall within this law. The only nod to this major issue, particularly when administered by managers demanding compliance, is that students will be unable to save and copy the whole recording of streamed audio lectures. The mistakes in interpreting the law are compounded through a miscomprehension of technology. Not only are there tools to rip streams, but the most basic of digital recorders like an iPod can create a good copy of streamed audio. The iPod or MP3 player can then be plugged into a USB slot to generate a wav file. This file can then be entered on the web, to be downloaded at will.

What is required is a logical discussion of research and teaching in sonic media, feedback about the process and correction when confronted by points of law. Instead, spin, spruik and advertising are the inadequate replacements. For example, the following 'scenario' is featured on the Curtin University website:

---

39 There are many issues to resolve in universities' management of intellectual property rights. When an academic accepts industry funding, there are profound questions about who owns the knowledge, research or product.

40 'I-lecture FAQ', http://ilecture.unsw.edu.au/FREQUENTLY%20ASKED%20QUESTIONS.CFM?DC=5, accessed on 7 July 2004.

41 S. Stokes, 'Some reflections on art and copyright', *Electronic Journal of Intellectual property Rights*, May 2004, http://www.oirc.ox.ac.uk/EJWPO604.html, accessed on 14 August 2004.

> A lecturer walks into a lecture theatre, turns on the microphone and delivers her lecture. An hour or so later, without any human intervention, an appropriately titled link automatically appears on the setup page for her unit, adding the just finished lecture to the list of lectures recorded for that unit. Shortly afterwards, a student logs into that unit's web page from anywhere in the world and clicks on the new link, bringing up a window with a streaming video and audio recording of the lecture. The student listens to the lecture in the background while typing notes in Word in the foreground.[42]

This is a scenario imagined by administrators and used to 'sell' this application to staff. No evidence or reference is presented. No feedback from staff or students is necessary, only an imagined narrative. With advertising replacing scholarship, it is important to work through and contextualize these imaginings.

Student learning: new ways to miss the point

> It is clear that the technology genie is out of the bottle, and there is no stuffing it back inside.[43]
>
> Mike Davis and Margaret Holt

> Universities are in the information dissemination business and computers are changing the way they work.[44]
>
> M. Gordon Hunter and Peter Carr

Hunter and Carr's statement is punchy, provocative and enticing. It is also wrong. Universities develop new knowledge, not only reproduce it. University academics have distinct functions and roles to other teachers in the educational sector. They not only disseminate information, but are involved in the creation of knowledge through research. Too often these functions of academic life are partitioned. Instead, research and teaching conflate, dialogue and spark innovative theories. Such a misunderstanding of scholarly functions serves to devalue the multiple sites of academics' knowledge production, including lectures. If scholars simply reproduced the information of others, then issues of intellectual property rights and cultural value would not be as significant.

Much of the i-lecture policy aims for obedience: staff must use the platform, rather than evaluating its quality or appropriateness for their discipline or pedagogical methods.

---

42 'ICT @ Curtin – for Staff', http://startup.curtin.edu.au/ict/staff/ilecture.html, accessed on 31 July 2004.

43 M. Davis and M. Holt, 'havingproblems@cm.com: new ways to miss the point', *Innovative Higher Education*, Vol. 22, No. 4, 1998, p. 312.

44 M. Hunter and P. Carr, 'Technology in distance education: a global perspective to alternative delivery mechanisms', *Journal of Global Information Management*, April–June 2000, p. 50.

I have found no quality assurance mechanism attached to any i-lecture policy. Without accountability, there is no way to ask who is served by i-lectures, and their purpose and effectiveness.[45] Lazy students who cannot attend lectures now have a software platform that gives them a right to miss sessions without accountability or consequences. In such an environment, it is important to assess the language of the i-lecture format, through the prototype/archetype provided by the University of Western Australia to 'sell' the platform.

Higher education has many definitions and functions. The sector is so large, fragmented and complex that the functions of teachers in this volatile workplace are difficult to monitor. D.D. Flannery explores the range of roles confronting the contemporary academic.[46] He shows the weakness of stressing personal empowerment as a universal, meritocratic goal.

> Universality must be avoided. Adult learning theory must include, along with self-directed learning, the place of other-directed learning, of collaboratively directed learning, of community-directed learning, of global processes of engaging in perspective transformation and other ways of learning that people and cultures use.[47]

Flannery demands that academics work much harder to understand the myriad contexts of teaching and learning. In standing against student-centred models – or any single model – he asks that academics ask deep and dense questions about the nature and form of emancipatory pedagogy. Further, he recognizes that 'empowerment' is a difficult word to map or monitor, and is difficult to assess in an academic setting. Notions of quality control and national standards – through the review of teaching practices and processes through the QAA or the AUQA, for example – can work against the complex plurality of a multicultural education.

Similarly, John Bennett acknowledges the diversity of students and staff in the current higher education sector.[48] He also argues that instead of placing the attention on learning, the current political emphasis not only cuts the costs of teaching, but moves money into the development of educational technology. Academic reward structures not only promote individualism, but compliance to directives about technological change.

---

45 Michael Bastedo and Patricia Gumport explore these questions of accountability through 'Access to what? Mission differentiation and academic stratification in U.S. public higher education', *Higher Education*, Vol. 46, 2003, pp. 341–59.

46 D. D. Flannery, 'Adult education and the politics of the theoretical test', in B. Kamol and P. McLaren (eds), *Critical Multiculturalism: Uncommon Voices in a Common Struggle* (Westport: Berghn and Garvey, 1995).

47 *Ibid.*, p. 156.

48 J. Bennett, 'Constructing academic community: power, relationality, hospitality, and conversation', *Interchange*, Vol. 34, No. 1, 2003, pp. 51–61.

Instead of intellectual inquiry into teaching and learning, a culture of conformity is created. Bennett confirms that technology is not the issue, but the funding of technology ahead of student training, libraries, facilities and staff needs is of great concern. His argument is verified by Jennifer Buckingham. In her study, she showed that 'the single most important influence on student achievement is teacher quality'.[49] If staff are overworked and quality suffers, then technology of any kind cannot assist students on their journey through learning.

A provocative research piece that frames the context of the contemporary university as a workplace was developed by Rachel Johnson.[50] She demonstrates the consequences of senior manager-academics being removed from daily contact with students. Because of this displaced reality, university management makes many assumptions about students, such as the demand for flexibility. Concurrently – and conveniently – 'flexible education' is a cheaper option than employing well-trained and credentialed scholars. International ranking systems, such as the Research Assessment Exercise in the United Kingdom or the Research Quality Framework in Australia, serves to increase the attention and value of research over teaching.[51] Research is becoming a resource input for a university, whereas teaching is a cost. The result of this ideology is that academic staff are being asked to do more with less money, and are valued less for the work that they complete. This is not the time or environment to demand that staff lose intellectual property rights and 'fit in' with administrative directives.

Through budget cuts in the last few years, I have had the great pleasure and also the challenge of conducting all the first year tutorials in my courses. Whereas in earlier years postgraduate tutors could assist me, budget cuts have meant that it has been me, a timetable and 120 first year students. While such a situation has left me (literally) running from room to room, session to session and course to course, it has presented some advantages. I have been able to monitor – at extremely close quarters – the new students arriving in our universities, paying attention to their expectations, goals, problems and hopes. In these tutorials each day, students grapple with difficult ideas. Good teachers are able to continually explain abstract concepts in different ways until

49 J. Buckingham, 'Class size and teacher quality', *Educational Research of Policy and Practice*, Vol. 2, 2003, p. 71.

50 R. Johnson, 'Talking of students: tensions and contradictions for the manager-academic and the university in contemporary higher education', *Higher Education*, Vol. 46, 2003, pp. 289–314.

51 Also noted is the value of the 'old' (often research-intensive) universities over the 'newer' universities. Stephen Sharp and Simon Coleman affirm that 'it is well enough known – and evidence is reported here to confirm this – that old universities dominate the panels in most Units of Assessment (UoAs)', from 'Ratings in the Research Assessment Exercise 2001 – the patterns of university status and panel membership', *Higher Education Quarterly*, Vol. 59, No. 2, April 2005, p. 156.

the specific experiences and context of the student are fused. In the true definition of the word, face-to-face education is the most flexible of all, creating a flexibility of the mind. There is an opportunity to align diverse forms of representation: from text to photography, video and music. Further, students need an opportunity to discuss the difficult problems of our era, such as racism and xenophobia, and to raise the issues and examples of interest to them, in an environment of safety and intellectual clarity.

Students who listen to an i-lecture have an opportunity to pause the audio stream, but not to ask questions. It is far easier to gloss over the difficult, the complex and the misunderstood. The reason why the lecture and tutorial format has survived for so long is not because academics are lazy or resistant to change, but because such structures and methods work. Students hear an argument presented in a lecture, think about it, conduct the reading for a week, and are then able to express concerns or confusions in the more intimate venue of a tutorial. Models of critical reflection and skill development are formed. This is an old system. It is also a functional system.

The i-lecture is a symptom of a financially starved university sector, employing over-worked staff, enrolling under-inspired students and cutting costs in teacher training. Instead of teaching staff developing – with time, precision and consideration – materials that utilize the specific attributes of the web such as hypertext links, the i-lecture is a cheap, inappropriate and low quality application for education. It confirms that the e-ducation revolution never arrived. The only managerial option was to upload already existing – analogue – lectures, ignoring intellectual property rights, and hope that no one would notice. By taking the creation, management and distribution of content out of the hands of academics, and deprioritizing the role of form in education, the language of teaching and learning changes. Suddenly 'web content management'[52] replaces well-theorized and delivered scholarship. Universities are making specific assumptions about students having home access to not only computers, but the literacy to manage the downloading of software and the management of the i-lecture stream. While forgetting about the class- and age-based inequalities manifested through the internet,[53] i-lectures are justified by the University of Western Australia as providing an 'equality of access, regional programs and expansion into international markets'.[54] Such justification is – obviously – nonsense. The digital divide accurately shadows analogue inequalities.[55]

---

52 'Web tools for teaching purposes', The University of Western Australia, http://www.staff.webct.uwa.edu.au/index/web_tools, accessed on 31 July 2004.

53 To monitor many of these injustices and inequalities in the most mature internet economy in the world, please refer to the PEW 'Internet and American Life Project', http://www.pew.org(.)

54 'i-lectures – enabling the collection & delivery of digital content on-demand', http://www.unsw.innovationxchange.com.au/page.print.html?article_id=00000000483, accessed on 31 July 2004.

55 Cushia Kapitzke monitored 'the digital divide along the same axes of gender, class, race, and geographic location that existed with print literacy', from 'Information literacy: the changing

Without a nod to, or recognition of, these concerns, a prototype for i-lectures was offered for public 'view'.

http://ilectures.uwa.edu.au/ilectures/ilectures.lasso?ut=726&id=33817

The University of Western Australia, which developed i-lectures, presented this link as the best practice and exhibition of their product. The example deployed was Paul Crompton's lecture on 'Inflation'.[56] The assumptions I brought to this review process before clicking open the sound file are important to recognize. I had predicted that the i-lecture presentation would be dry and inadequately utilize sonic media and literacies, but technologically competent. I intended to evaluate the i-lecture through the use of voice, the mixed media deployment of PowerPoint slides, the use of the visualizer and consider how the aural delivery was paced and structured. The criteria of assessment were derailed in a remarkable way. I am experienced enough to know that surprises emerge – particularly in unobtrusive research. Intentionally therefore I conducted all the research and analysis of the supplemental materials presented in this chapter before downloading the i-lecture. The shock of my displaced expectations was stunning.

I accessed this site from a dial-up connection at my father's house in regional Western Australia, rather than through the broadband connection at my university office so as to replicate student listening conditions. The resultant session horrified me. The sound dropped out through the streaming process. The lecture did not commence at the start of the session, but approximately 90 seconds into the recording. The 'visual component' was a graph which was drawn and augmented in scattered and irregular 'stream time', not real time. The prototype – either implicitly or explicitly – did not present copyrighted material or address the consequences of doing so. The choice of lecture topic – inflation – meant that the difficulties in gaining permission for the use of film or television extracts were not hinted or suggested.

The great surprise through this process was the extraordinarily poor quality of the streamed recording and the lecture performance itself. I had assumed that – considering that this prototype was being used to sell the application – it would be a gleaming example of a fine speaker, a riveting topic and a seamless presentation of the streamed session. Instead, the lecture was poorly structured and not well delivered. This example was used – I assume – because the lecturer deployed 'the visualizer', Once more the technology was prioritized over other questions of form, voice and topic. The application was deployed, but not well. It seems that within this model of educational discourse, the technology 'itself' is always enough, rather than evaluating the quality

library', *Journal of Adolescent and Adult Literacy*, Vol. 44, No. 5, February 2001, pp. 450–56.

56 A male academic voice – discussing inflation – was the prototype for this process. No recognition of the consequences of this choice, in terms of addressing or discussing social justice initiatives, was presented. Once more, a(nother) male academic was offering an authoritative presentation of an(other) educational technology.

of the use. The hand movements around the graph were jilted and distracting. The viewer never saw the lecturer, the students or anything that actually moved. Beyond the visual realm, the sound quality was dreadful. Hundreds of sentences were distorted through the dial-up connection – the connection that most students use from home. The scroll bar also encourages bad behaviour. Students – bored with the audio-only delivery – can move through the lecture without listening to it. Certainly this process is convenient, but it does not facilitate learning. With the application frequently chopping up the sound, it is no wonder that students would scroll through the form rather than suffering through a fragmented content.

Even the advertorial i-lecture presentation[57] had awkward streaming with multiple cutouts. A female voice was heard from Leitha Delves, but again she did not demonstrate expertise in reading text for the ear. It was a stilted and uneven delivery. The student testimonials all stress the use of i-lectures when sessions are missed because of work. There is no questioning of the context of education, suggesting that a student prioritizing paid work above university learning is not recommended or appropriate. The ease of use and the flexibility given to students are all stressed, not the ambivalent context for learning that makes the application necessary.

I expected the i-lecture presented by UWA to be smooth and slick. Much money and time has been spent developing this application. However, the inability to actually hear a continual streamed voice through the featured i-lecture was a complete surprise. Obviously through broadband many of these problems would be solved.[58] To assume this level of access amongst students is a clear example of elitism and an ignorance of how class, race and region impact on the use of the internet and the World Wide Web. Paradoxically, the justification of the i-lecture is through appealing to social justice initiatives and the desire to improve regional education.

The silent issue of the i-lecture discourse – beyond the bubbling talk of convenience and copyright – is how easily the community of scholars and the excitement of learning has been traded for flexibility. Education is about creating relationships. The question is how i-lectures forge these relationships. There is an implicit – and occasionally explicit – realization that the i-lecture will lead to compromises and the university authorities are prepared to accept this. Until I opened up the streamed lecture, I was not aware of the scale of these compromises. The i-lecture may permit viewing of PowerPoint slides. It may permit some graphs to be viewed through the visualizer. But the one attribute it does not permit is the clear and uninterrupted presentation of the human voice. The i-lecture can do a great many things, except present a lecture.

---

57 'The ilecture', http://ilectures.uwa.edu.au/ilectures/ilectures.lasso?ut=726&id=33816, University of Western Australia, accessed on 1 September 2004.

58 It is important to note that I wrote this chapter while resident in Australia, where vast areas of Australia's suburbs, regional hubs and rural zones do not even have the potential or opportunity to operate with broadband. It is simply not a technological option.

There is a reason for teachers' hostility to computer-mediated technology. We have seen the ridiculous distribution of resources in the last few years. Untested and untheorized applications have gained priority over other far more important teaching and learning needs. Jukka Husu – in one of the most intelligent readings of the current environment – confirmed the reasons for academic anger.

> The modern pedagogical task of teaching is ambiguous because contemporary policy perspectives and public discourses on education tend to focus on such issues that are largely external to teachers' everyday occupations; productivity, accountability measures, instructional technology, and so on.[59]

We all feel powerless when we are responsible for events over which we have no control. Curriculum design is more important now than ever in its history. Yet less time and credit is being given to those staff that spend effort on their teaching. There are pivotal questions to ask about the current funding of the university sector. The rationale needs to be unraveled for the purchase of technology, applications and platforms without research into their effectiveness. Currently, student and staff voices are absent from the i-lecture discourse.[60] With the prototype i-lecture stream being garbled, inadequate and incomplete, it remains a metaphor for the state of technology policy in educational settings.

The accelerated realities of university education are taking hold. Students expect lectures to be made available for consumption. They are our clients and have a right to demand service even if they are lazy, poorly motivated, bored or skewed in their priorities. A student – with some horror – asked me before a first year lecture in 2005, 'But what happens if we miss your lecture and it is not available on i-lecture?' My reply was curt, but tethers to the core of our current problems in teaching and learning. I replied – with a smile – 'if you make a decision to miss the lecture, then that is fine. But there are consequences for your actions'. Confusion filled her face. Without connecting student behaviour and scholarly consequences, teaching and learning will not function. Education is not convenient. Learning is frequently not pleasant. Asking students who are enrolled on a university course to be on campus for 150 minutes in a week is not

59 J. Husu, 'Constructing ethical representations from the teacher's pedagogical practice: a case of prolonged reflection', *Interchange*, Vol. 34, No. 1, 2003, p. 3.

60 This recognition is important in any discussion of social change and cultural difference. Janis Wilton stressed the importance of 'the meeting ground between theory, policy analysis, and the lived and remembered experiences of the people whose lives are subjected to the theory and the analysis', from 'Chinese-Australians talk, we theorise', in S. Gamage (ed.), *A Question of Power and Survival*, UNE Symposium Group on Assimilation, Pluralism and Multiculturalism (Armidale: UNE, 1993), p. 112.

curtailing their life choices. The opportunities for avoidance that we have created will not help these students in the long term. Let me explain.

I attended university during a kinder time for capitalism. There was still full-time and permanent work, universal healthcare coverage and a reasonably functional welfare state. Yet the education system in which I was enrolled was ruthless. If the assignment was late, then it would not be marked. I remember students on multiple occasions being expelled from tutorials for not completing the reading. We rarely saw our teachers outside of class time. We had to work it out for ourselves. It was an environment of fear: a fear of failure. At the very time that capitalism was benevolent, the university system was preparing us for the ruthless inequalities we would confront upon leaving the leafy campus.

Now that there are wars on terror, casualized workplaces, little union protection for workers and an economy based on credit card debt, universities are soft, kind and cuddly institutions, shielding our students from the dire reality of life. At the very time that we mouth the rhetoric that universities prepare students for the workplace, we are actually masking the sickening inequalities, injustices and disrespect that are the marinade of contemporary life. Actually, if we failed more students, expelled them from classrooms for not doing the reading, and demanded their presence on time and on topic, then we would be preparing them for the workforce. When bosses expect i-work for their i-salary, then i-lectures may have a place.

Chapter five

Popular culture and the sensuality of education

> I gave an in-service lecture to a group of secondary school English teachers in 1990. There and then, I was completely thrown off-guard by the gales of laughter prompted by the mere mention of the series, and especially its otherworldly anti-hero Freddy Krueger. It was certainly not affectionate laughter, but rather cruel, derisive, dismissive … These reactions to the *Nightmare on Elm St* films sum up for me, as in an absurdly recurring nightmare, just about all of the most retrograde, insensitive, superior, middle class assumptions about popular culture that one could ever encounter or imagine.[1]
>
> Adrian Martin

> Postmodern troubles cannot be adequately handled by modern means.[2]
>
> Zygmunt Bauman

Teaching culture is based on assumptions about standards and quality. Too often educators do not admit these assumptions to themselves, let alone to those who are being taught. We carry values in our minds that subtly but continually remind us of gradings and shadings of importance and significance. There are alternatives to repeating the cultural mantras and standards of our parents, colleagues and governments. Such alternatives are offered in this chapter to explore why, how and when popular culture – in its plurality and sensuality – is best deployed, and why such a discussion is even more relevant through digitization and the growth of e-teaching and i-lectures. It is also important to acknowledge that fine media teaching, teachers and pedagogy create networks of reflexive movements between the analogue and digital, providing models and methods for the rest of the academy. While the last chapter showed what is lost through uploading lectures, this chapter confirms the plurality and diversity of popular culture in the classroom.

---

1 A. Martin, 'In the name of popular culture', *Metro*, No. 89, 1992, p. 35.

2 Z. Bauman, 'Universities: old, new and different', from A. Smith and F. Webster (ed.), *The Postmodern University? Contested Visions of Higher Education in Society* (Buckingham: Open University Press, 1997), p. 24.

Throughout the history of universities and formal education, popular culture has been intentionally and actively excluded. The separation of pop from art, without overtly addressing embedded class-based notions of cultural value, served to disenfranchise generations of students from their own social frameworks and literacies. The strength of teaching the popular, to summon Stanley Aronowitz and Henry Giroux's phrase, is that it creates 'a language of possibility'.[3] Following their challenge, my goal is to transform Google into, not a static object for an investigation, but the matrix of an educational dialogue about the pathways from information to knowledge. Google is part of popular culture, not disconnected from it. Within this method, there is no separation of 'old' and 'new' media, but the active determination of appropriate media for the correct context.

If we grant culture a history and politics, rather than an intrinsic value and stability, then greater attention is placed on the function and circulation of representations. In pondering the stratification of cultural systems, literacy has a purpose, impetus and agenda. Such a goal was witnessed most poignantly in Richard Hoggart's *The Uses of Literacy*.[4] Born into a working class family in Leeds and educated at his home university, he went on to be the adult education tutor at the University of Hull. He taught literature to people who had been blocked from attending higher education. From such a context, *The Uses of Literacy* weaves Hoggart's personal experience into the text. Fascinatingly, and appropriately for his student cohort at the time, he deployed the tools used to study literature to a much wider range of cultural productions such as music, magazines and newspapers. There was an attention to sport, pubs and working men's clubs. Discussion of language was punctuated with family structures and gender roles. For Hoggart, culture became the method to link literary analysis and social inquiry, text and context, university and social justice.

Hoggart's example is important. Popular culture circulates ideas to a wide audience. While high cultural practices are associated with excellence, these standards are established and circulated through precise historical periods. Teachers often work with high culture rather than popular culture. The aim of good teaching, and the focus of this chapter, is to deny and decentre the easy and assumed division of art and pop. The trap of these categories is that teachers, writers and researchers spend too much time legitimizing their choice of topic against faceless forces of the elite, rather than exploring the political impact of these representational formations. If a discussion about the role and purpose of popular culture in education is not made, then our classrooms become museums. Teachers become guides through the dusty relics of texts and ideas. The conservative cry to go 'back to basics' is often code for returning to safe, seamless

---

3 S. Aronowitz and H. Giroux, *Postmodern Education* (Minneapolis: University of Minnesota Press, 1997), p. 181.

4 R. Hoggart, *The Uses of Literacy* (London: Transaction, 1998: 1957).

cultural formations that offer no challenge or argument against the current political order.[5] Conversely, popular culture is formed through the gritty transformations of economic and social structures through industrialization. It is a site of commerce and commercialization, but also play and transformation.

The emergence of popular culture in industrialized societies is tethered to the development of the print media in the eighteenth and nineteenth centuries. Serialized stories in newspapers and mass-produced novels became possible through the changes to consumer capitalism. Advertising reduced the cover price of newspapers, transforming them from an elite to mass media. Such pop imaginings summoned alternative dramaturgies and were dynamic. Opera, once popular, became infused with bourgeois ideologies through the nineteenth century. In the twentieth century, through the voice and presence of tenors like Pavarotti, opera once more entered popular culture. Il Divo is the confirmation of this principle with tenors part of the pop charts.

Such judgments and movements of value have profound consequences for the determination of legitimate knowledge. *Te Ara*, the Encyclopedia of New Zealand, while not mobilizing user-driven content like Wikipedia, maintains rigid notions of cultural quality. As Russell Brown revealed,

> If there is one part of the site that grieves me, it is the section on New Zealand music. The last 15 years have seen an emergence of national identity in our popular music that is as significant as the arrival of a characteristically New Zealand literature in the 1930s.[6]

Libraries, knowledge, education are embedded in the judgments and values of popular culture. Yet recent popular music – some of which is innovative and pivotal to the remakings of identity – suffers from the qualitative determinations of the powerful. Literature is framed as important to nation building. Music is youthful trash. Actually, New Zealand popular culture, through Flying Nun Records, Auckland electronica and the *Lord of the Rings* Trilogy, has transformed Aotearoa/New Zealand far more than the literature of cultural criticism. John Docker cut to the political chase when he realized that,

---

5 For example, the former Australian Education Minister, Dr Brendan Nelson, stated that 'I think too much of the curriculum is dominated by contemporary television and media … So you've got the kids studying Big Brother and Buffy the Vampire Slayer instead of T. S. Eliot and Thomas Hardy. Now I'm not suggesting they shouldn't study contemporary fads and the impact they have on our evolving society and cultural values. But I think we diminish and impoverish ourselves if we educate a generation of young Australians that are unfamiliar with Patrick White and Jane Austen and the great authors of the past 200 to 300 years', from C. Johnson, 'Bring back the three Rs: Nelson', *The West Australian*, 12 August 2005, p. 1.

6 R. Brown, 'Information Entrepreneurs', 2 September 2005, Public Address.net, http://publicaddress.net/print,2494.sm, accessed on 9 September 2005.

> Radical intellectuals who despise popular culture suffered from the pride of intellect: they believe in their bones that because working-class people are not formally educated then they lack consciousness, lack the ability to be critical, to make choices, to say no … Only the educated – which means only those of the middle and upper classes who have been university-trained – have the ability and the right to be rational conscious beings who can combine pleasure with discrimination.[7]

The neo-liberal emphasis tethering education and employment means that it is easy to attack schools and universities for their declining standards, mediocrity and place blame and responsibility for the economic downturn. It is also extremely easy to discredit music, film, television and the World Wide Web – or media studies generally – for causing the demise of civilization.[8] Actually new modes of living, thinking and writing are created on dancefloors, in darkened cinemas and through hypertext. Intellectual standards in research, writing and scholarship must not be confused with reactionary determinations of cultural 'quality' and 'value'.

A sad, but evocative example of how the teaching of popular music can change lives popped into my in-box in 2005.

> From:
> Sent: Thursday, 19 May 2005 12:30 PM
> To: Tara Brabazon
> Subject: A 'New Order' in my life
>
> Dear Tara,
>
> Well, it sure has been awhile! I have been wanting to write to you for awhile, but i have so much to tell you that i didn't know where to start!
>
> What made me get off my arse and finally write to you was something that happened last night... but i will start at the beginning. Over the past couple of months i feel like i have had a huge awakening, or an epiphany or something. it sounds so cliched but it is seriously like i have been born again! As you know, i have had a few issues over the past couple of years, and these all came to a head 2 months ago, when i attempted suicide. A couple of weeks after that i went to Melbourne to

7 J. Docker, 'In defense of popular culture', *Arena*, No. 60, p. 86.

8 For example, Janet Street-Porter, in *The Independent* of 27 August 2006, revealed in her column that 'I would never employ anyone with any qualifications in media studies: they are useless'.

stay with my step brother for a couple of weeks, and it was there that my whole outlook on life changed. i had many conversations with my bro and his housemate, and through these i came to finally accept myself as a person and the world as imperfect but full of amazing experiences. i have spent too long fighting life – complaining about things, being depressed about things and basically not taking responsibility for my own happiness. i used to have such a bleak and cynical outlook on life – i have never been religious so have never had that as a comfort blanket to give me meaning, so i basically just believed that its all pretty meaningless. But now, through reading and talking (and maybe experimenting with various substances!) i have discovered spirituality; not in religious terms really, just a peace within myself, and a peace with the universe. To put it simply, i guess i have am growing up. I am no longer self destructive – i eat healthily and exercise regularly, and i have stopped cutting myself for MYSELF, not for anyone else, because i finally see that more than anything i was hurting myself (and certainly not just physically).

So anyway, back to why i finally wrote to you... last night i was at my brother's house (who i couldn't be closer to) and we were listening to music, as we do. i have to admit, i used to be a bit of a music snob – i had my (narrow) likes and wouldn't really step outside the square. But, with the help of my brother, my new attitude and a few herbs, i am appreciating so much more music now. so last night, we were listening to New Order, which i have never liked until last night. i loved what i heard, but knew nothing about them, and when my brother educated me on ian curtis's suicide i finally realised the significance and the powerfulness of the music. it made me think of cultural studies and what you taught us about pop culture and i feel like i understand so much better now. i wanted to tell you all of this, as it feels as though the things you said to me back in first year, and the things we talked about both in class and out of class mean so much more to me now.

i always wanted someone to 'fix' me, to give me the answer, i didn't think i had the strength to do it myself, but here i am! This is all my own doing... the psych didn't do it for me – you were right- it was something i had to do when i was ready, and i did it.

It is often a cliché that a song saved our lives. In the case of this young woman, the cliché has a slice of truth. Even more significantly, it is education that provided an alternative path, a different way of thinking. Such an email serves as a reminder of the powerful and life-affirming capacity of popular culture. The difficulty in presenting the optimistic potential and role of popular cultural forms is that since Richard Hoggart wrote *The Uses of Literacy* in 1957, and since cultural and media studies' birth and development through the 1960s and 1970s, the political environment has changed. John Hartley captured the liberatory context that framed the paradigm during this earlier progressive time.

> Cultural studies is politically a child of the 1960s, when political radicalism was not only liberating but hip … when the boundaries between politics, music, sex and drugs became blurred, and when alternative, counter and sub cultures sprang up to claim attention like so many doggies in the window.[9]

Now that the long 1960s is over, pedagogical terrorism is patrolling the limits of acceptable teaching, learning and curriculum. There is a re-establishment of 'standards', 'basics' and 'fundamental principles'. Hewison noted this change: 'by 1975 the revolutionary optimism of the counter-culture had evaporated, its heroes arrested, overdosed or dead; their followers had taken their degrees, got their mortgages, moved to the country to sell antiques'.[10] The playful and excessive tackiness of popular culture has difficulty surviving in classrooms framed by such histories of disappointment. Literacy and technology snuff out analogue and popular culture alternatives.

Culture is integral to the building of neo-conservatism. Affirming an 'agreed' collection of literary texts is part of an ideology of tradition, religion, family and nationalism. Strange ideas, pictures, rhythms and sounds provoke a citizen to think outside of these structures and values. Popular culture is pivotal to the shaping of our identity, of building an image of ourselves, and the alliances that facilitate the creation of community. It is also sensual culture, affecting the body through the propulsion of laughter, the springing of tears or the dynamism of dancing. In offering narratives of emotion, transposing literacy beyond lettered representation, popular culture teaches and values different skills, senses and sensations. James Schwoch, Mimi White and Susan Reilly referred to this process as critical citizenship.

> We invoke a different way of reading media culture as a part of an alternative theory that opposes current trends in American education, trends that exclusively emphasize excellence, discipline, achievement, and quantitatively verifiable production.[11]

---

9 J. Hartley, *The Politics of Pictures* (London: Routledge, 1992), p. 16.

10 R. Hewison, *Future Tense* (London: Methuen, 1990), p. 37.

11 J. Schwoch, M. White and S. Reilly, *Media Knowledge: Readings in Popular Culture, Pedagogy, and Critical Citizenship* (New York: State University Press, 1992).

The goal of such a process is to create an environment of inquiry, questioning and critical thinking, rather than acceptance, denial or compliance. In recognizing that immersion in popular culture offers a framework of learning, change and thought, the purpose of schools and universities also changes in response.[12] The constitution of media knowledge, based on movements of the body or movements through mouse clicks via the World Wide Web, is not bowing to a culture of equivalence or denying cultural value. Instead new criteria is created to understand the changes to politics and how we commit to information. We must not deny pop, but create thinking pop. Through such a model, Google is not the domain of the elite, but the right of all to use in a way integrated with their lived experience and informed and shaped through training and scholarship.

A key strategy in our universities is not only handling or managing, but enjoying and caring for, students with learning difficulties. One strategy to assist those who may come from a range of cultural and linguistic communities is to mobilize popular culture with theoretical and pedagogical rigour. We all have learning difficulties, strengths and weaknesses. But those who can interpret and write a form of prose valued through formal educational testing are celebrated and validated through education and life. Those who can copy and develop dance steps or hold an encyclopedic knowledge of popular music are rarely celebrated for these skills. Learning difficulties are always diverse in origin, cause and orientation. Behavioural differences become overlaid with linguistic, cultural or familial dissonances.[13] When students are showing difficulties with more conservative or traditional literacies, and losing confidence through constant testing that reinforces their sense of inadequacy and failure, popular culture is incredibly important. Margaret Finders has recognized the relevance of this remedial role, confirming the function of popular culture in 'identity maintenance'. Further, she transforms her theory of critical literacy to incorporate 'both how to use and how one is used by popular culture'.[14] Perhaps there is no better statement of the profound, deep and ambivalent role of pop in the contemporary classroom. There is no point in celebrating students' popular culture without question or critique. There is a need to acknowledge, understand and

12 Henry Giroux and Peter McLaren confirmed in 'Media hegemony: towards a critical pedagogy of representation', that 'pedagogy occurs wherever knowledge is produced, wherever culture is given the possibility of translating experience and constructing truths, even if such truths appear unrelentingly redundant, superficial, and commonsensical'. This argument builds into a strong presentation of a critical pedagogy with attention to visions of and for the future. This chapter is included in Schwoch, White and Reilly (eds), *Media Knowledge*, p. xxiii.

13 Mary Rohl and Judith Rivalland monitored the complicated determination of these learning difficulties in 'Literacy learning difficulties in Australian primary schools', *The Australian Journal of Language and Literacy*, Vol. 25, No. 3, 2002, pp. 19–40.

14 M. Finders, '"Gotta be worse": negotiating the pleasurable and the popular', *Journal of Adolescent & Adult Literacy*, Vol. 44, No. 2, October 2000, p. 146.

contextualize these texts. Lisa Patel Stevens recognized the importance of this pop cult pedagogy.

> I was 11 years old when MTV (Music Television) burst onto the burgeoning scene of cable television in 1981. You would have been hard-pressed to find an adolescent more enraptured by the big hair, dreamlike plot sequences, and over-the-top fashions of music video than I was. However, this was a world that was distinctly separate and removed from the dialogues and actions found within my junior high school classrooms. This dichotomous relationship between school and popular culture was permeated by development and practices as a literacy educator.[15]

Throughout her career, Stevens worked between this disjuncture of school and popular culture. In a desire to converge these spheres, she assembled a checklist of questions for her students, to create a thinking pop through curriculum.

> For each portion of popular culture that we shared, we also modeled the inquiry process for students by answering six questions (a) What is the piece of popular culture? (b) Who is the intended audience? (c) Who is not the intended audience? (d) Who stands to benefit from it? (e) Who stands either not to advance in society or even to be hurt by it? and (f) What does this popular culture and its positioning say about U.S. society at large?[16]

Stevens has provided a succinct model for revealing the political complexity of these popular cultural texts. When I have used these questions – in fact her whole article – my students have responded with great enthusiasm, debate and discussion.[17] They learn critical literacy, and apply these difficult ideas and terms with greater ease because they are using and translating them into their own context. Teaching students must begin with a respect of their language, experiences and difficulties.

---

15 L. Stevens, 'South Park and society: instructional and curricular implications of popular culture in the classroom', *Journal of Adolescent & Adult Literacy*, Vol. 44, No. 6, March 2001, p. 548.

16 *Ibid.*, pp. 552–3.

17 Stevens' reflexive deployment of these critical questions has much to do not only with her immersion in MTV, but the tight relationship between Generation X and popular culture. For my broader discussion of the sociological and political connection between Gen X and popular culture, please refer to Tara Brabazon, *From Revolution to Revelation: Generation X, Popular Memory and Cultural Studies* (Aldershot: Ashgate, 2005).

Popping the web

> Poetry or potatoes? Culture and politics? Dancing or meat? These are not just t-shirt slogans … Asking neat, sharp and tasty questions like this raises issues of class, distinction and hierarchy while targeting polite society.[18]
>
> John Hutnyk

John Hutnyk's humour and pithy writing is always undercut by a sharp and tasty analytical edge. The World Wide Web is an outstanding site to ponder his questions. The speed at which the sociology of the internet is changing creates research on the run, making demands on those wanting to create a suite and context of literacies for this environment. Steve Redhead has aligned speed and pop. He stated that,

> Popular culture which is characterized not by content … but increasingly by the speed with which its products become outdated, and recycled, or by the speed with which the underground becomes overground … is one example of accelerated culture.[19]

The content – or indeed the audience – is not what makes popular culture popular. Instead, it is the pace at which it moves through discourses, spaces and times. This is an appropriate model through which to place the internet, web and Google into popular culture. Critics love to discuss the web's speed to popularity, and the wildfire of possibilities such rapid infiltration has instigated. However, as the excited expansion has slowed, there have been unusual consequences of web growth in its more mature form. The PEW Internet and American Life survey has tracked many of these surprises. There are two extraordinary findings from their research. Firstly, they discovered that the penetration of the internet in the United States has now reached a plateau. Former users – those who *were* on the internet and now choose not to be – outnumber new users.[20] Secondly, there is a section of the American population that does not use the internet, have never used it, and will never log on.[21] This digital subaltern see no reason or need for the construction of a digital avatar. Further research outside of the United States has demonstrated that, for the first time in 2004, less than 50 per cent of new internet

---

18 J. Hutnyk, *Critique of Exotica* (London: Pluto, 2000), p. 3.

19 S. Redhead, *Paul Virilio: Theorist for an Accelerated Culture* (Edinburgh: Edinburgh University Press, 2004), pp. 49–50.

20 A. Lenhart, J. Horrigan, L. Rainie, K. Allen, A. Boyce, M. Madden and E. O'Grady, *The Ever Shifting Internet Population: A New Look at Internet Access and the Digital Divide* (Washington: Pew Internet and American Life Project, 2003), http://www.pewinternet.org/report_display.asp?r=88, accessed on 5 July 2005.

21 *Ibid.* Also, the older a person, the less likely they are to be online. Please refer to S. Fox, 'Older Americans and the Internet', *PEW Internet & American Life Project*, 25 March 2004, pp. i–ii.

users speak English, with the Chinese dialects being the growing online languages.[22] The assumptions about American domination of the digital world and endless growth and expansion of the internet are not verified by current quantitative studies. Many citizens in the most mature digital economies in the world have disconnected or see no reason to ever connect. Meanwhile, the other nations who arrived later to digitization are not undergoing the rapid expansion of the United States, Europe, Australia and New Zealand of the late 1990s.

In such a time of flux, popular cultural representations of the web shadow this new history. How wired and unwired citizens think about the internet and web is framed and shaped by already existing popular culture. No longer trapped within the utopian and dystopian binary, the internet and web have become a thinking space for popular culture, allowing citizens to explore the movements in meaning between 'old' and 'new' media. The neophiliacs, those who approach the internet and web, let alone cyberspace, as new, innovative, distinctive and disconnected from all other media, do remain. The desire for media – particularly new media – distinctiveness is not (actually) new. Each 'new' media formation, the telegraph, radio, cinema, film and even Web 2.0, all preached revolution and change. Google, as the 'killer app' of the web, continues this ideology.[23]

By placing Google, the web and the internet in popular culture, rather than isolating 'technology' from 'culture', or even worse – assembling a barricade between old and new media – a more intricate, complex and accurate history of communication can emerge. Older media always provide information about the cultural formations that transcend it. Emails have 'CCs' – Carbon Copies. Websites have 'home' pages. Older ways of thinking about business and identity move from print to text and analogue to digital. As Homer confirmed on *The Simpsons*, 'Hmmm … they have the Internet on computers, now'.[24] For Homer, the intricacies of internet history are lost. In popular culture, the internet is merely one more application on a computer. Greater focus is required on how different modes and media of information encourage or discredit particular social values and groups. For example, young people fetishize mobile phone

---

22 In 1996, 80 per cent of the online population used English. By September 2004, this level had fallen to 35.2 per cent. In 2004, and for the first time, the United States accounted for less than half of all e-commerce transactions online. By 2007, China passed the United States in total broadband subscriptions. Please refer to 'China to Top U.S. in Broadband subscribers', *Electronic News*, 5 April 2005, http://www.reed-electronics.com/electronicnews/article/CA529685?nid=2-19, accessed on 6 August 2005, and Global Reach, 'Forrester projects 6.8 trillion for 2004', http://glreach.com/eng/ed/art/2004.ecommerce.php3, accessed 6 August 2005.

23 Charles Leadbeater has continued this celebration of 'the new' through his article 'Are you thinking what I'm thinking?', *The Times*, 13 October 2006, http://technology.timesonline.co.uk/printFriendly/0,,214-7-2400772-1867,00.html, accessed on 27 November 2006, and *We Think* (London: Profile, 2007)

24 *The Simpsons*, Director Pete Michels, Episode 192, 1998.

ring tones. Older men are the booming audience of the iPod. Wired senior citizens use email more than any other social group. More focus is required, not on the application itself, but the sociology and context of the user. The moment of a Fordist – one size fits all – internet is at an end. That is why much attention is required on educational policy, funding levels and the development of media literacy skills. There has never been a greater need for more specialized and subtle teaching and learning methods.

In expanding beyond the printed word, Google has offered a view of pedagogic convergence that models a potential for textual diversity. The long-term ideological bias in favour of the printed word also values sight over sound, and the eye over the ear. Instead, some of the most exciting and innovative research in the last five years has emerged in the areas of auditory cultures. The iPod, which is riding the wave of compression technology that facilitated the movement of audio files through the internet, is repainting sonic architecture and creating personalized soundtracks.[25] New aural literacies are developing, which will destabilize the hierarchical valuation of sight and sound.

Each media extends the senses. Books and cameras extended the potentials of the eye. Radio and listening devices such as mobile phone ring tones and the iPod extend the capacities of the ear. Television increases the convergent literacies of eye and ear. Gaming and computer applications more generally forge links between the eye, ear and hand, while also changing how we commit and understand information. As convergence increases, older technologies and literacies are not lost, but feed their values into the mixing desk of 'the next big thing'. Just as disco survives in house music, just as jungle lives in drum 'n' bass, so is the capacity to read print perpetuated in the iPod, enabling the negotiation of a menu on the illuminated screen. Aural literacies, from radio, mobile phone ring tones and other leisure technologies, allow the listener to rapidly recognize the song emerging through the headphones. Reading print is not lost as a skill, but is layered and enmeshed with other literacies and competencies, such as scrolling through text on a screen.

Popular culture emerges from these contradictions and confluences in media and social life, tracking how older social structures survive, are fragmented or changed. Literacies are formed and ranked when communities claim interpretations of symbolic forms. Some literacies are more important than others. Those in power claim their books, media and language as quality and part of educational curricula, while discrediting the rest. Those operating outside of these values may resist, or their literacies and texts

25 There is a gendered caveat to this analysis. Keir Keightley has affirmed that 'gendered access to leisure meant gendered access to leisure technology', p. 252. She argues that men have a different right to leisure than women, and have more time to gain technological literacies. She also suggests that sound technology in particular is 'a masculine bastion of high culture', p. 236. Please refer to 'Low television, high fidelity: taste and the gendering of home entertainment technologies', *Journal of Broadcasting and Electronic Media*, June 2003, pp. 236–59.

may be lost or buried by the dominant group. Yet struggle does not always result in resistance. Audiences, consumers and citizens seek out environments in which they are comfortable, and understand the signs and codes. Rarely do we gravitate to those images and ideas that make us uncomfortable or that we do not understand. The electronic revolution that Google has continued has made possible the reproduction and dissemination of cultural symbols, but also the careful filtering and selection of a digital environment to ensure that the empowered users of the web are comfortable and unchallenged.

Google is the metaphor, metonymy and the archetypal example of the need for higher levels of interpretation, comprehension and literacy in education. Because Google ranks its site returns on the basis of popularity, it is reasonably easy to influence the algorithms that display and rank results. Called Search Engine Optimization (SEO), all users must monitor not only the content of the sites returned, but their (lack of) diversity and the rationale for their ranking. Stephen Abram and Judy Luther discovered a clear example to demonstrate why we need to use Google to think with, not think through Google.

> If we fail to encourage highly formed multiliteracy skills in this generation, our democracies could be at risk. We have already seen the early results of manipulation of Google rankings in the U.S. Democratic primary race for President [in 2004] – especially in Howard Dean's campaign's use of blogs, which are valued fairly highly by Google's algorithms.[26]

Blogs are fascinating texts. They are – at their most overt – one person (over)valuing the minutia of their day. As a diary for public circulation, they make the writer feel important and published, without going through processes of refereeing, editing and proofing. They can also be – and frequently are – opinionated nonsense untempered by argument, research or analysis. Most bloggers demonstrate the self confidence of Dr Phil on steroids.[27]

> A Weblog is a contemporary form of communication, just like your mobile, email or instant messenger. No one 'needs' a Weblog – yet. But they are becoming more widespread and more essential because of the way they give you a constant presence on the internet.[28]

The confusion of needs and wants, access and significance, ephemera and the archive is very dangerous. Self-involved individuality of the already empowered and hyper-literate

---

26 S. Abram and J. Luther, 'Born with the chip', *Library Journal*, 1 May 2004, p. 35.

27 Russell Brown described bloggers as 'Information Entrepreneurs. Entrepreneurialism is the novel combination of resources that results in an increase in wealth', Public Address, 2 September 2005, http://publicaddress.net/print,2494.sm, accessed on 9 September 2005.

28 http://www.prasena.com/public/virtual_u/lectures/dct/eteckies.htm, accessed on 20 May 2005.

is justified through the 'service'. Blogs are available so the hyper-confident confirm their importance. Google then measures the popularity of these words. In anti-intellectual times, the lack of rigour, citation or scholarly protocols is framed as an advantage and strength, not an excuse for mediocrity. For example, Meg Hourihan stated that,

> What's important is that we've embraced a medium free of the physical limitations of pages, intrusions of editors, and delays of tedious publishing systems. As with free speech itself, what we ask isn't as important as the system that enables us to say it.[29]

The 'tedious delays' are the basis of quality assurance mechanisms. The refereeing and reviewing takes time, but also ensures the calibre of writing and research. Blogs are free from such 'constraints'.

Similar concerns are raised through Wikipedia. It is a 'free' encyclopedia that allows 'anyone' to edit it. The web literate and active can place information into the Wiki, and they often hold agendas. The famous example of these problems in quality control was the entry on the British pop star Jamie Kane. Actually Kane was fictional, a character in an online game launched by the BBC. A staff member of the organization had added the entry with the goal of viral marketing. When realized, the entry was corrected, but the original was not deleted.[30]

Such blogs and Wiki entries are returned through Google and are not a problem if re/searchers recognize that they are the words of one person and require interpretation, balance and discussion. One person – particularly on the web – is not popular culture. Without understanding the importance of this analytical matrix, a blogger's views could be granted as much value as a scholar's refereed research. There are some advantages in this user-driven content. When David Lange, former Prime Minister of Aotearoa/New Zealand, died, Russell Brown revealed that there was no online biography of him on *Te Ara*, the Encyclopaedia of New Zealand Online, the *Dictionary of New Zealand Biography* or the online *Encyclopedia Britannica*. It was Wikipedia that had the main entry for David Lange, and reported his death two hours after the public announcement.[31]

Significantly Wikipedia – the posterchild of Web 2.0 along with YouTube, MySpace and Flickr – is being challenged through Citizendium. Sick of the digital vandalism permitted through Wiki and appalling personal attacks on distinguished citizens such as John Seigenthaler Sr, Wikipedia has decided to 'fork', or break into two parts. While initially using Wikipedia's content, once an article has been changed in Citizendium, it will develop independently. The difference between the two sites in terms of process

---

29 M. Hourihan, 'What we're doing when we blog', Web Devcenter, 13 June 2002, http://www.oreillynet.com/1pt/a/2474, accessed on 20 May 2005.

30 R. Brown, 'Information Entrepreneurs', PublicAddress.net, 2 September 2005, http://publicaddress.net/print,2494.sm, viewed on 9 September 2005.

31 *Ibid.*

is stark. Citizendium's contributors will have to log in and use real names. Editors must have credentials, and expertise will be valued. Larry Sanger, the co-founder of Wikipedia and chief of the newly forked project, describes his manifesto as 'Citizendium will have a culture of real-world, personal responsibility'.[32] The online environment is part of popular culture: it is plural, complex, dynamic, reflexive and self-correcting.

The internet does not worry me as an artefact, medium or matrix, and neither do the web, Wiki or Google. What does concern me is the rise of these media sites and applications when teachers and librarians are demeaned and discredited. The information age requires information management. Citizendium is part of this project. Conservative critics are missing this point, blaming popular culture – television, personal computers, video games and DVDs – for obesity or the decline in literary standards. It continues the echo of the 1950s, where rock 'n' roll was held responsible for the loosening youthful morals. Greg Callaghan reports that,

> Children aged six and under spend an average of two hours a day watching television and DVDs and playing video games – and it's not only making them overweight, but increasingly illiterate. Kids with a TV or PC in their room are significantly less likely to read by the age of six, the Kaiser Family Foundation found in its study of 1000 children.[33]

Obviously, I am a believer in reading books. My life has been punctuated and enhanced by this practice. But I have also danced, sung, played music, watched television and spent far too much time mucking around with videos and DVDs. I have a dense dedication to my iPod and its burgeoning accessories. What Callaghan and the Kaiser Family Foundation have not grasped is that literacy has fragmented into multi-literacy. What was literacy 50 or 100 years ago is simply not sufficient to interpret an information-saturated and mixed media world. Print is no longer enough. Sean Cubitt, having watched the explosion of video recorders in the 1980s, realized that,

> Video's readers are already intensely 'literate.' The codes and conventions of moving-image media, now almost a hundred years old, are dense and complex. I would argue that there is a kind of Chinese Box effect in the history of twentieth-century media, TV subsuming film, video subsuming TV.[34]

The Chinese Box continues through digital television and DVDs. We need to teach children, adults, students and citizens how to be literate in many media and textual forms, and how to evaluate and balance their potentials, weaknesses and strengths.

---

32 L. Sanger in J. Schofield, 'Wikipedia reaches a fork in the road – and takes it', *The Guardian*, 21 September 2006, p. 6.

33 G. Callaghan, 'The way ahead', *The Weekend Australian Magazine*, 18–19 December 2004, p. 8.

34 S. Cubitt, *Timeshift: On Video Culture* (London: Routledge, 1991), p. 3.

These technological ensembles are interconnected media that are organizing society in new ways. Interpersonal relationships are being mediated by telephones, emails and instant messaging. There were similar mediations in the analogue environment by letters, cards and flowers. To repeat: the problem is not Google. The problem is not popular culture. The concern is that teachers and librarians are not being given a chance to instruct the literacies required to transform Google from a leisure application and into the starting point for a critical and reflexive research process.

Nearly 20 years ago, Carolyn Marvin published a fascinating book titled *When Old Technologies were New*. The title alone demonstrates the prescient nature of her argument. She showed that 'we are not the first generation to wonder at the rapid and extraordinary shifts in the dimension of the world and the human relationships it contains as a result of new forms of communication'.[35] Social change is always accompanied by a nostalgic desire for simplicity and continuity. Such a desire is understandable and carries forward an important lesson. Instead of stressing new and old media, teachers and librarians must focus on how we extend and develop already-held knowledge and competencies. Every 'new media' is based on another media. Every 'new literacy' is grafted from another analytical skill. Marvin mobilized this argument, confirming that 'the early history of electric media is less the evolution of technical efficiencies in communication than a series of arenas for negotiating issues crucial to the conduct of social life'.[36] Google, as a thinking space, is an opportunity to reassess our values, skills, commitments and literacies, and to test our desire to seek out alternative views and voices. To place Google in popular culture is to stress the inter-relationship between all media and the speed of change, fusing connections between historical and contemporary literacies, fears and desires. There is no 'revolution' in media technology, just revelations in ways of organizing society. Digitization has changed, and will continue to alter literacy and textual practice.

Unfortunately, money is being thrown at technology in education, not education in technology. Only when teacher-scholars unify and affirm our collective lifetimes of research will the complex and fascinating relationships between text-participants, text-users and text-analysts emerge.[37] Critical responsibilities are emerging. Curricula must change and the consequences of convergence be tracked. If this work is not completed, then 'new media' continues to overwrite minority cultures. The concern I have to resolve is that the multiple screens of our lives – television, mobile telephone, iPod and computer monitor – are creating disembodied information, a digital landscape

35 C. Marvin, *When Old Technologies were New* (New York: Oxford University Press, 1988), p. 3.

36 *Ibid.*, p. 4.

37 It is important to acknowledge the remarkable research work conducted by Cal Durrant and Bill Green. They predicted and explored many of these transformative possibilities in *Literacy and the New Technologies in School Education: Meeting the L(IT)eracy Challenge?* Discussion paper, New South Wales Department of Education and Training, 1998.

lacking tactility. The final stage of this chapter socializes Google into the corporeal environment of teaching media and popular culture.

Touching the screen

> Now film has traditionally (and institutionally) held a position of pre-eminence within the study of popular culture in Britain. The work of The British Film Institute (BFI) and the Society for Education in Film and Television (SEFT), in particular, has been of immense importance … television is, for them, a Cinderella area, ultimately of less importance than film. Other media have suffered from systematic lack of attention. Radio has been a long-neglected form.[38]
>
> Len Masterman

The great strength of convergent media is that it unsettles the assumed cultural value of dispersed media. Film and television feed into streamed media platforms. Radio and music distributors make their product available at a desktop. Nike advertising images and Van Gogh paintings are both available for reconstruction through Photoshop. Sound and vision, no matter what their source, are reconfigured in new ways. Such an environment makes it more difficult to establish and maintain a cultural hierarchy. Len Masterman's landmark study of media teaching in the mid-1980s demonstrates the growth, development and changes within this field. Through the 1970s and 1980s, media and popular culture were analysed in terms of domination, exploitation and imperialism. Through the 1990s, the embedded Gramscianism and Bakhtin's carnivalesque both provided alternative theories of power, negotiation and liberation. John Docker captured both these strains of analysis when he stated that 'there are an infinite number of things wrong with the contemporary world, but mass culture and the media are not the chief culprits'.[39] He argues that more emphasis should be placed on racism, colonialism, censorship, violence and war, rather than how it is mediated or 'blamed' on 'the media'. Google, and the web generally, are not to blame for the shoddy state of the higher education system. They simply document and track a decline in funding for libraries and a rise in a textbook culture, where publishers support those who synthesize already existing knowledge, rather than develop and challenge earlier truths.

The way in which web-based pedagogy is made corporeal is through its teaching. The exploration and discussion of literacy skills, while they can be discussed virtually, are best enacted through face-to-face engagement. Using popular culture is an ideal

38 L. Masterman, *Teaching the Media* (London: Routledge, 1990: 1985), p. xiii.

39 J. Docker, *Postmodernism and Popular Culture: A Cultural History* (Melbourne: Cambridge University Press, 1994), p. xvii.

mechanism through which to teach these skills.[40] Henry Giroux and Roger Simon recognized the consequences of *not* placing pop in our classrooms.

> By ignoring the cultural and social forms that are authorized by youth and simultaneously empower or disempower them, educators risk complicitly silencing and negating their students ... Educators who refuse to acknowledge popular culture as a significant basis of knowledge often devalue students by refusing to work with the knowledge that students actually have and so eliminate the possibility of developing a pedagogy that links school knowledge to the differing subject relations that help to constitute their everyday lives.[41]

If such an argument is taken seriously, if teachers recognize that by discounting the culture of students we discount the lives of our students, then media education becomes the pedagogic grammar that connects students to the curriculum, and assists their movement into new educational environments. In such a model, media studies is not a trivial elective to a serious academic programme of study, but the pivotal discursive translator between ways of learning and ways of living. This 'enacted curriculum',[42] explored in the first chapter of this book, allows a fluent movement between text and context and the establishment of an evocative, passionate and socially just literacy-learning environment. After the post-compulsory school years, there are too many assumptions that students can manage and coordinate multiple literacies, from oral conversations to reading advanced theory, writing analytical prose, interpreting diagrams and working through a diverse sonic and visual palette. The difficulty remains in the assumptions of prior knowledge, experience and expertise. Wyatt-Smith, Cumming, Ryan and Doig argued that 'if literacy focuses on only reading and writing, or if reading and writing are privileged over other forms of literacy, or if particular types of reading and writing are privileged over others, then the demands of speaking, listening, viewing

40 Perhaps the most significant role popular culture plays in the curriculum is to test and probe assumptions about cultural value. Jaroslav Pelikan, in *The Idea of the University: A Reexamination* (New Haven: Yale University Press, 1992), tells a story that 'at the outbreak of the First World War a group of patriotic Englishwomen who were going about the countryside recruiting soldiers swept into Oxford. On the High Street one of them confronted a don in his Oxonian master's gown who was reading the Greek text of Thucydides. "And what are you doing to save Western civilization, young man?" she demanded. Bringing himself up to his full height, the don looked down his nose and replied, "Madam, I am Western civilization"', p. 137.

41 H. Giroux and R. Simon, 'Popular culture as a pedagogy of pleasure and meaning', in H. Giroux and R. Simon, *Popular Culture, Schooling and Everyday Life* (Granby: Bergin and Garvey, 1989), p. 3.

42 This great phrase is derived from Claire Wyatt-Smith, Joy Cumming, Jill Ryan and Shani Doig, 'Capturing students' experiences of the enacted curriculum: the concept of curriculum literacies', *Literacy Learning: Secondary Thoughts*, Vol. 7, No. 1, 1999, pp. 29–35.

and critical thinking remain implicit'.[43] One of the great realizations of my teaching life, and outlined in chapter one, was that my understanding about reading, research and writing was not matched by my students. The next step in this revelation is even more important: to acknowledge my assumptions and teach them overtly. The development of literacy-related assessment necessitates a movement away from standardized testing thereby respecting student cultures and environments, but also constructing new scaffolds to innovative skills and ideas. Popular culture moulds the blocks that build this new knowledge.

Technology stretches our acceptance of unequal distribution of resources. Leu and Kinzer affirm the role of teachers and librarians in this environment.

> The literacies of today will not be the literacies of tomorrow. Literacy will not be measured simply by our ability to comprehend, analyze and communicate: instead, we expect literacy will be increasingly defined around our ability to adapt to the changing technologies of information and communication and our ability to envision new ways to use these technologies for important purposes.[44]

If adaptation and relevance become new determinants of literacy, then popular culture emerges into a significant testing ground for these skills. The integration of student's popular culture into the curriculum allows students to feel comfortable in their textual environment, while being challenged to develop new analytical skills. If both the text and literacies are foreign, then our students for whom a university is disconnected from the experiences of their family and friends are further alienated from the curriculum. There is a reason for perpetuating this disconnection. Shelly Hong Xu stated that 'teachers often shy away from student popular culture and feel that they have a moral responsibility of keeping popular culture out of the official school world'.[45] Such an assumption perpetuates the link between low literacy and social disadvantage. 'Flexible' learning reinforces this separation. Actually the point of pop – and the agenda of media and cultural studies – challenges the suppositions of teachers as much as students. Popular culture, when integrated into education and teacher training, prepares schools and universities for managing diversity. Gretchen Schwarz confirmed these challenges and potentials.

43 *Ibid.*, p. 34.

44 D. Leu and C. Kinzer, 'The convergence of literacy instruction with networked technologies of information and communication', *Reading Research Quarterly*, Vol. 35, No. 1, 2000, p. 118.

45 S. Hong Xu, 'Teachers' full knowledge of students' popular culture and the integration of aspects of that culture in literacy instruction', *Education*, Vol. 122, No. 4, 2002, p. 721.

> Today's teachers deal with diversity at every level. Many seem unprepared. Media literacy incorporated into teacher education and professional development may benefit teachers by helping them understand the 'other,' by helping them challenge media notions about gender, race, class, etc.; by introducing them to alternative pedagogies; and by offering them resources and techniques to empower their own students.[46]

Choices about media value are political decisions. Currently youth is a label to abuse and attack. Their media of choice is easily pathologized. Episodes of *Grumpy Old Men* complained about clothes, music, tattooing and piercings. Yet the warning from Janet Street-Porter should be noted:

> I accept that some people drink too much, hang around on street corners, threaten members of the public and create a nuisance. The rise of crime involving guns and knives is cause for concern. But don't assume that society's shortcomings are the fault of one group of people.[47]

The benefit of education is that it provides alternatives, answers, views and trajectories in an environment of blame and grievance. While these choices may not always result in economic benefits, it creates thinking space. The aim is to use the texts and contexts of our students and provide diverse ways of interpreting and shaping the history, geography and politics around them.

Grand narratives justified the oppressions of the twentieth century. By 1990, to cite Scott Lash, 'postmodernism is, patently, no longer trendy'.[48] The flattening of cultural differences and the valuation of popular culture were not forces to counter globalization, inequality and injustice. However, the right wing agenda of the 1980s and early 1990s from writers such as Allan Bloom, E.D. Hirsch and Pat Buchanan stressed heritage over history, literacy over literacies, censorship rather than transgression, regulation rather than empowerment and testing rather than learning.[49] Such a hierarchy valued sameness and homogeneity, rather than risking the potential of multiculturalism and diverse languages, religions and semiotic systems. In broadening out the concepts of education, the agenda of academics like Bloom – to reduce the definition of culture to a very narrow range of Western literary texts – is a way to exclude the working class, citizens of colour, gay and lesbian students and women from a comfortable, recognizable and

---

46 G. Schwarz, 'Media literacy prepares teachers for diversity', *Academic Exchange*, Spring 2004, p. 224.

47 J. Street-Porter, 'The politicians' fear of youth culture', *The Independent*, 7 April 2005, p. 39.

48 S. Lash, *Sociology of Postmodernism* (London: Routledge, 1990), p. ix.

49 Henry Giroux and David Trend investigated the consequences of this ideology in 'Cultural workers, pedagogy and the politics of difference: beyond cultural conservatism', *Cultural Studies*, Vol. 6, 1992, pp. 51–2.

conducive learning environment. Teachers need to move beyond cultural tourism – getting hip with the kids – and actually contextualize and theorize the sphere of pop.

Learning is socially transformative. That is why the stress on technical competency and basic literacies necessitates more attention and greater critique. We require more of our schools and universities than students being able to mobilize Photoshop or to justify the market economy. We need new goals and structures to address systematic and structural exclusions in schools and universities.[50] To explore and renew a commitment to media education and popular cultural studies is a reminder of the revelatory impact of the best education in teaching differences.

From:
To: t.brabazon@murdoch.edu.au
Subject: Intro to Cultural Studies
Date: Tue, 03 Aug 2004 22:39:44 +0800

Ms. Brabazon,

Today's tutorial was so excited...

I didn't have tutorial systems at my university in Japan.

So, I'm enjoying uni life here.

Today's topic was difficult for me, but I could think many things. Especially about culture or 'cultures'..

I wanted to say about that question..., but I was so shy, I was stupid... So, now I want to say my opinion a bit here... sorry.

I think each person has each culture, even though they're same nationality. Cause we live our own life by ourselves and we're different person. No one can live same way with me.

50 Barbara Comber revealed in 'Literacy, poverty and schooling', *English in Australia*, Vol. 119, No. 30, 1997, that 'the myth that youth unemployment, poverty and crime are largely the result of low levels of literacy have come to be heard as the "truth" in contemporary Australia. Admitting to being a teacher or teacher-educator frequently unleashes a series of uninvited verbal attacks about what a lousy job teachers are doing and how young people can't spell, don't know what a verb is, and so on. Taxi drivers, shop keepers, TV current affairs hosts and casual acquaintances all have horror stories to offer as evidence', p. 23.

> So, we should discuss about difference of cultures and we should know each other. I had stereotypes before I come here, still now, I think I have. Therefore, I'd like to change my mind and make wide my horizon.
>
> That's all.... I'm interested in your lecture and tutorials. So, as much as possible, I'd like to try to say my oponion in tutorial. Teacher is the job of my dreams!!! I want be a teacher (lecturer?!) like you, tara!
>
> I'm looking forward to attend next lecture and join next tutorial.
>
> Thank you for your kindness.

The pathologization of popular knowledges has repressed our students for too long. We have continued to isolate schools and universities from the lived experience of the people we are meant to be educating. As Jon Lewis confirmed, 'if the point of a critical media literacy is to meet students halfway – to begin to take seriously what they take seriously, to read what they read, to watch what they watch – teachers must learn to love pop culture'.[51] Pop is a medium and method to manage classroom diversity and facilitate a critical interpretation of texts and contexts. There is a need to find a strategy to assist students who are not prepared for higher level writing, reading and research skills. With care and good curriculum, Google can smooth the passage from information to knowledge, but the first step is to transform consuming pop into thinking pop.

51 J. Lewis, 'Practice what you preach', *Afterimage*, Summer 1996, p. 26.

Section Three
Critique

Chapter six

Exploiting knowledge?

I have rarely been embarrassed that I do not have internet access at home. For most of my teaching life, I have lived across the road from the university, walking to work each day, including weekends, to handle the emailed micro-traumas as they arrive. These days, when emails arrive at such a speed and in such a number, daily attention is required or else the inbox festers into an uncontrollable shambles of mis/organization. In such an environment, universities as workplaces, let alone sites of learning, are not what they once were. At the end of 2004, my old craggy work computer, still running Windows 98 and featuring such hardware innovations as a zip drive, stuttered through its final reboot. My university, in shutdown for the Christmas holidays, did not replace this computer for seven weeks. During that time, I was drafting and administering the submission of three PhD theses, the proofs and indexing of a book, and the publicity and marketing of another. I was managing one of my courses from an off-shore campus, writing the curriculum for honours students and supervising 14 postgraduates. To 'manage' this load without a working computer or an internet connection, I was borrowing web time from my father, who lives 60 kilometres from my home, and pinching some access at my gym. It was dreadful. Two hundred emails were arriving each day, with a backlog from 21 December, and I could only grab 20 minutes to 'handle' the most urgent queries. I was frustrated, angry, but bemused at the blasé suppositions of my employer.

There was the assumption that the loss of a work computer was not an inconvenience, because obviously I had web access at home. Surely everyone does. Living two minutes' walk from work, and desiring to occasionally get away from paid employment to actually have a life, I never installed dial up or broadband access. When sharing this information with techno-crats and administrators, it was the first time in my professional life that I felt ashamed, a weird person who deserves pity and concern. I nearly considered getting the internet put in the family home. But I was staunch, and no matter how many others I inconvenienced, I held on to the thought that the workplace has a responsibility to ensure internet access to complete *their work*. I already print, photocopy, scan and design too much course material at home, at my expense. If I bent to this final privatization of the workplace, then life would be radically changed, and certainly not improved. This digital distraction would finally sever the blocks of research and teaching administration – and leisure – that I have been able to pinch from a workplace.

Welcome to the knowledge economy, a world of expectations and arrogance, of budgetary crisis and making do. Education, teaching and learning is about adding value to goods and (re)skilling labour for the development of an efficient, modern industrial economy. Production in the new economy utilizes computers, information, communication and multimedia technologies as its tools. The profound inefficiencies of the contemporary university sector, where emails and memos circulate without precision or relevance, create workplaces of distraction, boredom and irrelevance. Through the mask of speed and convenience, an intricate and provocative tension is emerging between globalization and localization, universality and individuality, competition and equality. Most importantly, decisions are being made about the role and place of the market in universities.

While neo-liberals welcome McUniversities, New Labour is more tortured in its relationship with the educational sector, still maintaining the meritocratic dream of schools and universities salving societal ills. As Colin MacCabe argued,

> Having explicitly abandoned the goal of economic equality, it [New Labour] needed education to bear the entire weight of the Labour Party's historic mission of social justice. But the question of social equality and justice cannot be solved simply by education and in attempting to do so we are currently destroying a first-class university system.[1]

Postmodernity is often blamed for the downfall of civilization, history and truth.[2] Critics gave this theoretical school too wide an influence. An incredulity of metanarratives and the desire for overt exploration of cultural value was a mechanism to critique modernist totalizing solutions to social difficulties. But the postmodern moment has been 'over' for at least 15 years.[3] Emerging from these debates about knowledge, education and value, this chapter concentrates its attentions on three nodes of focus. Firstly, there is a tracking of information and the knowledge economy in its many guises, followed by a consideration of post-work theory. Finally, the role and place of universities in 'value adding' to the new capitalist project rounds out the chapter. The goal is to ask why universities have been gutted at the very moment that knowledge has seemingly never held a greater economic value.

---

1 C. MacCabe, 'Set our universities free', *The Observer*, 13 March 2005, http://observer.guardian.co.uk/comment/story/0,690,14650,00.html, accessed on 14 March 2005.

2 For example, Eric Hobsbawm argued that postmodern historians were claiming that 'there is no clear difference between fact and fiction. But there is, and for historians, even for the most militantly antipositivist ones among us, the ability to distinguish between the two is absolutely fundamental. We cannot invent our facts', from E. Hobsbawm, 'Fact, fiction and historical revisionism', Higher Education Supplement, *The Australian*, 8 December 1993, p. 35.

3 S. Lash, *Sociology of Postmodernism* (London: Routledge, 1990), p. ix.

Post knowledge in the information age

On 18 May 2003, the then Australian Minister for Education and would-be Prime Minister, Brendan Nelson, appeared on the Channel Nine *Sunday* programme. The Yoda of political journalism, Laurie Oakes, attacked him personally and professionally. He disclosed to viewers that the then Minister had suffered a false start in his own education, enrolling in one semester of an economics degree that was never completed. The following year, he commenced a medical qualification and went on to become a practising doctor. He did not pay fees for any of his university courses. When reminded of these events, Dr Nelson became agitated, and stressed the importance of a 'cap' on governmentally subsidized places, at five years for each student. He justified such a decision with the cliché that taxpayers do not want 'professional students completing degree after degree'.[4] The Minister confirmed that the primary – and perhaps the only – task for university academics was to 'train' young people for the workforce. The fact that nearly 50 per cent of students in many Australian universities are over the age of 25 had not entered his vision. He wanted young people to complete a rapid degree and start working, to commence paying taxes and the debt or loan required to fund a full fee-paying place. He holds a nostalgic vision of who attends university while concurrently maintaining a neo-liberal ideology of how curricula and degrees should be structured for the workplace. It is an odd combination.

The curbing of the time available to complete undergraduate courses during the Liberal Party's last term in office, and their subsequent re-election on that platform, makes plain the primary assumption of the new funding model: that a student/worker can attain all required competencies, skills, attributes, motivations and ambitions from a single three-year degree. It is also significant to note that while attention is placed on the changing sources of income for universities, from governmental to private sector, there have also been major shifts in the pattern of expenditure, focusing on branding, marketing, recruitment, 'regional' campuses and off-shore courses. Similarly, the short-term funding goals of university research agendas encourage projects required by industry, rather than socially necessary concerns that are beneficial in the long term. There is little that is inevitable about teaching, research and education in the current environment, except that no government will create a fully funded model for life long learning. The task for those involved in education is to probe the form and rationale for a (post) publicly funded university. I am also interested in why governments – even though they will not pay for it – spout the significance of continuing education. To move beyond the empty promises of just-in-time learning, on-the-job training, graduate attributes and generic skills, we must reorder our assumptions and ask difficult questions of those who frame the context in which education takes place.

4 B. Nelson, talking to L. Oakes, *Sunday*, Channel Nine, 18 May 2003.

After the Second World War, and intensified through to the 1990s, significant social transformations emerged in post-industrial economies. At their most basic, these changes included an ageing population, 'efficient' technologies which reduced the labour force in manufacturing sectors, greater numbers of women staying in the workforce, new organizational cultures of work and leisure, immigration, movements and changes to the market labour structure. Janet Street-Porter presented the speed and scale of these cultural shifts.

> A couple of generations ago the British workforce stood on assembly lines in draughts and dirt. We were a country with a manufacturing and engineering industry at our core. With the collapse of Rover, it's more evident than ever we are a nation of shopkeepers, leisure park attendants and heritage ticket collectors. The truth is, most people grow up with unrealistic expectations of what life has in store for them. They don't bother to pay any attention at school, and then are astonished to discover that work is boring and not too wonderfully paid.[5]

For Street-Porter, stress and disappointment is triggered in the post-school workforce by a gulf between expectations and aspirations, and experiences and reality. She also has an agenda of blame in her article: those who do not work hard – at school or the formal workplace – deserve the boredom of their lives. Meritocracy is a seductive ideology, but further precision is necessary in ascertaining the difference between access to education, and the context in which this 'access' has been offered.

Education is implicated in economic, social and political change. It is also a subtle facilitator of these movements, with a shift in expenditure as the population ages from the education of children and young adults to an increase in (re)training schemes to ensure that the adult labour market has 'flexibility'. There is also a more significant transference of educational expenditure, from the public to the private sector. Busse, Wurzburg and Zappacosta reported that 'one effect of spreading learning over the lifetime, particularly into the working years, is to change the likely allocation of financing responsibility between public and private sources'.[6] In other words, to remain viable and employable in the contemporary workplace, workers must use private funds from their household economy to prevent obsolescence. In such an environment, it is no surprise that skill attainment and competency-based training, delivered through short-term courses and 'flexibly' through computer-mediated platforms, is the cheapest method to 'solve' these structural changes to the workplace.

---

5 J. Street-Porter, 'Stress? I'll give you Stress', *The Independent on Sunday*, 10 April 2005, p. 24.

6 R. Busse, G. Wurzburg and M. Zappacosta, 'Shaping the societal bill: past and future trends in education, pensions and healthcare expenditure', *Futures*, Vol. 35, 2003, p. 13.

The great imponderable for complex economic systems is how to manage fluctuations in labour and the market. The unstable relationship between need and supply necessitates flexibility in staffing solutions, and short-term supplementary labour options. When productivity and profit are the primary variables through which to judge successful management, then the alignments of education and employment are viewed and skewed through specific economic imperatives. The library profession is an obvious occupation that has confronted these contradictions. It is ironic that the occupation that orders knowledge is experiencing a volatile and disordered workplace. In the past, it had been assumed that librarians held a degree while technicians did not, and that technicians would not be asked to perform – unsupervised – the same duties as librarians. Such distinctions are increasingly redundant. Training packages, structured through competency-based training principles, have ensured technicians and librarians share knowledge systems which are taught through incremental stages. Mary Carroll recognized the primary questions raised through this change.

> If it is now the case that these distinctions have disappeared do we need to continue to draw them between professional and para-professional education? Does this mean that all sectors of the education community are in fact learning/teaching the same skills but at different levels so that no unique set of skills exists?[7]

With education reduced to skills, thereby discrediting generalist degrees that were the foundation of many librarians' intellectual experiences, the needs of 'industry' have corroded professional standards and status. Certainly, the abilities of library technicians are finally being valued, but it is too convenient that one of the few professions dominated by women has suffered a demeaning of its knowledge base into a collection of competencies. Lifelong learning, in this context, has collapsed high level abilities in information management into bite sized chunks of 'skills'.

The ideology of lifelong learning – which is rarely discussed – is that it serves to devalue prior abilities and knowledges into an ever-expanding imperative for 'new' skills and software competencies. For example, ponder the consequences of Hitendra Pillay and Robert Elliott's words:

> The expectations inherent in new roles, confounded by uncertainty of the environment and the explosion of information technology, now challenge us to reconceptualise human cognition and develop education and training in a way that resonates with current knowledge and skills.[8]

---

7 M. Carroll, 'The well-worn path', *The Australian Library Journal*, May 2002, p. 122.

8 H. Pillay and R. Elliott, 'Distributed learning: understanding the emerging workplace knowledge', *Journal of Interactive Learning Research*, Vol. 13, No. 1–2, 2002, p. 95.

Neophiliacal urges jut from their prose. The stress on 'new roles', and 'uncertain environments', the 'explosion of information technology', 'challenges', 'reconceptualisations', and 'current knowledge' all celebrate the present, the contemporary, and the now. The phrase 'reconceptualise human cognition' is also noteworthy, meaning – at its most basic – changing thinking patterns. Knowledge and expertise that have taken years to develop, nurture and apply are not validated through this educational brief. The demands and injustices of family, work, leisure, lifestyle, class and sexuality stretch the skin taut over these economic and social contradictions. To ease these paradoxes, lifelong learning should stress pedagogy rather than applications, and context rather than content.[9] Put another way, instead of affirming the link between (the 'wow' of) technological change and (inevitable) workplace restructuring and redundancies, consideration is required on the relationship between change-managing workplaces to attain verifiable educational outcomes, rather than the spin and promises of reconceptualizing human cognition.[10]

Short-term vocationalism in educational policy speaks to the ordering of priorities in public culture, requiring rapid profits and a tight mesh between education and immediate workplace needs. Extending this logic, if education 'creates' employment, then it also 'creates' unemployment. In an environment that focuses on the multiple identities and roles of citizens, students are reduced to one label – 'future workers'. Obviously education is always marinated in the political directives of the day. The industrial revolution introduced a range of technical complexities to the workforce. Fordism necessitated that a worker complete a task with precision and speed, requiring a high tolerance of stress and boredom.[11] Now, more skills are 'assumed' by employers at the time that workplaces are off-loading their training expectations to the post-compulsory education sector. Therefore 'lifelong learning' is a political mask to empower the already empowered and create a low-level skill base for poorly paid and vulnerable workers,

---

9 Stan Aronowitz stressed the importance of context in teaching. He stated that 'mostly when I don't make connections, it's because I haven't tried hard enough', *The Knowledge Factory* (Boston: Beacon Press, 2000), p. 193.

10 Claudia Meister-Scheytt and Tobias Scheytt recognized this problem, arguing that 'managing change in universities is an odious task: it tends to be carried out in periods of decreasing budgets and must deal with unclear goals of the organization. The motivations behind the actions taken by the individuals involved are for the most part not obvious to others. In addition, hierarchies are ambiguous and unreliable, and governance structures are weak', from 'The complexity of change in universities', *Higher Education Quarterly*, Vol. 59, No. 1, 2005, p. 76.

11 The landmark article that investigated the relationship between industrialization and changing notions of time is E. P. Thompson's 'Time, work and industrial capitalism', *Past and Present*, No. 38, December 1968, pp. 56–97.

with the promise of competency-based training.[12] Such ideologies are not stated overtly. The ever-bubbling celebration of 'the new' shrouds this task.

Diane Coyle realized the dense problems in collapsing education into work: 'at a time of rapid and tumultuous economic change, it is impossible to predict what workforce skills employers will need'.[13] The talk of generic competencies and transferable skills chatter over the reality that capitalism is becoming a twenty-first century avant-garde experiment that is unpredictable in its applications. Google, and the internet more generally, is a transitory techno-mask for under-prepared students moving through an education system without clear long-term goals, funding models or contextual dynamism in reconfiguring a productive relationship between education and economics. An information economy requires the development of an information infrastructure and therefore, planning and policy. John Wills, a decade ago, predicted the challenge of this environment to a university. Being modernist formations, universities were unable to hybridize effectively with phrases like applied knowledge and professional competency.[14] Cutting away public funding from universities – demanding that money be raised from industry – has not made this alignment any smoother, but created a two-tiered sector, one affirming scholarly standards and the other vocational competency. To put it another way, one system focuses on knowledge, the other information.

Phrases like the information society, information overload and the information revolution raise questions about how information is communicated and organized. Derived from the Latin *informare*, which describes the imposition of a form or structure, an order is implied in the etymology. Google is one method to create order and organization to improve the access to information. While the quality of information is not evaluated, the ranking of sites by popularity provides the level and model of categorization appropriate for a celebrity-satiated age.[15] Google is a reminder that the world is awash with information, but the goal is to obtain relevant information in the correct place at an appropriate time. The key corrective to Google is an understanding

12 David Ashton, of the Centre for Labour Market Studies at Leicester University, confirmed that 'For some companies, skills are an essential part of their competitive strategies ... For other companies – and I would think a good proportion of British companies – skills are very low on the agenda because business strategy is focused on reducing costs and on production of standardized goods and services', from P. Kingston, 'A journey for the workers', *The Guardian*, 22 August 2006, p. 4.

13 D. Coyle, 'How not to educate the information age workforce', *Critical Quarterly*, Vol. 43, No. 1, 2001, pp. 46–54.

14 J. Wills, 'The post-postmodern university', *Change*, March/April 1995, pp. 59–62.

15 For an investigation of celebrity and tabloidization, please refer to Graeme Turner, 'Tabloidization, journalism and the possibility of critique', *International Journal of Cultural Studies*, Vol. 2, No.1, April 1999, pp. 59–76.

of the context in which the information is received, or where the Google ranking is returned, and to whom.

Information has no value in and of itself. It must be sorted, contextualized and evaluated. When information is the aim, when information becomes a commodity, the interests of those groups already in power are reinforced. Google replicates this initiative. That is why there are profound social consequences of educational research materials moving from public goods to commercial commodities, as libraries increasingly have to negotiate the rights to obtain important refereed articles and books. Information management requires not only attention to content, but retrievability.[16] Intervention is necessary in increasing the tight alignment of hardware, software and wetware, or technology, applications and literacies. With a concentration on technology, platforms and its applications, digital literacy and illiteracy is actually more relevant to creating knowledge than the distribution of programmes, screens and keyboards. For librarians and teachers, the costs of this new environment were great. Carla Stoffle outlined the consequences on librarians.

> The combination of too much change, too much to learn, too little staff to do it all, and no new money generally means that library personnel are worn down and demoralized rather than excited and energized.[17]

The consequences of digitization are that it increases the speed and spread of information. Yet the quantity of trivial data that survives also increases. The crap of a culture is stored on multiple hard drives and endlessly returns through Google. As Robert Sutton confirmed,

> Companies have spent hundreds of millions of dollars on compute hardware and software, on hiring knowledge-management experts and on maintaining data warehouses of best practices and past experiences. The designers of these systems imagined they were inventing electronic libraries that would provide every employee quick and easy access to a firm's collective wisdom. The reality is that most information warehouses have become junkyards, databases cluttered with forgotten information.[18]

---

16 N. Swartz, 'The "Wonder Years" of Knowledge Management', *The Information Management Journal*, May/June 2003, pp. 53–7.

17 C. Stoffle, 'The emergence of education and knowledge management as major functions of the digital library', Follett Lecture Series, University of Wales, Cardiff, 13 November 1996, http://www.ukoln.ac.uk/services/apers/follett/stoffle/aper.html, accessed on 11 July 2004.

18 R. Sutton, 'Knowledge management is not an oxymoron', *Computerworld*, 3 January 2000, http://www.computerworld.com/nws/2000/story/0,11280,40500,00.html, accessed 11 July 2004.

The most effective metaphor to explore models of useable information or the difference between the availability of hardware and the development of wetware, is the iPod. It has a clean and intuitive navigational screen. It is simple to move around the musical database and hours of pleasure can be derived from digitally exploring a musical collection gathered over decades. But explore another person's iPod. The same clean interface welcomes the user, but there is frequently no music of interest. Hours are wasted hearing the aural musings of another person's lived soundtrack. The hyper-personal nature of popular music means that the best methods of information management are pointless if there are no criteria for information relevance within a precise context. As workplaces are washed clean of staff with institutional memory, being replaced by human resources departments with regulations and a weight of emails confirming the agenda of now redundant meetings, there is a glugging of the great potentials of digitization, such as mobility, speed, convergence and accessibility.

Being a student of higher education at the moment is like living in someone else's iPod. The transference from a manufacturing to an information-driven economy necessitates permanent reskilling. The cost of labour market flexibility is educational standards and scholarly excellence. If competence is the goal of schools and universities, then higher levels of attainment are discredited. This focus on quite basic skills and competencies is being overlaid by the changing economic environment. Clearly, capitalism has morphed into capitalisms. While low-order competences are necessary for under-employed (post) workers, knowledge is a commodified asset for those educated at higher levels of the sector. Put another way, Rob Kling confirmed this difference by asking a provocative question: 'why are women more likely to be found feeding data into computer systems, while men are more likely to be in the position of specifying requirements for, and designing, computer-based systems?'.[19] These skill sets of data entry and database design overlap. Yet the power and credibility accorded to these literacies are distinct. Knowledge is an asset, building not only personal reputations, but relationships. John Daley termed this 'the intangible economy'.[20] In marking these new forms of work organization, old orders of power, hierarchy and difference are reinforced. While – after industrialization – most workers can read and write, few are given the chance to complete a doctorate. The consequences of both globalization and technological change are that few jobs are generated for a more qualified labour force. This is the context in which Stanley Aronowitz developed his theories of post-work. Vocational training is a way to create proto-redundant competencies for a job sector requiring less labour.[21] Retraining is a relanguaging of unemployment and underemployment. Therefore education and

19 R. Kling, 'Social controversies about computerization', from R. Kling (ed.), *Computerization and Controversy* (San Diego: Academic Press, 1996), p. 12.

20 J. Daley, 'The intangible economy and Australia', *Australian Journal of Management*, Vol. 26, August 2001, pp. 3–19.

21 S. Aronowitz, *The Knowledge Factory* (Boston: Beacon Press, 2000), p. 158.

educators are implicated in meta-exploitation, training generations of brilliant people to settle for less and suffocate their dissatisfaction and dislocation with consumerism.

Post work and the exploitation economy

> Technological change is primarily to the benefit of the same class that not so long ago forced people off the land and into factories, destroying whole ways of life in the process.[22]
>
> James Brook and Iain Boal

It did not take long for the 'labour' in labour-saving devices to transform from a verb to an adjective and then into a compound noun. Actually, computer-punctuated workplaces have not reduced workloads or increased productivity because this technological innovation has been concurrent with a reduction in the workforce – labour-saving indeed – and vertical integration of employee functions. Fewer people are doing more work. I spend much of my time at universities answering emails and entering data into university systems. These functions were not required of academics until the mid-1990s. There were other staff responsible for handling student queries and entering data. These others positions and jobs have now disappeared. Most of the 'new' jobs created in the 'new' economy are in the low wage sector, and completing low skill, repetitive tasks often in the service industries.[23] Flexible jobs are the most inflexible in terms of their content. Concurrently for 'managers', the use of mobile phones, pagers, blackberries and wireless laptops means that work colonizes all available time. The cultural standards of a good day's work are being split between the overworked and the underemployed, with consumption being the only connective justification for these workplace structures.

Theories about identity and work require stable models of both careers and capitalism. Interestingly women, who through much of the twentieth century were the residual workforce summoned to do a man's job when the men were unavailable through wars, entered post-Fordism before their male colleagues. Wajcman and Martin conducted a study of what this 'new' capitalism, or reflexive modernization, means for men and women in terms of their aspirations for a family and career. In studying managers in six companies, three in the financial services sector and three in the manufacturing engineering sector, they discovered that men were able to clearly

---

22 J. Brook and I. Boal, 'Preface', from J. Brook and I. Boal (eds), *Resisting the Virtual Life: The Culture and Politics of Information* (San Francisco: City Lights, 1995), p. viii.

23 Please refer to Monty Neill's 'Computers, thinking, and schools in the "new world economic order"', from J. Brook and I. Boal (eds), *Resisting the Virtual Life: The Culture and Politics of Information* (San Francisco: City Lights, 1995), p. 182.

establish the boundaries between work and family. Women were not.[24] When delving into the social consequences of these statements, the researchers realized that

> While well over a third of the men have partners who were not in paid employment, almost a third of the women managers are currently single or divorced, while virtually all those with partners are in dual-career households.[25]

This situation reveals what I term 'the dry cleaning problem'. Much can be determined about a marriage, long-term partnership and the household economy by who is able to pick up the dry cleaning. If men have partners without the deadening responsibility of paid employment and long hours, then they do not have to worry about picking up the dry cleaning. For the women, one third without partners and the remaining majority in dual-career households, there is a daily debate about who is actually able to leave work and get the dry cleaning before the business closes at 6pm. This is the consequence of work consuming life. The alternative to the dry cleaning problem is the minimum wage job sector, which is vulnerable to the restructuring of global capital. They can get to the dry cleaner because of split shifts, but cannot afford the bill. In 'decentering the worker'[26] there is a disconnection between the labour force and the work they complete.[27] The imperative of labour market flexibility, when placed in the context of neo-liberalism, uses consumerism to salve the volatility and antagonism of employment relations.

Such exploitative patterns and relationships matter. The oppressive nature of most workplaces, including universities, is increased through technological surveillance. Through the 1990s new management policies facilitated not only changing employment contracts but a growth of job insecurity. The diverse, dynamic and intriguing work is conducted by upper levels of management who have the advantages of upskilling and professional development. The movement from a leadership to management model means that it is difficult to both define and measure an individual's labour time,

---

24 This is what Keir Keightley referred to as 'gendered access to leisure', from 'Low television, high fidelity: taste and the gendering of home entertainment technologies', *Journal of Broadcasting and Electronic Media*, June 2003, p. 252.

25 J. Wajcman and B. Martin, 'Narratives of identity in modern management', *Sociology*, Vol. 36, No. 4, 2002, p. 995.

26 S. Aronowitz and W. DiFazio, *The Jobless Future* (Minneapolis: University of Minnesota Press, 1994), p. 85.

27 This disconnection is an unravelling of modernity. Alain Touraine stated in *Critique of Modernity* (Oxford: Basil Blackwell, 1995), that 'the idea of modernity was the assertion that men and women are what they do, and that there must therefore be an increasingly close connection between production, which is made more efficient by science, technology or administration, the organization of a society governed by law, and a personal life motivated by both self-interest and the will to be free of all constraints', p. 1.

contribution or responsibility.[28] In such a volatile context, the rhetoric of team bonding and a caring family of workers generates what Douglas Ezzy described as 'the new corporate workplace['s] … simulacrum of trust'.[29]

Technological change lubricates these corporate conditions. As Aronowitz acknowledges,

> For politicians and most commentators on American social mobility, the new frontier is technology. The electronic revolutions in computers, fiber optics, and lasers have inspired an outburst of utopian thinking … no social problem is exempt from the technological fix; it is just a matter of time before educational and income inequality will be a memory.[30]

In this environment, any protection of a worker's rights that blocks this technotopia is quashed as hampering economic progress. Free trade is a way to open markets that had been restricted through the right to a minimum wage. Individual employment contracts create a culture of blame, insecurity, competition, secrecy and confusion. Education becomes a (desperate) attempt to protect the self against the ever-increasing vagaries of capitalism.

In such a context, learning is a big business. This is panic education, a desperate attempt to understand why the movement from life to lifestyle has not created happiness or satisfaction. Whether discussing the University of the Third Age, personal development courses, self-help bestsellers or hard-edged vocational qualifications, definitions of learning – let alone education – are expanding. Concurrent with this growth, governments are reducing centralized funding and 'promoting' alternative revenue streams. The diversity of student interests – or to use the language of the time, clients' learning goals – is transforming higher education into more than the provision of undergraduate and postgraduate degrees. The expansion of the student body beyond the 18–25 age group and the desire to 'service industry' has reordered the form and purpose of formal education. The number of potential students has expanded extraordinarily. [31]As Lee Bash realized,

---

28 F. Bowring, 'Post-Fordism and the end of work', *Futures*, Vol. 34, 2002, p. 159.

29 D. Ezzy, 'A simulacrum of workplace community', *Sociology*, Vol. 35, No. 3, p. 635.

30 S. Aronowitz, *How Class Works* (New Haven: Yale University Press, 2003), p. 20.

31 Australia has shown an extraordinary growth in student numbers. As Deborah Tranter and Robert Sumner have shown, 'the pattern of higher education participation in Australia has changed markedly over the latter half of the twentieth century, moving from an elite system catering to less than 4 per cent of the 17 to 22 year age group of the population in the 50s, to a mass system with 30 per cent of that age group participating by 1995 … In fact, in recent years, Australia has experienced one of the highest growth rates of any OECD country with an 80 per cent increase in enrolments between 1983 and 1996', *Tertiary Education and Management*, Vol. 8, 2002, p. 81.

> Today, some estimates suggest that as many as 47 per cent of all students enrolled in higher education are over 25 years old. In the future, as lifelong learning becomes more integrated into the fabric of our culture, the proportion of adult students is expected to increase. And while we may not yet realize it, the academy is already being transformed as a result.[32]

Lifelong learning is the major phrase and trope that fuels and justifies these changes. Such expansive economic opportunities, where more students cyclically return to campus, trigger the entrepreneurial directives within universities. If lifelong learning is taken seriously, then the goals, entry standards, curriculum, information management policies and assessments need to be reconsidered. Attention must be placed on words and phrases like 'access' and 'alternative entry'. Even more consideration must be placed on 'outcomes' and 'accountability'.

Lifelong learning is a catchphrase for this change in purpose and agenda of the workplace, government and employment patterns. Courses are developed from a wide range of education providers so that citizens can function in, or at least survive, the agitation of the post-work world. Both neo-liberal and Third Way models of capitalism require the labelling and development of an aspirational class, a group who desires to move 'above' their current status. Such an ambiguous economic and social goal always involves more than the vocational education sector or universities, with the aim being to seamlessly slot just-in-time training into a 'lifestyle'.[33] The difficulties with this discourse are two-fold. Firstly, how effectively can these aspirational notions be applied and translated into a real family and a real workplace? Secondly, does this scheme increase the information division between rich and poor, the Eloi and the Morlocks? There are many characteristics of an effective lifelong learner including high personal motivation, self-esteem, confidence and intellectual curiosity. In a double shifting, change-fatigued population, the enthusiasm for perpetual learning may be difficult to summon.

With the casualization of the post-Fordist workplace, it is no surprise that policy makers and employers are placing the economic and personal responsibility for retraining on to individual workers. Instead of funding a training scheme in the workplace, there has been a devolving of skill acquisition and personal development. Through the twentieth century, and particularly after 1945, education was the map for social mobility. The difficulty now – with degree inflation and the loss of stable, secure, long-term employment – is that new modes of exclusion and disempowerment are being perpetuated through the education system. Field recognized that 'the new adult education has been embraced most enthusiastically by those who are already relatively

32 L. Bash, 'What serving adult learners can teach us: the entrepreneurial response', *Change*, January/February 2003, p. 35.

33 An evocative article critiquing the unproblematic and clichéd use of lifestyle is N. Maycroft, 'Cultural consumption and the myth of life-style', *Capital and Class*, No. 84, Winter 2004.

well qualified'.[34] This is a significant realization. Motivation, meta-learning skills and curiosity are increasingly being rewarded when found in the already credentialed, empowered workforce. Those in work undertake lifelong learning. Adult education operates well for members of the middle class who are doing well and wish to do better. Those who 'choose' to ignore such credentialing are blamed for their own conditions and 'failures'. The concern, through the internationalization of managers, technological change and privatization of national assets, is that 'failures' in formal education create waves of social exclusion and immobility.

Besides being forced into classrooms, there are few options for those who do not wish to learn in a learning society. Those who 'choose' not to be a part of the national project of individual improvement, increased market share, company competitiveness and international trade are not relevant to the economy. But there is a personal benefit – that may have long-term political consequences – from being 'outside' society. Perhaps the best theorist of the excluded is not sourced from a university, but from fictional writing. Irvine Welsh, author of the landmark *Trainspotting*, has stated that,

> People who are in work have no time for anything else but work. They have no mental space to accommodate anything else but work. Whereas people who are outside the system will always find ways of amusing themselves. Even if they are materially disadvantaged they'll still find ways of coping, getting by and making their own entertainment.[35]

A blurring of work and learning, and work and leisure, may seem to create a borderless education, a learning framework uninhibited by curriculum, assessment or power structures. Google perpetuates this endless access to data. But lifelong learning aims to place as many (national) citizens as possible in 'the system', striving for success – or at least a pay increase – which will facilitate the purchase of more consumer goods. Through any discussion of workplace training and vocationalism, it is important to remember those who choose *not* to choose life, who choose something else, who will not follow orders.

The increasing importance of the 'new' economy means that, amidst the fear of downsizing and redundancy, there is a concurrent desire for individual creativity to (re)fuel economic productivity and competitiveness. Richard Caves defined this 'new' sector:

> 'Creative' industries supply goods and services that we broadly associate with cultural, artistic or simple entertainment value. They include book and magazine publishing, the visual

34 J. Field, *Lifelong Learning and the New Educational Order* (Stoke on Trent: Trentham Books, 2000), p. 105.

35 I. Welsh from S. Redhead, 'Post-punk junk', *Repetitive Beat Generation* (Glasgow: Rebel Inc, 2000), pp. 145–6.

> arts (painting and sculpture), the performing arts (theatre, opera, concerts, dance) sound recordings, cinema and TV films, even fashion and toys and games.[36]

His use of 'simple' and 'even' is quite significant. High cultural values are embedded in creative arts policy, and spill over into creative industries initiatives. So instead of popular music, there is discussion of sound recordings. Instead of blogs and e-zines, there is mention of book and magazine publishing. These assumptions of cultural value are significant. Britain's biggest export earner in 1998 was the Spice Girls, not the London Philharmonic Orchestra. Alongside such a recognition, it is difficult to be precious in the qualitative parameters of creativity. Really, the only interest of 'the industrialists' in 'the creative' is the products which fall under intellectual property law, encompassing patents, copyrights, trademarks and designs.[37] There is a universalizing of the success and achievement of the creative industries that is unsettling. For example, John Howkins stated that,

> It is about a new way of working. The whole point of the creative economy is that it involves everyone, from engineers, lawyers, IT professionals, teachers and artists.[38]

If these five professions includes 'everyone', then we live in a world without electricians, carpenters, mechanics, waiting staff, roof tilers, hairdressers and fitness instructors.[39] This 'new way' of working involves cutting out and ignoring those who build, shape, fix and buff. Obviously this 'new economy' incorporates 'new' technologies and digitization because of its convergent qualities and the capacity to render ideas mobile.[40] Analogue skills and knowledges are redundant in these narrowly defined creative industries.

---

36 R. Caves, *Creative Industries: Contracts between Art and Commerce* (Cambridge: Harvard University Press, 2000), p. 1.

37 This issue of copyright was noted by the British Academy's report in January 2004, '*That Full Complement of Riches': The Contribution of the Arts, Humanities and Social Sciences to the Nation's Wealth*. It was stated in this report that 'a great many of the products of teaching and research in the arts, humanities and social sciences are covered by copyright, providing the basis on which the intermediary industries such as publishing, analogue and digital, broadcasting, film, sound recording, and retailing of the products to consumers operate', p. 15.

38 J. Howkins, 'The competitive process of creativity', *FORM Magazine*, Perth, FORM Contemporary Craft and Design, 2005, p. 13.

39 Aronowitz confirmed that 'industrialism transforms the life world in its image of instrumental rationality – the sharp division of intellectual and manual labor, the distinction between nature and culture and with it the division of labor in the knowledge domain', *Roll Over Beethoven* (Hanover: University Press of New England, 1993), p. 241.

40 Kieran Healy noted that 'the new economy is a global system based on information technology, knowledge, and innovation. It has created a new corporate form that is flexible and

The arts – whether music, tourism or film – do not matter in and of themselves. Actually, it is their capacity for movement, to transfer products and ideas that generates the revenue. Content must be created and proliferated, moved, bought and sold. Such a paradigm and theory has little to do with education or work, but more to do with leisure and consumerism. John Howkins confirmed that 'the British, Americans and Japanese spend more on entertaining themselves than on clothing or healthcare'.[41] How class-based inequalities impact on such a realization are unclear. Most startling though is who is conducting this research in creative industries. Steven Jay Tepper noted that 'what is most striking to me about these claims and arguments [about the new economy] is that so few are made by economists. In fact, virtually all the writing on the subject has been done by scholars in communications and cultural studies, as well as pundits and consultants with expertise in media, education, intellectual property, and information'.[42] With economists not writing about the creative changes to the economy, it is appropriate to pin point the other great absence in this debate: how the educational sector will 'manage' this expansion of the service economy and an interest in 'the creative.'

In an environment where supposedly everything is creative – cities, clusters, the economy and classes – how the knowledge in this new economy is not only formed but sustained becomes significant. The ever-present Richard Florida's belief that 'people are the critical resource of the new age',[43] has rarely been matched by an interest in education to ensure a strategic and lasting funding stream for scholarship. Only in 2006 was a report released, funded by the Heinz Endowments, titled *The University and the Creative Economy*.[44] While he lists teachers in his creative class, the function of education,

---

network-like', from 'What's new for culture in the new economy?', *The Journal of Arts Management, Law and Society*, Vol. 32, No. 2, Summer 2002, p. 96.

41 J. Howkins, *The Creative Economy: How People Make Money from Ideas* (London: Allen Lane, 2001), p. xv.

42 S. Tepper, 'Creative assets and the changing economy', *The Journal of Arts Management, Law and Society*, Vol. 32, No. 2, Summer 2002, p. 161.

43 R. Florida, *The Rise of the Creative Class* (New York: Basic Books, 2002), p. 6.

44 An exception to this statement was Richard Florida's *Cities and the Creative Class* (New York: Routledge, 2005). There was one chapter – 'The university, talent, and quality of place' – that offered a convergent analysis with some of the concerns raised in this book. Florida noted that 'during the 1980s and 1990s, the university was posed as an underutilized weapon in the battle for industrial competitive and regional economic growth. Even higher education stalwarts such as Harvard University's then-president Derek Bok argued that the university had a civic duty to ally itself closely with industry to improve productivity. At university after university, new research centers were designed to attract corporate funding, and technology transfer offices were started to commercialize academic breakthroughs. But we may well have gone too far. Academics and university officials are becoming increasingly concerned that greater involvement in university research is causing a shift from fundamental science to more applied work ... Universities have been naively viewed as engines of innovation that pump out new ideas that can be easily translated

curriculum and literacy theory are not part of his methods or modes to develop creativity. In other words, he has performed the movement tracked by Ted Tapper: 'from the politics of education to the economics of education'.[45] The point of all learning, but particularly lifelong learning, is to move beyond economic advancement. We need to bring politics back to our learning.

Post creativity and the loss of literacies

> EHE [The Enterprise in Higher Education Initiative] was a response to concerns that HE was failing to provide graduates who were employed or enterprise oriented. Attention was focused on the need for effective supply of higher skills into the workforce; on the employability of graduates; and on the role of personal or transferable skills in making graduates effective contributors at work. Although based on funding for individual institutions, the ultimate aim was to influence the culture and practice of HE, across sectoral, instructional and disciplinary divides.[46]
>
> Stephen Burniston, John Rodger and James Brass

> The main concerns about graduate quality expressed by employers relate to some job applicants' lack of relevant work experience.[47]
>
> Geoff Mason

Why researchers such as these offer 'Research Briefs' to governments is a mystery. Besides naturalizing ahistorical notions of employability and enterprise, they repeat the hypocrisies and ruthlessness of the job market. Employers express concern about a lack of work experience amongst *graduates*. Let us be clear here: graduates have spent three years of their life, mortgaging their present for a better future, to expend time researching, writing, thinking and learning. Then, after (only) three years at university,

---

into commercial innovations and regional growth. This has led to overly mechanistic national and regional policies that seek to commercialize those ideas and transfer them to the private sector', pp. 143–44. In addressing this concern, Richard Florida, Gary Gates, Brian Knudsen and Kevin Stolarick produced a 2006 research project funded by the Heinz Endowments, *The University and the Creative Economy*.

45 T. Tapper, *Fee-paying Schools and Educational Change in Britain: Between the State and the Marketplace* (London: Woburn Press, 1997), p. 201.

46 S. Burniston, J. Rodger and J. Brass, 'Enterprise in higher education – changing the mindset', Research Brief No. 117, Department for Education and Employment, United Kingdom, September 1999.

47 G. Mason, 'The Labour Market for engineering, science and IT graduates: are there mismatches between supply and demand?', Research Brief No. 112, Department for Education and Employment, March 1999.

employers want work experience as well.[48] Surely employers are responsible for work experience, and educators for education.[49] What makes such statements even more inappropriate is that they are published under the guise of governmental reports, validating an excessive market ideology without any respect for the history of education and different models of scholarship.

The last 20 years have witnessed an expanding jurisdiction and justification of the market through all levels of education. As part of Tony Blair's Third Way, the creative industries and the knowledge economy became catchwords to demonstrate that cultural concerns are not only economically viable but a necessity in the digital, post-Fordist, information age. Concerns with intellectual property rights, copyright, patents, and ownership of creative productions predominate in such a discourse. Described by Charles Leadbeater as *Living on Thin Air*, this new economy is 'driven by new factors of production and sources of competitive advantage – innovation, design, branding, know-how – which are at work on all industries'.[50] Such market imperatives offer both challenges and opportunity for educationalists and students. Knowledge is also a resource for both political democracy and the bedrock of struggles for social justice and human rights.

In continually 'reskilling' the workforce, lifelong learning is a pivotal accoutrement to the creative industries project. Learning cities and communities are the foundations for design, music, architecture and journalism. In British policy, and increasingly in specific states in Australia such as Queensland, attention is placed on industry-based research funding to address this changing environment. In 2000, Stuart Cunningham and others listed the eight trends that configure education, information teaching and learning in this new environment.

The changes to the provision of education
Globalization
The arrival of new information and communication technologies
The development of a knowledge economy, shortening the time between the development of new ideas and their application

48 I particularly want to note the landmark critique of this ideology of work readiness by John Clarke and Paul Willis in their 'Introduction' in *Schooling for the Dole? The New Vocationalism* (Houndmills: Macmillan, 1984).

49 In 1918 Thorstein Veblen was ruthlessly precise in the jurisdiction of a university's purpose. He believed it was a place for a scholarly inquiry into knowledge and nothing else. He stated that 'training for other purposes is necessarily of a different kind and is best done elsewhere. It does not become university work by calling it so and imposing its burden on the man and equipment whose only concern should be the Higher Learning', from *The Higher Learning in America* (New York: Viking, 1935), p. 17.

50 C. Leadbeater, *Living on Thin Air: The New Economy* (London: Viking, 1999), p. 10.

The formation of learning organizations
User-pays education
The distribution of knowledge through interactive communication technologies (ICT)
Increasing demand for education and training
Scarcity of an experienced and trained workforce

Source: S. Cunningham, Y. Ryan, L. Stedman, S. Tapsall, K. Bagdon, T. Flew and P. Coaldrake, *The Business of Borderless Education* (Canberra: DETYA Evaluation and Investigations Program [EIP], 2000).

This table reverberates with the current challenges confronting education. Mobilizing such changes requires a translation of university mission statements and the promotion of a learning culture, while also acknowledging the limited financial conditions in which the educational sector is placed. For university scholars facilitating the creative industries approach, education is 'supplying high value-added inputs to other enterprises',[51] rather than holding a value or purpose beyond the immediately and applicably economic. The assumption behind this table is that the areas of expansion in the workforce are the creative and service industries. In fact, the creative industries *are* the new service sector. This new economy makes specific demands of education.

Education in the 'old economy' and the 'new economy'	
Old Economy	**New Economy**
Four-year degree	Forty-year degree
Training as a cost	Training as a source of competitive advantage
Learner mobility	Content mobility
Distance education	Distributed learning
Correspondence materials with video	Multimedia centre
Fordist training – one size fits all	Tailored programmes
Geographically fixed institutions	Brand named universities and celebrity professors
Just-in-case	Just-in-time
Isolated learners	Virtual learning communities

Source: T. Flew, 'Educational media in transition: broadcasting, digital media and lifelong learning in the knowledge economy', *International Journal of Instructional Media*, Vol. 29, No. 1, 2002, p. 20.

There are myriad assumptions lurking in Flew's fascinating table. The imperative is short courses on the web servicing the needs of industry. He described the product of

51 J. Hartley and S. Cunningham, *Creative Industries – from Blue Poles to Fat Pipes*, Department of Education, Science and Training, Commonwealth of Australia, 2002, p. 5.

this system as a 'learner-earner'.[52] This 'forty-year degree' is based on lifelong learning ideologies. However, Flew's ideas are undermined by the current government higher education agenda, through the capping – through time – of courses. The effect on the 'learner-earner' in having to earn more to privately fund a continuance of learning – to ensure that they keep on earning – needs to be addressed. There will be consequences to the housing market, family structures and leisure time. The costs of education will impact on other sectors of the economy and private lives. There is little attention to the groups who are outside this taken-for-granted commitment to learning. Flew noted that,

> barriers to greater participation in education and training at all levels, which is a fundamental requirement of lifelong learning in the knowledge economy, arise in part out of the lack of provision of quality technology-mediated learning, and also from inequalities of access to ICTs, or the 'digital divide.'[53]

In such a statement, there is a misreading of teaching and learning. Once more there is a confusion of technology with literacy, or hardware with wetware. Such uncertainty is fuelled by the untheorized gap between 'student' and 'consumer'. The notion that technology (which in this context too often means computer-mediated platforms) is a barrier to education does not explain why conventional distance education courses, utilizing paper, ink and postage, were also unable to welcome or encourage groups disengaged from formal learning. Flew and others do not confront the issue of motivation, or the reason why citizens choose to add or remove the label of 'student' from their bag of identity labels. The stress on technology as both a panacea and problem for lifelong learning may justify theories of convergence and the integration of financial, retail, community, health and education provision into a services sector, but does not explain why students desire to learn, beyond economic necessity and employer expectations.

Education is distinct from training. Often creativity is a word that blurs these categories. For example, the Queensland University of Technology launched the world's first creative industries faculty in 2001. It replaced a failing arts faculty facing the threat of declining student numbers. John Hookham and Gary MacLennan, lecturers in film and television studies in this new faculty, stated 'there was also a commitment to new, digital technology that, it was argued, would enable greater creative freedom'.[54] Digitization was therefore not only conducive to, but enabling, creativity. Technology

52 T. Flew, 'Educational media in transition: broadcasting, digital media and lifelong learning in the knowledge economy', *International Journal of Instructional Media*, Vol. 29, No. 1, 2002, p. 50.

53 *Ibid.*, p. 51.

54 J. Hookham and G. MacLennan, 'Let's unlock our creative potential', *The Australian*, 11 May 2005, p. 32.

also became a battleground between the staff. There was a standardized provision of audio-visual equipment: 'all the equipment was to be of a cheap domestic standard'.[55] Not surprisingly, the pedagogy, methods and ideologies of education followed this Fordist framework.

> Particularly damaging was the illusion that the new technology had brought us to an era where to become creative all one had to do was log on to the network. Instead of finding ways to combine the old and the new technology and to make them work creatively for and with each other, the old technology was effectively banned. Such was the extent of hostility towards the old media that at the start of 2004 academics arrived in classrooms only to discover that the overhead projectors had all been removed in accordance with a central fiat.[56]

This division between old and new media is unhelpful in any context, but debilitating in classrooms. Particularly in education, presenting the continuities between books and web pages, railways and the World Wide Web, demonstrates that many of the problems, fears and inequalities that exist in and through digitization are a continuation of many earlier analogue injustices. Good teaching looks for connections, synergies and relationships. To snap away the education past is to demean and deny all the great teachers who have developed contemporary knowledge.

The pathologization of overhead transparencies is underestimating the flexibility that good analogue platforms can provide. Transparencies are cheap, mobile, flexible, quick and convenient. No time is necessary to set up a projector, or check for system compatibility. PowerPoint is not the solution to all educational problems and difficulties. It encourages poor public speaking and little preparation of educational materials. Too many teachers prepare PowerPoint slides, assuming that a lecture, tutorial or presentation can be bounced off the headings. Actually, good print- (or text-) based media should be constructed *after* the educational session has been researched and written, and after the learning outcomes have been determined and structure has been configured. PowerPoint slides are one medium for educational presentation, but there are hundreds of others. To compress the complexity and plurality of the material world into one software programme is a bastardization of not only teaching and learning, but public speaking.

Digitization and creativity are not synonyms or synonymous. Often, they are not even convergent. Yet the language of creative industries education aligns a suite of terms and phrases into a tight, commercialized techno-package. For example, monitor Stuart Cunningham's response to the criticisms of his faculty.

---

55 *Ibid.*

56 *Ibid.*

> Queensland University of Technology's creative industries faculty was formed in 2001 as a way to reinvent approaches to research and teaching in a traditional arts environment. We took talent-based creative arts with their conservatorium approaches, placed them together with the disciplines serving the industrial-age mass media, and turned them both towards the challenges of a knowledge based economy.[57]

In such a model, there is no other time but now, and no alternative model, trajectory or theory of capitalism except the 'knowledge based economy'. However, if the recent work of Zygmunt Bauman is taken seriously, then the multiple modernities and capitalisms within post-Fordism require a much more complex approach. There is no singular progressivist (and linear) historical model stretching from creative arts to industrialization to post-Fordism. Instead the economy, culture and social structures are operating in and through multiple times, loops, spaces and narratives.

The QUT creative industries faculty based its structure and ideology around Tony Blair's first cultural mapping exercise in 1997. Even by the time that these tropes and paradigms were institutionalized into curriculum through 2001, global trends and improvements had overtaken and critiqued the language being taught. Yet with so much government money sunk into the faculty, the language of Leadbeater and Florida punctuated mission statements and strategic plans. While it is perhaps possible – through copyright and patents – to live on thin air, we cannot teach on thin air. For example, ponder this literacy double-speak from Stuart Cunningham describing the pedagogy in his faculty:

> We're not just trumped-up econometric-speak people … We've got a social agenda that is part and parcel of the extension of multimedia literacies to the broad population.[58]

The last sentence, even on multiple readings, is unclear in its meaning. If a social agenda is part of multimedia literacies, then the precise determination of both 'multimedia' and 'literacies' is required. As has been argued throughout this book, any discussion of literacy requires a smooth transition between analogue and digital, the cultural and the critical, text and context. 'Multimedia literacies', if such a formation exists beyond the production of Hypertext Markup Language, is not self-standing, but organically derived from other skills. Perhaps, in their quest for a social agenda for the 'broad population', there will be a recognition that there are more important issues, goals and educational outcomes than the extension of 'multimedia literacies'. In the quest for social justice, there are more fundamental educational initiatives to initiate.

---

57 S. Cunningham, 'Precinct seen as an innovative hub', *The Australian*, 18 May 2005, p. 31.

58 S. Cunningham, in D. Illing, 'Humanities gets a centre of excellence', *The Australian*, 22 June 2005, p. 34.

Based on these assumptions of expanding creative industries, multimedia literacies and lifelong learning, the shape of education is warping. John Halliday confirmed that 'lifelong learning may be seen as a means of legitimizing a capitalist requirement for a flexible and low-skills workforce'.[59] This educational cost will be privatized. When coupled with immigration flows, technological changes and alterations to market and labour structures, lifelong learning presents a profound and personal cost. An instrument for economic and social progress has been individualized, customized and privatized. The consequence of the ageing population in many nations is that there will be fewer young people in schools or employment. Such a shift has consequences for the workplace and the taxation system. Similarly, those young workers who remain will be far more entrepreneurial and less loyal to their employers.

Public education is now publicly assisted education. Jane Jenson and Denis Saint-Martin realized the impact of this change.

> The 1980s ideological shift in economic and social policy thinking towards policies and programmes inspired by neo-liberalism provoked serious social strains, especially income polarization and persistent poverty. An increasing reliance on market forces and the family for generating life-chances, a discourse of 'responsibility,' an enthusiasm for off-loading to the voluntary sector and other altered visions of the welfare architecture inspired by neo-liberalism have prompted a reaction. There has been a wide-ranging conversation in the 1990s and the first years of the new century in policy communities in Europe as in Canada, among policy makers who fear the high political, social and economic costs of failing to tend to social cohesion.[60]

There are dense social restructurings initiated by neo-liberalism and changing the notions of learning, teaching and education. There are yet-to-be tracked costs to citizenship. The legacy of the 1980s and 1990s is that all organizations must behave like businesses. In such an environment, there are problems establishing social cohesion and connectiveness, let alone social justice. To stress the product – and not the process – of education contradicts the point of lifelong learning. Compliance and complicity replace critique.

Tony Blair, summoning his best Francis Fukuyama impersonation, signalled the triumph of liberal democracy over other political and economic systems. His Third Way was unrecognizable from the Labour Party ideals of Clement Attlee. Probably his policies needed to be. In his second term, he was not focused on probing the specificities of the market-orientation of education, health and social welfare.

---

59 J. Halliday, 'Who wants to learn forever? Hyperbole and difficulty with lifelong learning', *Studies in Philosophy and Education*, Vol. 22, 2003, p. 196.

60 J. Jenson and D. Saint-Martin, 'New routes to social cohesion? Citizenship and the social investment state', *Canadian Journal of Sociology*, Vol. 28, No. 1, 2003, p. 78.

> The Cold War has ended. The great ideological battle between communism and Western liberal democracy is over. Most countries believe both in markets and in a necessary role for Government. There will be thunderous debates inside nations about the balance, but the struggle for world hegemony by political ideology is gone. What preoccupies decision-makers now is a different danger. It is extremism driven by fanaticism, personified either in terrorist groups or rogue states.[61]

Decision makers such as Gordon Brown remain preoccupied with war and terrorism. Such conflicts seemingly justify large defence budgets at the expense of social programmes. There is no recognition by empowered world leaders that 'high-tech' armory and warfare is generally impotent to the terrorist's weaponry of cars, bodies and bombs. After the rapid and successful 'shock and awe' tactics of Iraq War II, terrorism was neither annihilated nor slowed by the Coalition's victory. Instead, suicide bombers in Saudi Arabia, Morocco, Indonesia, Israel and 'post war' Iraq have snuck through defences, requiring little more than a car and explosives. More Americans have been killed since the war 'ended' than during the conflict.

Wars are useful when establishing a political order. They sort out good and evil, the just and the unjust. Education policy will never provide the 'big win' or the visible success of toppling Saddam Hussein's statue. The victories of retraining, literacy, competency and knowledge can never succeed on this scale. As Blair confirmed, 'these are new times. New threats need new measures'.[62] These new measures include – by default – a user-pays education system. While the next chapter addresses the global movements and models for education, there is a fear that in a (post) information age lifelong learning cannot succeed. It requires a dense financial commitment in the long term. A learning society requires a new sort of war, using ideas not bullets.

61 T. Blair, 'Full text of the Prime Minister's speech at the Lord Mayor's Banquet', 10 Downing Street Newsroom, 12 November 2002, http://www.number-10.gov.uk/output/Page6535.asp, accessed on 13 November 2003.

62 *Ibid.*

Chapter seven

Deglobalizing education

> An important fact of the world we live in today is that many persons on the globe live in such imagined worlds (and not just in imagined communities) and thus are able to contest and sometimes even subvert the imagined worlds of the official mind and of the entrepreneurial mentality that surrounds them.[1]
>
> Arjun Appadurai

Globalization, like sex, is seemingly everywhere. Just as a compliant woman with breast implants is sold with an ever-increasing range of products, so is globalization the excuse, mantra and answer to social change, political struggle and economic challenge. Swimming through Coke and supersizing McDonalds, capitalism seems sustained as much by calories as free trade agreements. While critics from wide-ranging political agendas saturate their cursors with the potential and problems of globalization, it is clear that they summon different meanings, goals and objectives through this word. The contestation of these 'imagined worlds', which share vocabulary but not ideology or discourse, is a fascinating, but terrifying, consequence of post-industrialization and post-Fordism.[2] A war on terror has only added the ghostly shadow of xenophobia to discussions of the free market. As Arjun Appadurai confirmed, we need to unpick the relationship between globalization and homogenization. The movement in ideas and images demonstrates that meanings and interpretation are not the same at origin and destination. The boundaries, margins and interdependencies of culture triggers fascinating studies. Too often, one word – globalization – blocks the complexity of such a study emerging. For example, Subramani confirmed the extraordinarily complex and intertwined relationship between the nation state, Pacific and Oceanic imaginings of globalization. He realized that 'writing in English has already played a vital role

---

1 A. Appadurai, 'Disjuncture and difference in the global cultural economy', from F. Lechner and J. Boli (eds), *The Globalization Reader* (Oxford: Blackwell, 2004), p. 103.

2 The extraordinary influence of Benedict Anderson's *Imagined Communities* resonates with my work here. The emergence of print capitalism, which permitted the emergence of vernacular print languages, was furthered through the teaching of these literatures that then unified dialects for middle class readers. Print capitalism and Protestantism solidified identity formations around nationalism. Please refer to *Imagined Communities: Reflections on the Origin and Spread of Nationalism* (London: Verso, 1991).

in imagining Oceania'.[3] However, he recognizes that oppositional cultures create adversarial interpretations of European history and the English language,[4] with new vernacular iconographies and imaginings emerging through the dialogue.

Google is a 'global' search of the World Wide Web. In our often-typed 'www.shoptilyoudrop.com' discourse, we rarely consider if the 'www' in the URL is the acronym for two adjectives and a noun or three nouns. What we are surfing is a web, a structure over the internet. It is wide, moving through space at speed. It is also constructing an ideological world that emphasizes some parts of the planet and excludes or ignores others. Effective and challenging education on and offline must probe these three words, asking who is not represented, over-represented or misrepresented in the dialogue between analogue and digital. Google makes possible globalizing knowledge. This permeation of popular data is emerging at an historical moment of waging fundamentalisms between Islam and Christianity that is destroying lives and killing the debate about ideas. The source of this 'problem' is not found in the Americas, Europe or the Middle East. The solution remains in education. Hanif Kureishi, besides being a fiction writer who changed fiction, is also an incisive commentator about the volatile identity of British-born children of Islamic parents.

> When it comes to teaching the young, we have the human duty to inform them that there is more than one book in the world, and more than one voice, and that if they wish to have their voices heard by others, everyone else is entitled to the same thing. These children deserve better than an education that comes from liberal guilt.[5]

While commenting about the place of Islam in a supposedly multicultural nation, Kureishi's words apply to any faith. A belief without question and thought is a fascism of the mind. It corrodes desire, hope, aspiration, creativity and knowledge. It also makes teaching a very dangerous and difficult profession. This chapter takes on the challenge of pluralism, diversity and difference, situating education in debates about space and power. This discussion is necessary as it provides the connector between easy celebrations of creative industries outlined in the last chapter and the dense changes and challenges of education and literacy after September 11 that is explored in the final chapter of this book. It is a place to measure the width of the web being searched by Google.

---

3 Subramani, 'The Oceanic Imaginary', *The Contemporary Pacific*, Spring 2001, p. 158.

4 Clearly the English language is the new Latin. It is the most studied foreign language and the most used second language. It is also the language of publishing and therefore digital aggregation.

5 H. Kureishi, 'The carnival of culture', *The Guardian*, 4 August 2005, http://www.guardian.co.uk/religion/Story/0,2763,1542252,00.html, accessed on 4 August 2005.

Glocal ed

There is no google.com.us.[6] In fact, there is no 'us' in domain names.[7] The default setting of global web addresses is that they are all based in the United States of America.[8] If a non-American digital nationalism is summoned, then a couple of initials are added to the URL. Other nations clamber for digi-space, recognition and specificity. There is a power in these domains. The George W. Bush-led Government turned off the domain suffix for Iraq – .iq – before the invasion of the country. This act of digital erasure can be enacted to any other country domain.[9] Therefore, the virtual 'US' is enormous, extending far beyond the physical landscape of the country. More positively, Google has made possible the ability to explore domains in territories other than the United States, and it is a useful service when searching for precise information from governments, community organizations and regional popular culture. When entering google.de or google.co.uk, the speed increases in finding precise documents that are distinctive to a nation. Yet a particular version of the nation is summoned. It is possible to go to Google Canada – google.ca – but the specificity and cultural sensitivity stops at that point. It is not an option to then enter French or English speaking Canada. Similarly, virtual New Zealand can be searched at google.co.nz, but there is no recognition of the dual identity, histories and allegiances of this bicultural nation. New Zealand has another name that is tethered to these antipodal islands: Aotearoa. The Treaty of Waitangi, signed in 1840, ensured that the rights and privileges of the Maori, the indigenous peoples of

---

6 The .us domain does exist. It was reserved for government bodies below the federal level and higher education institutions offering less than a four-year degree. In April 2002, the .us domain name was opened up to non-government entities and individuals in the United States, but is rarely used. Google remains branded as Google.com.

7 This lack of a national suffix parallels British postage stamps during the height of the British Empire. They also did not have – or need – a named place of origin. The absence of place spoke identity.

8 The Internet Corporation for Assigned Names and Numbers (ICANN) and the World Wide Web Consortium (WC3) have recently had their control of the domain name registry questioned by nation states at the World Summit on the Information Society. VeriSign is a private company that controls the distribution of the .net domain name based in the United States of America. Please refer to M. Rimmer, 'Virtual countries: internet domain names and geographical terms', *Media International Australia*, No. 106, February 2003, and D. McCullagh, 'ICANN "Disappointed" in VeriSign', *News.Com*, 27 February 2004, <http://news.com.com/2100-1-38_3-5166818.html>, accessed on 15 July 2005.

9 In 2005, the United States Government announced that it would not hand over control of the domain name system to ICANN, which was planned to occur in September 2006. The justification was national security concerns. Please refer to D. Morgenstern, 'Feds won't let go of internet DNS', *EWeek.Com*, 1 July 2005, http://www.eweek.com/article2/0,1895,1833928,00.asp, accessed on 5 August 2005.

Aotearoa, would be preserved. Within the nation, this Treaty is maintained at the level of domains, with 'iwi' – loosely translated into 'tribe' – being available for Maori sites. However Google only permits a search of New Zealand, not Aotearoa. Colonial truths are perpetuated in and through digitization.

In this Googlescape, nationalism is morphing and twisting. It is a complex and contradictory political era. While neo-conservatives wage a war to preserve democracy, heterosexual marriage, families and nationalism, neoliberal market agendas crush through legal, temporal and spatial barriers. Often the tight internality of neo-conservatives, imprinting a particular political vision on the world, and the expansionist externality of neo-liberals clash and education is often the site of this conflict. As Aronowitz and Gautney have realized, this mode of globalization is based on the view that 'there are universal values that supersede the old nineteenth century notion that the prerogatives of nation-states are inviolable, changing both the liberal and the Marxist theories of imperialism'.[10] Through the nineteenth century, industrialization required colonization to increase and maintain the rate of capital accumulation.[11] The rise of modern corporations in a postcolonial environment has created 'imperial globalization',[12] charged with regulating the movement of capital, not people. Privatization, deunionization and free range capitalism are no longer cultural forces to discuss or moderate, but to accept and embrace. The consequences of such a system were that, by 2000, 51 of the world's 100 largest economies were corporations. Only 49 were countries.[13] This economic integration has consequences for the distribution of wealth. In such an environment, the word globalization is too easy an explanation and justification of macroeconomic imbalance. There are profound social costs for this social distribution. Such results were reported in the United Press International (UPI).

> In globalised countries, people lived longer, healthier lives, and women enjoyed the most social freedom, educational and economic opportunities. One troubling aspect of the survey was that 50 per cent of the world's population lives in the 10 least globalized countries: Brazil, Kenya, Turkey, Bangladesh, China, Venezuela, Indonesia, Egypt, India and Iran.[14]

---

10 S. Aronowitz and H. Gautney, 'The debate about globalization: an introduction', from S. Aronowitz and H. Gautney (eds), *Implicating Empire: Globalization and Resistance in the 21st Century World Order* (New York: Basic Books, 2003), p. xii.

11 Leslie Sklair stated that 'capitalist globalization is an historical form but not the only possible viable form of globalization', *Globalization: Capitalism & its Alternatives* (Oxford: Oxford University Press, 2002), p. 5.

12 Aronowitz and Gautney, p. xvii.

13 M. Marable, '9/11 Racism in a time of terror', from Aronowitz and Gautney, p. 7.

14 D. Haddix, 'Globalization survives by tourism and tech', *United Press International*, 24 February 2004, Expanded Academic Full Text.

In globalized (mobile, affluent) countries, citizens have access to the internet and travel. They are healthier and have economic and social options. For most of the world's population, these lived alternatives are not possible.

Similarly, something odd has transformed the local. The rapid decolonization of the globe through the twentieth century was met and matched by words like Americanization, Westernization and cultural imperialism. I have never watched Martha Stewart on television or bought a book or magazine featuring her name or photograph, but the soggy image of beige wallpaper and crisp linen permeates my vista through media convergence and branding. The tension between the local, national and international can be eased by demonstrating – particularly through leisure, the workplace and education – both respect and sensitivity to local knowledge. The bias of digital media, which cuts through space and time compression, means that the axis of diversity is changing. Without challenge or questioning, citizens can live in a gated local community of the mind, assuming their values are shared by others. Consumerism, religion and the media are three cultural forces that move ideas through boundaries.

Globalization is a contested and volatile term because a myriad of problems are attached to it, most precisely the unequal distribution of wealth. As a term, it underplays the changes to capitalism, where a citizenry is no longer reliant on government, but transnational corporations. There is a horror in this disparity. David Held and Anthony McGrew reported that 'estimates of the cost of providing basic health care for all those presently deprived of it amount to $13 billion a year, some $4 billion less than is spent annually on pet food by European and Japanese consumers'.[15] However unjust such spending may appear, the shifting organization and application of power is not a new problem.[16] Often forgotten is that globalization is a process that has a long and dense history entwined with modernity.[17] The alignment, following on from Weber, of

---

15 D. Held and A. McGrew, *Globalization/Anti-Globalization* (Cambridge: Polity, 2002), p. 77.

16 Many theories of globalization focus on current injustices and imbalances of power. Fredric Jameson marked this disappearance of the past, let alone critical and interpretative history, as a postmodern reaction to high modernism. He stated that 'the disappearance of a sense of history, the way in which our entire contemporary social system has little by little begun to lose its capacity to retain its own past, has begun to live in a perpetual present and in a perpetual change that obliterates transitions of the kind which all earlier social formations have had in one way or another to preserve', from 'Postmodernism and consumer society', in H. Foster (ed.), *Postmodern Culture* (London: Pluto Press, 1985), p. 125.

17 Al-Qaeda, Al-Jihad, Lashkar-e-Toiba, Harkat-ul-Mujahideen and Laskar Jihad offer fascinating interventions in discussions of both globalization and modernity. Even when the national government of Afghanistan – the Taliban – collapsed, Al-Qaeda continued. William Tow described these organizations as 'driven primarily by grievances directed against religion, power establishments and modernity itself', from 'Apocalypse Forever? International relations implications of 11 September', *Australian Journal of Politics and History*, Vol. 49, No. 3, 2003, p. 318.

capitalism and the protestant work ethic, marks the point of difference between the traditional and the modern. The collapse of the Twin Towers only made this discussion of change more intricate and difficult. The unipolar power of the United States is comparable to Ancient Rome. By the tail end of the Cold War, Allan Bloom could state (seemingly without qualms) that 'America tells one story: the unbroken, ineluctable progress of freedom and equality'.[18] That is why the terrorist attack was such a shock. As Walden Bello realized,

> Then came September 11, and with it a massive effort on the part of the pro-globalization forces, who now saw the whole thing as a war, to turn the tide by trying to extend the range of terrorist action to include the civil disobedience tactics of anti-corporation globalization activists, and, even more important, by manipulating the anti-terrorist hysteria to ram through the liberalization agenda at the Fourth Ministerial of the WTO in Doha, Qatar.[19]

Bello's percussive and persuasive prose has its excesses, but his analysis of the consequences of free flowing trade liberalization is convincing. He searches for alternative forces of community that are not based on the dollarization of the world. Perhaps most appropriately, he confirms and promotes the existence of alternative Americas, where an anti-terrorist campaign is not used as a shield for a domestic agenda managing a corrosive division between conservatives and liberals that was captured best in the knife-edged mid-term elections in November 2006. The Democrats regained the Senate by one seat. More concretely, Mark Beeson and Alex Bellamy confirmed that the greatest error by the lone American superpower was a misreading of 'the implications that flow from massive international inequalities of wealth and power'.[20] The tools for the damage to American property and lives were American, delivered on legally scheduled domestic flights. Such reflexive interiority was reinforced when Hurricane Katrina destroyed New Orleans. The confidence in the American models of democracy and freedom were shaken. As Adrian Wooldridge stated in the aftermath of the disaster:

> The big losers among Republicans will be the neocons… The hubris of thinking America could reshape the world, creating a democracy in hostile territory, when it can't even keep order in an American city – that hubris has just been punctured in a big way.[21]

As black faces jutted out from television screens, the costs and consequences of privatization and deregulation were shown. The affluence of some was built on the

---

18 A. Bloom, *The Closing of the American Mind* (London: Penguin Books, 1987), p. 55.

19 W. Bello, *Deglobalization: Ideas for a New World Economy* (New York: Palgrave, 2002), p. 17.

20 M. Beeson and A. Bellamy, 'Globalisation, security and international order after 11 September', *Australian Journal of Politics and History*, Vol. 49, No. 3, 2003, p. 339.

21 A. Wooldridge in J. Freedland, 'The levee will break', *The Guardian*, 7 September 2005, p. 21.

poverty and loss of others. This internal order presented a contested and contestable model to export to the rest of the world.

I-ntervention

Anger emerges from this nest of excess. Fifty thousand demonstrators protested in Seattle about the free trade policies of the World Trade Organization in December 1999. Inequality created this resentment and anger. Displacement triggered disenchantment. Yet, as Appadurai realized, global culture does not have to create a homogenizing culture. When films, music and websites move through space, they also change in meaning. The concern is, when overlaying computer-mediated communication, that a digital divide only further polarizes the rich and poor, in relation to their access to digitized platforms.[22] These cycles of deprivation require intervention, facilitated by increasing the rate and scale of social interactions.[23] Technology is an agitator of and for cultural change. There are wide-ranging disparities in the access to internet infrastructure, and massive resources are necessary to address this inequality. Douglas Houston confirms that 'not surprisingly, nations with little income have little Internet access or use'.[24] The confluence of capitalism, social progress and technical progress builds barriers in the way of critical consciousness. Through the facilitation of both connections and mechanisms for translation, 'transnational social movements'[25] are possible. While information transfer is a characteristic of digitized media, the process of translating and understanding that data development is a cultural process necessitating attention to literacy and education.[26] Even if the internet infrastructure was global, the knowledge

22 An important corrective for diasporic communities is that – upon leaving a nation – they may continue involvement with their homeland after immigration. The new information technologies allow transnational political organizations to operate and increase in spread and scale. Globalization, in this context, can facilitate the spreading of political cultures. Please refer to Paul Rowe's analysis of this issue in 'Four guys and a fax machine? Diasporas, new information technologies, and the internationalization of religion in Egypt', *Journal of Church and State*, Vol. 42, Winter 2000.

23 A fascinating analysis of the relationship between nationalism and globalization was conducted by Sylvia Walby, 'The myth of the nation-state: theorizing society and politics in a global era', *Sociology*, Vol. 37, No. 3, 2003, pp. 529–46.

24 D. Houston, 'Can the internet promote open global societies?', *The Independent Review*, Vol. 7, No. 3, Winter 2003, p. 354.

25 S. Scalmer, 'Translating contention: culture, history, and the circulation of collective action', *Alternatives*, Vol. 25, No. 4, October–December 2000, p. 491.

26 Translation – as an agenda and project – is incredibly important in the postcolonial environment. Tejaswini Niranjana offered one of the most complex and evocative analyses of translation believing it not only raises issues of representation and power, but 'produces strategies

to understand the information upon arrival is not so pervasive. All translations take place in (a frequently formerly colonized) context.

Information ethics sets new agendas for (post)colonialism. Digital communication permits the movement and exchange of ideas not possible (or at least slowed) through analogue channels. Digital stalking and rampant plagiarism are two negative consequences of the free movement of bytes. Yet the information poor are invisible at the digital frontier, disconnected and irrelevant. They cannot gain visibility through the screen. Without internet literacies, the screen and keyboard are an impermeable barrier. The cost-intensive nature of the information infrastructure means that the context of knowledge and the processes involved in the development of literacy are often discounted. A public library is not only a collection of books, but a social institution for sharing ideas. The World Wide Web does not have the openness of a library. The costs of buying equipment and attaining the necessary literacies are high. For those literate in these discourses, digital documents are easy to manage and dynamic. As more documents become digitized, those who lack the infrastructure and experience will be less visible or relevant to the building of a democracy, and less able to hold political leaders accountable.

Fast communication, like fast capitalism, is flexible and fluid. However, it creates competing and dissonant information worlds. While some citizens are able to live trans-local lives, gaining new data at great speed, other communities and groups are rendered increasingly isolated through digitization. Marginality is increased. Langdon Winner described this process as social structures and cultural artefacts 'going liquid'.

> Digital liquefaction is also liquefying economic structures, educational institutions, and communities. Whole vocations – secretaries, phone operators, bank tellers, postal clerks – have been abolished or drastically reduced.[27]

The loss of jobs and expertise in the name of progress has increased the unequal nature of decision making. Individual choice and agency has shifted the relationship between accountability and responsibility. Organizations like the World Bank, the International Monetary Fund and the World Trade Organization hold extraordinary power, validating the views of shareholders, not citizens. The WTO was formed to manage global trade, not moderate civil society. As Aronowitz confirms,

---

of containment', from *Siting Translation: History, Post-structuralism and the Colonial Context* (Berkeley: University of California Press, 1992), p. 3.

27 L. Winner, 'Who will be in cyberspace', *The Network Observer*, Vol. 2, No. 19, September 1995, http://dlis.gscis.ucla.edu/eople/page/no/september-1995.html#who, accessed 24 August 2002.

> Globalization was forged on a widened wage and unemployment gap. Living standards in the vast developing world have actually declined for many since the new phase of accelerated global capital investment began in the 1980s.[28]

The question is how to move questions of global economic governance beyond the profit imperative.[29] If the World Wide Web is embedded in the matrix of the market economy, then the consequences of this masking need to be monitored. As Troy Schneider has suggested, much has been promised in this digital revolution.

> Since at least 1996, technophiles have been promising that the Internet would revolutionize politics: that it would provide issues over attack ads; virtual town hall meetings to replace the six-second sound bite; real-time campaign-finance disclosure; cyber-coalitions; online voting; and more. In short, plugging in could offer purer, more productive politics and a more direct democracy.[30]

Few of these initiatives have entered mainstream culture. The information elite continue to talk to the information elite, but in more media. The online environment has, since 1996, been commercialized, useful to shop for products but not to debate ideas. The enlightenment narrative, where progress initiates liberation, is not addressing the unequal nature of analogue communication and the subsequent distribution and development of literacies. As Abhijit Sen confirmed, 'reassertion of religious beliefs and Islamic fundamentalism could possibly be a backlash to the pervasive nature of American and Western symbols'.[31] Global culture is an ideology of developed, urban areas, where well educated and affluent citizens talk to their contemporaries. Deterritorialization, and the attendant development of virtual communities, can disorient and exclude those who cannot celebrate or welcome plurality, hybridity and diversity.[32] The internet, as a context for social change and identity formation, can create (cyber)spaces for governments in

---

28 S. Aronowitz, *How Class Works* (New Haven: Yale University Press, 2003), p. 30.

29 An outstanding analysis of the changing theories of representation, accountability and responsibility through globalization is Shareen Hertel's 'The private side of global governance', *Journal of International Affairs*, Vol. 57, No. 1, Fall 2003, pp. 41–50.

30 T. Schneider, 'Online in 2000: call off the revolution', http://www.findarticles.com/cf_0/m1548/5_14/56065498/print.html, accessed on 16 May 2003.

31 A. Sen, 'The impact of American pop culture in the Third World', *Media Asia*, Vol. 20, No. 4, 1993, p. 216.

32 Fiona Allon argued that 'cosmopolitanism appears ... less a marvelous spectacle of diversity than as the ground for the intensification of inequality and social division and the revival of a defensive localism seeking to protect "places" of recognition and identity', from 'Nostalgia unbound: illegibility and the synthetic excess of place', *Continuum*, Vol. 14, No. 3, 2000, p. 276.

exile, such as in Tibet,[33] but can also reinforce the rationale for ethnic cleansing, such as in the Sudan.[34] Spaces can be provided for indigenous languages and literatures, such as the role and place of the Maori and Maoritanga in the cyber-Aotearoa/New Zealand, or the Nation of Hawaii, which was established as a presence on the web in December 1994.[35]

Internet sociology, when aligned with history and education studies, allows us to understand how the local, national and global conflate in convergent, digitized space. Jon Anderson has undertaken some of this important work:

> The international Internet is not culture free or culture transcending but a special precinct of the already cosmopolitan. It magnifies that cosmopolitanism, provides it with new sinews, even enhances its realities. Still, it is not cosmopolitanism that the Internet fosters, nor parochialism, but creolization.[36]

The greater issue is if the internet fosters increasing corporatization, with the exchange of information becoming less relevant and significant than the exchange of goods. Privatization and free market forces will not – inevitably – increase the range and scope of telegeography in the developing world. The confusion of dueling freedoms – freedom to shop and Google with democratic freedom and the right not to purchase consumer goods – is perpetuated through the virtual environment.

Moving knowledge

The impact of globalization on higher education is far more difficult to track than the transfer of capital or commercial opportunities. Through the movement of staff and

33 Scott Crawford and Kekula Bray-Crawford discuss these cyberspace-facilitated governments in exile in 'Self-determination in the information age', http://www.hawaii-nation.org/sdinfoage.html, accessed on 16 May 2002.

34 Nils Zurawski reported that the World Wide Web home page for the Sudan perpetuates the ruthlessness of the political order in that country. He states that 'here the impression is created that this is the perfect country for a family vacation, as though there were no civil war – accompanied by massive ethnic cleansing – going on in the south of Sudan. We learn nothing about the different groups living in the country, but get instead a lot of links to Arabic – and Islamic oriented servers that mirror the situation of domination and power in the Sudan', from 'Ethnicity and the internet in a global society', http://www.isoc.org/isoc/whatis/conferences/inet/96/proceedings/e8/e8_1.htm, accessed on 16 May 2003.

35 The Nation of Hawaii, http://hawaii-nation.org(.)

36 J. Anderson, 'Middle East Diasporas on the Internet', http://www.isoc.org/isoc/whatis/conferences/inet/96/proceedings/e8/38_2.htm, accessed on 13 May 2003.

ideas, best practice is grafted to already existing structures. Philip Altbach confirmed that,

> the structure of the American university itself, so influential worldwide, constitutes an amalgam of international influences. The original colonial model, imported from England was combined with the German research university idea of the 19th century and the American concept of service to society to produce the modern American university. Foreign models were adapted to domestic realities in creative ways. As the European Union moves toward the harmonization of national higher education systems in the 'common European space,' foreign influences again emerge – degree structures, the course-credit system, and other elements in modified form combined to produce evolving academic patterns. Just as Japan adapted German academic models and some American ideas as it built its modern university system after 1868, the European Union looks to 'best practices' worldwide.[37]

Throughout their history, universities have balanced national and international models within local conditions. Students have traveled to conduct their fieldwork. Scholars move countries to continue their work and attend conferences. Most of us publish with companies not within our nation. Through distribution, our books are read in many places. Via transnational education, our courses are offered on off-shore campuses.[38] Web-based education is therefore increasing the speed of this movement in teaching and learning. It is not initiating it. Ideas have always moved, but not as quickly.

In transnational education, regulation and quality assurance is difficult. The mobility of institutions and increasing demand for skills and retraining is creating a host of new providers. Sergio Machado Dos Santos realized that,

> The conditions are therefore ripe for the emergence of alternative providers outside the official higher education, who are quickly grasping the opportunities for a potentially lucrative market. These new providers target the new and left-behind areas which were neglected or poorly served by the traditional institutions, often filling niches and making use of flexible approaches to adapt to clients' needs. The new information and communication technologies facilitate different and more decentralized ways of organizing education, providing easier access to courseware. Many new providers are therefore technology-driven, characterized by high capital investments but low-cost operations.[39]

---

37 P. Altbach, 'Globalization and the university: myths and realities in an unequal world', *Tertiary Education and Management*, Vol. 10, 2004, p. 4.

38 There are many interpretations of these campuses. It can be a form of franchising, or a more integrated scholarly environment, sometimes referred to as 'twinning'.

39 S. Santos, 'Regulation and quality assurance in transnational education', *Tertiary Education and Management*, Vol. 8, 2002, p. 100.

The marketing of educational services across national boundaries can build the basis of intercultural communication, but it can also raise revenue for institutions. The concern is that these alternative providers do not conduct research and build original and innovative knowledge. They simply transmit and deliver learning outcomes, not changeable and hybrid ideas and ideologies. They generate 'courseware' but not knowledge. This sale of educational materials and models is not sufficient. As ideas travel, they must change.

In an attempt to organize these diverse transnational institutions, education is administered and managed. It is an 'audit culture'.[40] Berit Askling and Bjorn Stensaker confirmed that,

> Focus tends to be on procedures and outcomes of institutional leadership, governance, and management rather than the concerns of 'front-line academics' struggles to improve teaching and learning. In other words, the higher education institutions and their leaders and staff members face inconsistent expectations.[41]

In such an environment, notions of leadership are in conflict. Leaders in the classroom speak a different language to managers. Such dissonance is made more convoluted and conflictual in a globalized environment. Powerful universities, based mainly in the United States and the United Kingdom, have transformed into logos and brands to be exported. Yet within these countries, inequality and disparity also emerge. Of the 3,200 American postsecondary institutions, only 100 could be considered research universities.[42] These institutions receive more than 80 per cent of government research funds. Even within centres, there are peripheries.

The globalizing expansion of trade and commerce has aligned with the internationalization of education. Managing culturally-diverse students and teachers moving across borders creates new environments for communication and education. Formal education constructs and teaches topologies of knowledge. Transforming universities into teaching factories producing graduates has forged a segmented sector and a modularization of degree structures. Yet this hyper-hierarchization of universities into league tables is under challenge. Sander Gilman argued that 'the boundaries between the older models that divided the world into separate spheres for the creation and dissemination of knowledge will begin to alter'.[43] In such a time, classroom encounters can be unsettling. Particularly with diverse nationalities, religions and languages in the

---

40 T. Tapper and D. Palfreyman, 'Understanding collegiality: the changing Oxbridge model', *Tertiary Education and Management*, Vol. 8, 2002, p. 57.

41 B. Askling and B. Stensaker, 'Academic leadership: prescriptions, practices and paradoxes', *Tertiary Education and Management*, Vol. 8, 2002, p. 115.

42 Altbach, p. 7.

43 S. Gilman, 'Collaboration, the economy, and the future of the humanities', *Critical Inquiry*, Vol. 30, Winter 2004, p. 390.

same room, diverse world histories spark in our tutorials. These educational travels open up new ways to both position and write knowledge. Working *with* this diversity will improve our education, sharpen our teaching and improve universities. This is a productive globalization, which counters xenophobia and insularity.

Globalization and technological changes are both symptoms, rather than causes, of capitalist restructuring of social and economic relationships.[44] This globalizing technocapitalism not only increases inequalities, but also offers the potential for new resistances. Such interventions require access, time and care in the deployment of literacies. Such phrases as the digital divide cannot represent or monitor the complexity and dynamism of these inequalities. Without tracking analogue injustice, digital divisions will only confirm and continue systems and structures established through colonization. The final chapter explores both the horror and hope of this new environment. We walk through the ashes of terrorism.

---

44 Douglas Kellner works through these changes to capitalism in 'Globalization, technopolitics and revolution', *Theoria*, December 2001, pp. 14–34.

Chapter eight

Burning towers and smouldering truth: September 11 and the changes to critical literacy

The truth is that force alone cannot end terrorist violence.[1]

John Gray

Images still scar the mind: of skyscrapers sliced open like sardine cans, bilious black smoke erupting from concrete and iron, of grey streets and people, stained by tonnes of expelled paper, ash and dust. I was not in New York when this iconographic tragedy actually 'happened'. Like most experiences of social and political change in the post-industrial era, my relationship with September 11 was mediated by television, newspapers and the internet. There were no 'real' Twin Towers to witness: only endless interpretations circulating in the semiosphere.

Cut to three years later. I am in a university committee meeting trying to stress the importance of studying communication and cultural studies during this difficult time. Colleagues frame the paradigm as too abstract, needing to make way for courses in public relations, journalism, film and radio production. Certainly my case and cause was made more difficult because I was 'managing' a curriculum that had barely changed in 20 years because of managerial disregard for the humanities. Course titles appear spliced from a bad 1970s sociology conference: Culture and Everyday Life, Sexuality and Culture, Cultural Difference and Diversity, Television and Popular Culture. This is redundant knowledge, derived from a kinder era for the humanities and social sciences when phrases like social justice and social responsibility were validated and affirmed, rather than mocked as liberal pluralism or political correctness. While arguing for curricula revision, I realized none of the decision makers held teaching qualifications. There is a common lack of professional development in Australia, but in the global university environment it is a startling absence, particularly when compared with expectations in the United Kingdom and the United States. The notion that staff can make determinations about curricula, the knowledge economy and critical literacy without credentials in these

1 J. Gray, 'Appeasement: should we strike a deal?', *New Statesman*, http://www.newstatesman.co.uk/nscoverstory.htm, accessed 23 April 2004.

fields is an indictment of Australian universities, and demeaning of the expertise held by education faculties and the academics within them. These times of diverse student backgrounds and changing parameters of knowledge necessitate formal training in education, and the ability to construct curricula with relevance and appropriateness in difficult times. It is a cliché that September 11 changed the world. More rarely discussed is how it changed universities. Right now, an awareness, knowledge and application of critical literacy and information management theory is an imperative, not a luxury.

After September 11, teaching students became more difficult. The humanities and social sciences attract a diverse cohort of international students, mature-aged scholars, and those with disabilities. Scholars are derived from many classes, races and sexualities. Teaching race, religion and cross-cultural communication in such an environment requires intense concentration. A decade ago, I could discuss political resistance in reasonably clear terms. Now, the confluence between resistance and terrorism haunts my tutorials. Such definitions and discussions are even more complex when visiting Christian, white, American students and Muslim Malaysian scholars are in the same classroom.

For example, one of my first year students, a visiting scholar from the United States, was placed in an 8am tutorial. One week, we were addressing the definitions of terrorism and their difference from the concept of resistance. One of my Australian students asked her about her thoughts. She replied that, when preparing for the tutorial, she tried to remember what she thought about terrorism before September 11. This young woman stated that she had no memory of her definitions before that time. It was as if the ash of the Twin Towers had smudged all recognition of history before that dreadful day. The most effective (and dangerous) ideology is able to erase the past, to make us believe that how we live now is how people have always lived. Perhaps the greatest task of teachers is to use intricate and precise theories of literacy to summon – gently and with compassion – the ghostly visage of this history. By giving our students metaphoric footnotes – references to prior belongings and knowledges – we offer reminders of how we have lived life differently.

The intensity of teacherly focus, and the changes to curriculum required to balance these diverse imperatives, is of a high order. Such judgments are assisted through attention to curricula development and literacy theories. Since September 11, many aspects of a humanities education have changed. Yet there has never been a greater need to provide a strong voice of critique and questioning amid political contradictions. Remembering the words of John Gray, force will not end terrorist violence. Education and the development of plural and reflexive literacies is a necessary facilitator of the process.

This chapter focuses on a very precise relationship: the moving of students from a cultural literacy to a critical literacy. I argue that – after September 11 – teachers need to be more methodical and precise in assisting students to transfer, with reflexivity, between their truths and contexts, and the lived experiences of others. Through an application of literacy theory, curricula can provide a space for discussions of difference. The War on Terrorism that provides a framework for our educational system and students requires translation, care and precision. Two issues dominate my investigation. The first component explores the changing understandings of news, truth and identity, and how these movements impact on the construction and framing of education. The second section brings forward the discussion of information and knowledge deployed throughout this book, to probe the mobilization of critical literacy in this environment.

Choose freedom

We need freedom from choice.[2]
Irvine Welsh

It is neither glib nor rhetorical to argue that the world has changed since the collapse of the Twin Towers.[3] Jonathan Schell, in his book *The Unconquerable World*, revealed how the modern system of warfare was formed. It was based on four conflated histories: the democratic revolutions which brought greater numbers into the political system, the scientific developments that facilitated military technologies, the industrial revolutions that allowed these technologies to be manufactured, and colonialism which spread a European war system around the world.[4] He showed the consequences of European nations, between 1870 and 1900, grasping control over 10 million square miles of global real estate, where 150 million citizens lived. Schell realized that nuclear weaponry signaled an end to this global war system. The gulf in power between the imperializing West and the alternative structures and systems of the formerly colonized created disparities, subjugations and highly conflictual ideologies. Being in control of the most advanced technologies of war is no longer enough to ensure domination. While the smoldering World Trade Centre is the most visible manifestation of the disempowered, deglobalizing formation of Al-Qaeda 'winning' over the greatest military power the world has known, such a mode of resistance has a history. In the late 1930s, Chinese communist guerrillas fought against the Japanese invaders. Similar strategies and tactics

---

2 I. Welsh, 'Post-punk junk', from S. Redhead (ed.), *Repetitive Beat Generation* (Edinburgh: Rebel Inc, 2000), p. 145.

3 Michael Galvin, following on from Paul Virilio, argued that the phrase 'twin towers' has added to the scale and scope of the tragedy. He stated that 'if only one of the two towers had been attacked or destroyed, then it is suggested that the impact of the event could have been quite different', from *Continuum*, Vol. 17, No. 3, 2003, p. 305.

4 J. Schell, *The Unconquerable World: Power, Non-violence and the Will of the People* (London: Allen Lane, 2004).

were deployed in the war between Vietnam and the United States. This model provides a shape for the (post)war waged in Iraq. Describing the struggle against terrorism as a 'war' permits the thunderous and violent history of the twentieth century to bleed into the next: the justification of pre-emptive strikes, the deployment of an industrial-military matrix, and the construction of a hierarchy that values one form of economic and political system – one mode of 'freedom' – over others.

The notion that 'war' is required to 'destroy' terrorism has become an assumed slogan of the last few years. There are alternatives to this neo-conservative imagining. Spain's Prime Minister, Jose Luis Rodriguez Zapatero, pulled his national forces out of Iraq. Much talk of weakness and appeasement ensued. However John Gray realized that this alternative strategy – of dropping the tug-of-war rope – has merit.

> In this neoconservative fantasy world, only an uncompromising refusal to have any truck with terrorism stands any chance of defeating it, but in the real world things are done rather differently. Appeasement has been present wherever terrorist violence has been controlled successfully. It was an essential ingredient in the mix of policies implemented by successive British governments in Northern Ireland – one of the few genuine success stories in the history of counter-terrorism – and it is a major element of the process that has been made in ending decades of terrorist murder and suicide bombing in Sri Lanka. Appeasement is only another name for the willingness to negotiate.[5]

Media reporting has been complicit in this denial of alternatives. On 10 April 2004, it was becoming obvious that at least 600 Iraqis had been killed and 1,700 wounded in Fallujah. Yet only three days earlier, the British ITV Lunchtime News granted six minutes to the story, focusing on the killing of twelve US marines – which was mentioned eleven times. The reported 66, rather than 600, Iraqi deaths – which included civilians – were mentioned twice.[6]

In such a context, the internet was able to capture at least some plurality in reportage. John Schwartz believed that, 'the 2003 war in Iraq may well be referred to in the future as the "Internet war"'.[7] It crystallized an already existing shift in the relationship between credibility, truth and popular culture. It was September 11 that altered the way in which already existing web users managed new sources. As Lee Rainie, Susannah Fox and Mary Madden realized,

---

5 J. Gray, 'Appeasement: should we strike a deal?', *op. cit.*

6 D. Edwards and D. Cromwell, 'Fallujah – when the moral crusaders fell silent', *New Statesman*, Monday 26 April 2004, http://www.newstatesman.com/200404260015, accessed on 28 July 2004.

7 J. Schwartz, 'A cast of thousands', *Australian Screen Education*, No. 32, 2004, p. 54.

> Do-it-yourself journalism has been a staple of Internet activity for years and the terrorist attacks gave new prominence to the phenomenon. In the days after the attacks, the Web provided a broad catalog of facts and fancy related to 9/11.[8]

Such digital deployment of opinion and argument increased after September 11. During Iraq War II, 77 per cent of already existing users deployed the web to discover information about the conflict. Intriguingly, war opponents, rather than supporters, reported that they increased the access and time on the internet.[9] While the reasons for this discrepancy are debatable, one interpretation is that opponents to the war were seeking out alternative views and truths to 'mainstream' news sources. Yet multi-platforming and cross marketing, where already existing 'mainstream media' converge with emerging technology, are creating a media-glugged – rather than fertile – environment. In such a context, great emphasis should be placed on the development of a critical literacy that can deploy semiotic methods to probe and question regimes of visuality and aurality, and text and images.

Further attention is necessary on the configuration of a new digitally savvy citizenry and those not active in this environment. An April 2003 survey in the United States found that younger, upper class, white, well-educated, urban and suburban parents were more wired than other groups.[10] Further, the researchers revealed that most non-users of the internet stated that they had no intention to enter the online environment,[11] and that 'basic literacy in any language are (sic) another barrier to full Internet use'.[12] In the context of this report, 'literacy' is being defined as encoding and decoding text, rather than the deployment of interpretative skills.

Access to these alternative sources of information is important at a time when news and current affairs is conflated with entertainment. This change means that critical literacies are necessary to sift data, ideologies and discourses. Particularly with the proliferation of blogs, an individual's opinions may be granted equivalent standing

---

8 L. Rainie, S. Fox and M. Madden, *One Year Later: September 11 and the Internet*, 5 September 2002, http://www.pewinternet.org/, accessed on March 10, 2004.

9 This data is derived from a report by Lee Rainie, Susannah Fox and Deborah Fallows, *The Internet and the Iraq War*, PEW Internet and American Life Project, 2003, http://www.pewinternet.org/, accessed on 10 March 2004. What particularly interests me in this report is that the writers referred to 'war opponents'. The question is if they meant opponents to Iraq War II, or those who are pacifists by political allegiance. I am also interested in their finding that 'Men with Internet access are much more likely than online women to be getting news from the Web both before and after the war broke out', p. 3.

10 Amanda Lenhart, *The Ever-shifting Internet Population: A New Look at Internet Access and the Digital Divide*, The Pew Internet and American Life Project, 16 April 2003, accessed on 20 March 2004, p. 4

11 *Ibid.*

12 *Ibid.*, p. 5.

to a scholar's detailed research.[13] Intriguingly, in such an environment of digital fog, politicians are actively combating against teaching practices that encourage thinking, not conforming. For example, a Minister for Education in Queensland, Australia was critical of the 'mumbo jumbo' being taught in English classrooms. At his most dogmatic, he stated that 'nothing will leave this department that I don't understand'.[14] When a politician becomes the arbiter of appropriate curriculum and knowledge, education is bent to the vagaries of elections. Journalists reinforce the limited vision of such politicians, misrepresenting critical literacy:

> Critical literacy, which is heavily influenced by postmodern theorists that rose to prominence in the 1980s, has influenced the English curriculum in all states and territories but particularly those of Queensland, Western Australia and Tasmania. Opponents of critical literacy argue that it takes away the enjoyment of reading, squeezes classic works off the syllabus and politicises the classroom.[15]

Supposedly, 'politics' in the classroom critiques the value and quality of 'the classics'. Obviously postmodernity and critical literacy, while sharing some theorists and theories, have distinct origins and disciplinary frameworks. Without these caveats, politicians and journalists initiate a fear of losing 'standards' because of critical and interpretative theory.[16] The response from educators to this misreading of intellectual history was shock, horror and humour.

> Congratulations, Luke Slattery. Despite citing no evidence regarding Australian literacy rates and armed with only a handful of wowserish examples, you were able to achieve a populist

---

13 The proliferation of blogs – or web logs – is also having a consequence on journalism. Mark Fisher reported that 'we've made it all the easier for consumers to spurn our products because we've bought into the notion that all voices are equal, that a blowhard on talk radio has as valid a reading of political events as does the Washington bureau chief of the *New York Times*, or that opinions dumped into a random Web site are as useful as a story written by a reporter who knows every deputy secretary in the agency he covers', from 'The metamorphosis', *American Journalism Review*, November 2002, p. 22.

14 R. Welford, in L. Slattery, 'Mumbo jumbo teaching to end', *The Australian*, 4 August 2005, p. 1.

15 L. Slattery, *ibid.*

16 Another example, also on the front page of a newspaper, was Bethany Hiatt, 'No books needed in OBE English', *The West Australian*, 17 September 2005. The first paragraph of the article was 'Students may be able to pass Year 12 English without reading a book when the controversial outcomes-based education system is introduced into high schools next year', p. 1.

> shift in education policy. That's the sort of intelligent process that will keep Australia on the right track. Who needs informed opinions? Keep up the great work.[17]

Once more 'postmodernity', without content or specificity, is used to demonize popular culture, affirming literary 'quality' and discrediting the skill and professionalism of educators. There has been a confusion between cultural value and educational value, or class bias and critical thinking.

In such an ideas-thick – rather than rich – environment, a pre-emptive war on Iraq was not only waged but justified. In this context, the internet offers alternative sources and ideas, but there is also greater space for ideologues to perpetuate their message. It allows fast, frequently unchecked rumour to gain currency over verified and credible journalism. As discussed through this book, there are consequences in relying on research shortcuts for news and information. This sound bite culture has a major impact on the calibre of political debate. In 1968, the political sound bite was 43 seconds, which reduced to 9.8 seconds in 1988 and seven seconds by 1996.[18] The speed at which ideas are expressed, and the truncated vocabulary utilized to convey complicated ideas, makes it difficult to encourage researched, theorized interpretations and intellectual rigour. This accelerated culture creates an impetus for accelerated literacy. There is no time to move – with reflexivity – from operational literacy, decoding signs, through to critical literacy, which interprets and contextualizes signs and codes to create knowledge. John Horrigan and Lee Rainie reported that 'the dissemination of the Internet has transformed how many Americans find information and altered how they engage with many institutions'.[19] In developing curricula to facilitate critical literacy and interpretation, questions must be asked about the impact, relevance and value placed on web-based information when compared to other platforms such as television, or print on paper.

Community borders of otherness and difference have calcified through the events of September 11. The emotional responses to those burning buildings mean that it is difficult to critically evaluate how these events have been represented. Three thousand people lost their lives on that day. But 250,000 lost their lives in the Bosnia conflict, and up to one million people were killed in 1994 during the genocide in Rwanda. Every day, 24,000 people die from malnutrition and 30,000 children under five die from preventable causes. The symbolic power of September 11, through the destruction of the World Trade Centre as the embodiment of neo-liberalism, and the Pentagon as the basis of the US military, grants this date a resonance beyond the sheer number of deaths. Until

---

17 S. Farry, 'Grasping concepts of postmodernism is to be applauded', *The Australian*, 5 August 2005, p. 17.

18 These statistics are derived from Fisher, *op.cit.*

19 J. Horrigan and L. Rainie, *Counting on the Internet*, Pew Internet and American Life Project, 29 December 2002, http://www.pewInternet.org/, accessed on 20 March 2004.

September 2001, foreign stories occupied half the time they did in 1989. This lack of global content created an inward focus to American, Canadian, British, New Zealand and Australian news. Jennifer Lawson, a Washington DC-based independent producer stated that,

> We as a nation were so surprised by what happened with 9/11. Had we known more about how others view us and our policies, I don't think we would have been so surprised. We get very little coverage from Indonesia or the Philippines, and almost no backgrounders, even though there are links to al Qaeda-type organizations. The news is always crisis-oriented, and then it drops off the radar screen. Even our coverage of Afghanistan dropped off.[20]

Fox News Channel solved the problem of few foreign bureaus by reducing non-American news stories and the literacies to understand them. They spend little time on international material and stress domestic news. The station chose to be different from CNN or BBC World by promoting a patriotic and narrow performance of Americanness. Their programme style is colloquial, ideological, insular and anchor heavy.

The consequence of this cultural shift is that few public figures speak in full sentences anymore. A detailed argument is redundant. Slogans become facts. Perusing abstracts and extracts replaces reading full books. Ponder these phrases:

> Weapons of mass destruction
> Coalition of the Willing
> Regime change
> Axis of Evil
> Asylum seekers
> Pacific Solution
> War against terror

Ideologies are carried through these phrases so that alternative trajectories are silenced. What was the Australian problem that caused a 'Pacific Solution'? If there is an Axis of Evil, then is there a parallel Axis of Good? What is this Coalition willing to do? Technological change has increased the speed through which 'news' is proliferated, often encouraging unchecked rumour and gossip to overwrite and decentre journalistic standards of ethics and reporting. Clichés swarm informed commentary. The reduction in time between information availability and the creation of news narrative triggers a 'rip and read' mentality challenging standards of newsworthiness and accuracy.[21]

---

20 J. Lawson in N. Fleeson 'Bureau of missing bureaus', *American Journalism Review*, October/November 2003, p. 35, http://www.ajr.org/article.asp.?id=3409.

21 Elisia Cohen raised some concerns with online journalism in 'Online Journalism as market-driven journalism', *Journal of Broadcasting and Electronic Media*, December 2002, pp. 532–48.

In liberal democratic theories, a news system maintains a vital role in providing information for citizens to be rational and construct thought-out political judgments. Positioned as a Fourth Estate, news organizations must be independent of government and business. As news organizations have become big businesses themselves, they are subject to the same economic concentrations of the wider economy. The permeation of the free market system has validated and increased structural inequalities, with access to news becoming synonymous with an ability to pay for this service.[22] Concurrently, tabloidization has permeated all sectors of news, with entertainment and celebrity valued over information and debate.

The attacks on the World Trade Centre and the Pentagon morphed international politics and journalism. How September 11 transformed education is a question posed less frequently. Not only have vocabularies and literacies shifted, but so have our capacity to interpret, debate and think. Definitions of terrorism are determined within the dictionary of the definer. Terrorism challenged the sovereignty and solidarity of 'us' and 'them'. Great military ascendancy after 'winning' the Cold War did not remove or eradicate vulnerability. September 11 demonstrated that the primary concepts through which international relations are run – such as core and periphery, first and third worlds – no longer function. Such a division leads to sloganized answers to difficult questions. The closures of language, like Axis of Evil, Operation Enduring Freedom and Freedom-loving People, fabricate a solid enemy rather than a vague or unsubstantiated threat to security. George W. Bush was clear on such a division. On CNN he stated that 'you are either with us or against us'. [23] Organizations such as Al-Qaeda are anti-globalizing and trans-national, operating between the spaces of nations, cities and citizens. Their ideas move as freely as an email or SMS, and their finances follow already established pathways of international capital. Instead of affirming good and evil – or us and them – we need more subtle approaches and methods to understand the networks of anger, resistance and hate that render binary oppositions both inadequate and redundant explanations for global problems. Anne-Marie Slaughter stated that the war against terror is 'all about language'.[24] Focusing on those images from September 11 and fear of the future means that students and teachers are less likely to ask questions about the cause and context for the attacks. The link between global inequalities and terrorism is rarely highlighted. The discourses of terrorism as currently framed ensure that anything is valid or appropriate

---

22 Dan Schiller has written an outstanding early analysis of news and how electronic sources were challenging the relationship between entertainment and news. Please refer to his 'Transformations of News in the US Information Market', in P. Golding et al., *Communicating Politics: Mass Communications and the Political Process* (Leicester: University of Leicester Press, 1986), pp. 19–36.

23 G. Bush, *CNN*, 6 November 2001.

24 A. Slaughter, 'Beware the trumpets of war', *Harvard Journal of Law and Public Policy*, Vol. 25, No. 3, Summer 2002, footnote 17.

if it is countering terrorism. The language of terrorism organizes social relationships, creating floating and unsatisfying solutions to stark injustices and distributions of wealth. Meanings do change through time: Nelson Mandela and Menachem Begin have both been termed terrorists, only later to become statesmen. Therefore, new questions need to be asked. Deferring the inquiry into 'What is terrorism?', teachers and students may probe how the vocabulary, language and ideologies of terrorism function. Such a project moves teachers and students away from cultural literacy and towards critical literacy. The key is to reduce the fear, and increase the understanding. As one of my students described it, the goal is to naturalize 'Islam in the west'.

Date: Fri, 3 Sep 2004 15:37:17 +0800
From:
To: Tara Brabazon <tbrabazon@central.murdoch.edu.au>

Subject: islam in the west...hmmmm

peace,

dearest tara, thank you soo much for today, it was both interesting and quite shocking....just the fact that you will discuss this fear of the difference with me is great, because obviously you yourself are one of the many white australian women of this world...but you have developed an appreciation for the different instead of a fear .... absolutely amazing!

i will proberbly come see you on monday....maybe 4–5ish...? is that ok? just cos i love talking to you, and i am still a little unsure on how to approach this topic, as i am obviously from a particular attitude....

i will see you monday then, if that suits...

ALLAH hafiz

may ALLAH protect you

Len Unsworth provides a strong model with which to negotiate these changes to literacies by stressing historical continuities and making multiple definitions and arguments complementary rather than antagonistic. He sees no digital divide, instead recognizing that 'written texts have always been multimodal',[25] with distinct typefaces, layouts and graphology. He also affirms that no singular literacy operates across the curriculum. This is a revelatory argument, as universities in particular are being shaped by generic skills and mission statements, not specific or targeted knowledges. Such phrases allow the proliferation of Teaching and Learning Committees without educational qualifications. In such a context, 'experience' – however that is determined – substitutes (and perhaps replaces) the need for credentials, scholarship and research. Instead, as Bill Cope and Mary Kalantzis realized, 'the globalization of communications and labour markets make language diversity an even more critical local issue'.[26] This means that cultural and linguistic difference must be negotiated in a particular context, and requires precision and care in the construction of curriculum, assessment objectives and pedagogy.

Marlene Asselin and Elizabeth Lee argue that the key for contemporary education is to teach people how to independently interpret information.[27] The development of interpretative capital requires resources and precise methods. The ideological crunch of September 11 and a war on terrorism has only made this imperative more urgent. The next section of this chapter investigates what the study and use of critical literacy theories can offer in the current educational environment. Many of the discussions in this book are tethered to this, the final section.

Critical Digital

> So, the question for teachers should not be: what is the best way of teaching reading and writing?[28]
>
> Allan Luke

The term critical literacy has become an aspirational phrase for a mode of 'reading' students should be actualizing. Yet concise definitions and applications remain ambiguous. Mary Macken-Horarik suggests that it 'problematises the relationship between meaning making (reading and writing) and social processes'.[29] She constructs a model of literacy that moves through the educational process.

---

25 L. Unsworth, 'Changing dimensions of school literacies', in *Teaching Multiliteracies across the School Curriculum* (Melbourne: Macmillan, 2001), pp. 7–20.

26 B. Cope and M. Kalantzis, 'Putting "multiliteracies" to the test', *Education Australia*, Vol. 35, 1997, p. 17.

27 M. Asselin and E. Lee, '"I wish someone had taught me": information literacy in a teacher education program', *Teacher Librarian*, Vol. 30, No. 2, December 2002, pp. 10–17.

28 A. Luke, 'Getting over method: literacy teaching as work in "New Times"', *Language Arts*, Vol. 75, No. 4, April 1998, p. 306.

29 M. Macken-Horarik, 'Exploring the requirements of critical school literacy: a view from two classrooms', from F. Christie and R. Mission (eds), *Literacy and Schooling* (London: Routledge, 1998), p. 75.

Everyday	**Applied**	**Theoretical**	**Reflexive**
Diverse and open-ended	Attaining a particular expertise	Gain disciplinary knowledge	Negotiation of social diversity
Confluent with spoken language	Use of spoken and written words to enable activity	Production and interpretation of epistemic texts	Probing assumed and specialized knowledge systems
Moving through roles and relationships in the family and community	Skill-based literacy	Situated in educational learning environments	Finding alternatives
Personal growth literacy		Specialized literacies	Challenging commonsense
		Assimilating and reproducing knowledge	Meaning determined through diverse media
			Critical literacy

Table based on Mary Macken-Horarik, 'Exploring the requirements of critical school literacy: a view from two classrooms', from F. Christie and Ray Mission (eds), *Literacy and Schooling* (London: Routledge, 1998), p. 78.

Mary Macken-Horarik argues that critical literacy is not an 'add on' to literacy debates, but does require the initial development of instrumental modes. In other words, an everyday familiarity with spoken language cannot seamlessly (and concurrently) facilitate an awareness of ideological gaps and silences in a discourse. Macken-Horarik argues that there is a linear and progressive relationship between literacy modes, disagreeing with those who argue that students can simultaneously learn to read *and* challenge what they read. The difficulty with her model is determining the level of competency in one mode that allows students/citizens to move to other theories and paradigms. Macken-Horarik argues that when students/citizens are able to place questions in context, a level of literacy has been mastered. Therefore specific techniques and assessment structures are required to move students from their current literacy mode to another knowledge system. Falk confirmed this intricate weave of social and cultural context in defining literacy competence.

> It is not the ability of the educator to impart skills which will determine the outcome in the learning situation but the ability of the educator to relate the learning to the learners'

> changing perception of literacy and how the learners can take charge of its use in the newly constructed life picture which they should start to own as a result of the interaction.[30]

The consequences of this powerful analysis to curriculum development are clear. Literacies cannot be imparted or transferred from teacher to learner. Instead, there must be multiple paths through readings, assignments and writing, allowing a diverse cohort of students to travel through knowledge in a way that has resonance for their social environment and experiences. In enacting such a method, literacy is not a 'problem' to be solved, but actualizes specific abilities to address and develop in context. Barbara Comber and others refer to this as 'the literate repertoire'.[31]

The context of September 11 permitted transitory electoral survival of neo-conservative governments in the United States and Australia. Both these governments summoned 'back to basics' literacy programmes. Luke believed that such a framework 'builds and connotes a selective, interest-bound version of culture'.[32] The encoding and decoding of print becomes an endpoint rather than the start of another stage or mode of literacy. Such a model encourages conservative, insular and retrospective knowledge proliferation. Higher levels of literacy competence are then locked away from the disempowered as they 'master the basics', perpetuating the distribution of knowledge and power in society. Literacy in a communication-rich environment needs more than an invention of tradition or a re-creation of supposedly timeless standards. Tired and inappropriate determinations of literacy are being circulated by these conservative governments. Literacy is not only about reading and writing, but activating a diversity of communication skills in context. These skills in reading, thinking and recognizing the developments in learning of others are, at its most basic, the point of education.

---

30 I. Falk, 'The social construct of adult literacy learners' needs: A case study', *Language and Education*, Vol. 7, No. 4, 1993, p. 236.

31 B. Comber, L. Badger, J. Barnett, H. Nixon and J. Pitt, 'Literacy after the early years: a longitudinal study', *The Australian Journal of Language and Literacy*, Vol. 25, No. 2, 2002, p. 10.

32 A. Luke, 'The social construction of literacy in the primary school', in L. Unsworth (ed.), *Literacy Learning and Teaching Language as Social Practice in the Primary School* (London: Macmillan, 1993), p. 3.

From: Ngan
Sent: Monday, 15 November 2004 4:35 PM
To: Tara Brabazon
Subject: cultural studies: note/novel from ngan

Hi Tara, it's ngan from cultural studies here.

This message may sound a little sucker uperish, if that is even a word and I apologise for that Because I dislike ppl who have their head up someone's arse, but if you feel the need if even out of sympathy to lift my grade, feel free. My morals are flexible.

This is just a little note to say that I really enjoyed your unit. I know it's been a few weeks over now. I thought to myself, should I send a msg or is it too late? Is there a time rule? Will I feel like a dickhead writing to my tutor? Maybe I will. I put that all behind me.

Anyway, I really did enjoy the unit. Although not the best student nor the most vocal person in the tutes , in case you had'nt noticed and at mosttimes sat there with what could be described as an emotionless face (sorry bout that), but I honestly did enjoy the discussions. I know, hard to believe huh? but you betta believe it.

It was good to see that people with different opinions were accepting and understanding of each other. I have a problem with some aspects of society, without going into detail, but it seems to me that society does not want to tackle issues that matter or accept them. If these issues are not talked about or brought forward to the ppl that have the potential to make a difference, than there obviously can't be change and that sucks and I don't want to move backwards.

I thank you for being open, honest tolerant and genuine and I'm sure you have had an impact on each student's life in some way. I appreciate your help and time. You and your unit have left an imprint on my life.

Cheers Xx

and

Be Well

This is literacy in a post-Fordist knowledge economy. It is much more than reading and writing. It is to open eyes and ears to difference, not to judge or ridicule, but to think and explore. Effective learning is able to captivate students with multiple learning strategies that move through the analogue and digital, through text and print, through sound and vision. There are many ways of knowing, and so many ways of thinking.

Allan Luke realized that 'the ways that literacies are shaped have uneven benefits for particular communities and, unfortunately, the outcomes of literacy teaching continue to favor already advantaged groups in these communities'.[33] This means that middle class children have already existing literacy skills developed in the home reinforced at school.[34] For disempowered groups, there is a need to make educational expectations explicit. If literacy is framed as a singular set of standards then, as Diane Coyle realized, 'education systems inevitably produce first- and second-class citizens'.[35] Literacy practices build cultural capital, which then provides the framework for the development of more advanced interpretative skills. Luke argues for a 'critical social literacy'[36] which incorporates the capacity to manage and mobilize diverse texts for decision making and facilitates the development of critical thinking.

The attention to quality assurance in higher education, framed through public speculation about falling academic standards, has created debate about acceptable levels of achievement and performance. Brendan Nelson, on behalf of the Australian Federal Government, released the ministerial discussion paper, *Higher Education at the Crossroads*, in 2002.

> Over the years there have been allegations that university standards are falling. Some critics contend that some universities now offer courses lacking intellectual rigour and that there has been a 'dumbing down' of universities. There are also concerns about deterioration in the calibre of students entering universities but the available evidence does not support this. There have been claims that 'soft marking' has become common practice, and the quality of education has generally been compromised.[37]

33 A. Luke, 'Getting over method: literacy teaching as work in 'New Times,' *Language Arts*, Vol. 75, No. 4, April 1998, p. 306.

34 Viv Edwards stated that 'children who do best academically come from homes where the literacy practices are very similar to the school', from 'Literacy or literacies?' in C. Modgil and S. Modgil (eds), *Educational dilemma: debate and diversity* (London: Falmer Press, 2000), p. 190.

35 D. Coyle, 'How not to educate the information age workforce', *Critical quarterly*, Vol. 43, No. 1, 2001, p. 53.

36 Luke, 'The social construction of literacy in the primary school', *op. cit.*, p. 7.

37 B. Nelson, *Higher Education at the Crossroads: an overview paper,* Canberra: Department of Education, Science and Training, 2002 http://www.dest.gov.au/crossroads/pubs.htm, accessed on January 5, 2003.

The rhetorical devices in this extract are evocative. The Minister chooses not to critique the unreferenced claims of 'soft marking' or 'dumbing down', but does caveat the argument that there has been a lowering of entry requirements to universities. The 'quality' of education has not been compromised but like all determinations of quality, it has changed. When I started at an Australian university in 1987, I rarely saw my lecturers outside of formal class time. Such a lack of contact did not worry me. I went to the library, attended lectures and tutorials, completed my assignments, worked hard and finished my degree. I respected – and still do respect – those academics enormously. They taught me lessons by example, about professionalism, respect and scholarship. My fellow students were young, white, affluent and from university-educated families. This is a completely different educational environment to the one in which I teach. My cohort is of mixed race and heritage, diverse in class background, and frequently the first member of their family to attend university. Nearly half of my students are mature-aged scholars. Most are in paid employment, with a university education low on their list of priorities.

These social changes in the student cohort do not signify a deterioration of student 'quality'. There are great benefits in teaching such a diverse community. Media and cultural studies comes alive as the theories of difference speak to the lived experience of scholars. However, these students require much more time, effort and initiative from academic staff. Curricula must be precisely crafted and honed, 'unspoken assumptions' about reading, writing and critical thinking are overtly articulated, and pedagogical methods deployed with precision. The older modes of a university education – the sage on a stage – no longer function. Neither can the abrogated responsibilities of a reified student-centred learning. Instead, academics must become proactive and experienced teachers, trained in pedagogy, curriculum and action research, to ensure reflexive deployment of academic standards. The economic and political changes to the world in the last five years have had a wide impact. The benefit of internationalization is the rapid transfer of knowledge, but there are also effects on the diversity of higher education. Affirmations of standards may mask an imperative for homogeneity. Education based in Perth *should* be different from that offered in New York, Brighton or Osaka. As discussed in the last chapter, some of the most significant theories emerging since September 11 have mobilized the trope of deglobalization.[38] There is important theoretical and applicable research to be conducted affiliating critical literacy, localism and deglobalization, rather than a simplistic affirmation of standards, sameness and homogeneity. Wittgenstein critiqued the impetus of globalization, confirming a 'contemptuous attitude toward the particular case'.[39] The local, specific and particular

38 For example, David Held and Anthony McGrew, *Globalization/Anti-Globalization* (Cambridge: Blackwell, 2003), Walden Bello, *Deglobalization* (London: Zed, 2002) and Ankie Hoogveld, *Globalization and the Postcolonial World* (Houndmills: Palgrave, 2001).

39 L. Wittgenstein, *The Blue and Brown Books* (Oxford: Blackwell, 1958), p. 18.

holds value for critical literacy theory, offering a way to problematize and stop the easy movement of information and capital.

While 'empowerment' was the cliché of 1980s education,[40] debates in the 2000s are punctuated by 'flexibility'. The irony is that – while flexible learning is a goal – concurrent surveillance of standards and rigid administrative and managerial protocols encircle education, stiffening structures and reducing the capacity for curricula change and development. Coyle realized the consequences of this paradox.

> For bureaucrats to pretend they can set out an appropriate curriculum and standards in every detail is both dishonest and an appalling failure of their responsibilities to the public. Bureaucratic planning failed as an economic system under Soviet communism and now it is failing under Western capitalism too. Yet it clings on grimly in ministries of education the world over, at the expense of our children.[41]

This managerialism in education is particularly inappropriate in encouraging a transfer from operational to cultural and critical literacy, transforming vocabulary into language, and meaning into context. The environment after September 11 has validated Green, Hodgens and Luke's earlier realization that 'literacy debates are fundamentally a contest of social visions and ideologies'.[42] Those on the right wish to affirm 'basics', thereby maintaining the political status quo and deflecting critique, while those on the left wish to encourage critique and questioning, moving beyond rudimentary skills of encoding and decoding. Literacy education is always a reminder and monitor of how these differences in class, religion, region, gender, race and age are configured and constructed in a particular historical moment. As Anderson and Irvine realized, 'people are not poor because they're illiterate: they are illiterate because they're poor'.[43] Social and economic conditions are determinants of literacy. Therefore, the surveillance of literacy, and the monitoring of 'standards' at schools and universities, normalize and homogenize a discussion of 'learning outcomes', not contextual causes for inequality.

The issue is how to critique the notion that there is a literacy 'problem'. Individual teachers, students and schools are monitored for low standards and punished through threats to funding. Barbara Comber argued that 'the anxiety about illiteracy goes beyond media induced public panic; it is also manifested in federal and state government policy and funding allocations, where the primary goal often appears to be to ascertain "how

---

40 Luke, 'The social contruction of literacy in the primary school', *op. cit.*, p. 15.

41 Coyle, *op. cit*, p. 54.

42 B. Green, J. Hodgens and A. Luke, 'Debating literacy in Australia: history lessons and popular f(r)ictions', *The Australian Journal of Language and Literacy*, Vol. 20, No. 1, 1997, p. 10.

43 G. Anderson and P. Irvine, *Critical Literacy: Political Praxis and the Postmodern* (Albany: SUNY Press, 1993), p. 82.

bad things really are'".[44] She argues that all teacher education requires an attendant sociology of the communities in which learning takes place. Such socio-cultural initiatives show that singular definitions of literacy and curriculum are not helpful. Each media requires specific attention in determining its strengths and weaknesses in the framing and shaping of information. The core concern in such a political/educational environment is how to create cycles of reflection, to move beyond the reproduction (and recycling) of words through cut and paste, and create a bolder and bigger perspective.[45] While the internet surfer has control over the sites they choose to visit, how they gain the skills to evaluate the material they access remains a concern.[46] The capacity to read text on the screen is not enough.

The ideology of skill development deflects and decentres more precise probing and testing of critical literacies. With employers demanding transferable skills and competency, surface knowledges are celebrated. Yet such an imperative also means that education can be assessed and quantified in terms of cost and benefit.[47] It seems too convenient – politically and socially – that at a time of war, violence and excessive consumerism that 'lifelong learning may be seen as a means of legitimizing a capitalist requirement for a flexible and low-skills workforce'.[48] Just-in-time learning validates the role of the workplace in determining the goals of education. A focus on critical literacy changes this inflection, to arch beyond reskilling, flexibility and competency.

The revelatory capacity of these ideas to teachers and students is of a grand scale. In my first year courses, while teaching cultural and media studies, I now teach this diverse model of literacy directly to students. We discuss – overtly – the politics of education in the first lecture. The responses are startling.

---

44 B. Comber, 'Literacy, poverty and schooling', *English in Australia*, Vol. 119, No. 30, 1997, p. 23.

45 This core concern was raised by Len Unsworth, 'Changing dimensions of school literacies', *op. cit.*, p. 15.

46 Y. Liu and L. Shrum raised this concern in 'What is interactivity and is it always such a good thing', *Journal of Advertising*, Vol. 31, No. 4, Winter 2002, pp. 53–64.

47 For a discussion of the consequences of terms such as competency, flexibility and lifelong learning onto education, please refer to John Halliday, 'Who wants to learn forever? Hyperbole and difficulty with lifelong learning', *Studies in Philosophy and Education*, Vol. 22, 2003, pp. 195–210.

48 *Ibid.*, p. 196.

From: pansy2002
Sent: Monday, 29 August 2005 8:50PM
To: Tara Brabazon
Subject: thank you, Tara

Hey, Tara!

How are you? I am one of the students who studies cultural studies at the moment and I have to say I really enjoyed your lecture on Monday (19th August). That was awesome and I particularly liked the part when you mentioned that in this unit students were taught how to think critically. I think it's really really important for our studies. Maybe I am a dumb student, I didn't realize how important this unit was until this morning and I also found out it is a very interesting unit. Thank you so much for the lectures you've given us so far and for our very special personality.

By the way, Tara, I want to ask you a question. I am an overseas student, sometimes I find it's hard for me to get into this unfamiliar community. What kind of things do you think I should do in order to know Australia and its people better?

I'm lookin forward to hearing from you again and thank you so much for your time.

from: yi

Yi was a special student, managing English as a second language and a new country concurrently with her education. Yet allowing all students – and particularly first years – to see behind the Wizard's curtain and understand the layers and levels of literacy is integral to further education, in the many meanings of that phrase.

Two years after September 11, John Tiffin and Lalita Rajasingham published *The Global Virtual University*. The ease with which three nouns transformed into two adjectives and a noun did not warrant comment in the book. Instead, neo-liberalism, techno-celebration and globalization aligned to crush the social justice imperatives of education.

> This leaves us with a question that many people who have attended a university must at some time have asked themselves. As long as a person can read and write and has some self-

> discipline, why bother going to classes? To societies seeking to reduce the costs of tertiary education the question then becomes; instead of using transport systems to bring people together to communicate in classrooms, why not use the postal service? Better still, today, why not use the Internet?[49]

Even in a text written in 2003, literacy is reduced to the ability of a person 'to read and write'. The idea that a university develops critical literacy that requires more than self-discipline to be actualized – the notion that students learn as much through form as content – is beyond the vision of Tiffin and Rajasingham. What these writers do not address is how the student cohort is changing, requiring more precise teaching and curricula development alongside attention to motivation and pedagogy. At a time when Blackboard and WebCT are standardizing education, academics are 'managing' a socially diverse classroom.

Further, Tiffin and Rajasingham have not referenced the intricate body of critical literacy theory. Mary Macken-Horarik's argument that literacy is a multi-layered formation, requiring the development of encoding and decoding skills before higher levels of interpretation may be developed, is ignored by the writers of *The Global Virtual University*. They argue that the 'new' mode of internet-mediated teaching means that 'instruction can focus on whether a student can apply knowledge as distinct from whether they can write a lot'.[50] As someone who does 'write a lot' – and is fascinated to see this practice pathologized by fellow academics – I am concerned that they are suggesting that 'application' of knowledge can supposedly emerge independently of writing. Actually, more attention needs to be placed on the many modes and modalities of writing and reading. Without reading and writing, research and interpretation, higher order skills – let alone expertise – will not materialize.

My other critique of *The Global Virtual University* brings this chapter back to its beginning. By stressing standardization in the teaching process and creating the awkward anagram/avatar of JITAITs – Just in Time Artificially Intelligent Tutors[51] – there is no recognition that after September 11, the requirements of education have shifted. They discuss building a university curriculum responsive to global needs, unsupported by national government funding and based on commercial principles. However, 'the world' is also deglobalizing, shredding back to the local, the specific and the particular. The reason why terrorism exists is because values *do not* move freely through space without consideration of context, difference and history.

Teachers cannot assume that there is a single method to construct curriculum, assemble a reading list, or express an ideology. Generic competencies undervalue and

49 J. Tiffin and L. Rajasingham, *The Global Virtual University* (London: RoutledgeFalmer, 2003), p. 24.

50 *Ibid.*, p. 48.

51 *Ibid.*, p. 58.

unravel the social diversity and plural complexity of our classroom. Unless discussed and valued, these differences will fester into xenophobia, isolation and fear. We all will lose perspective. As Edwards and Cromwell suggested,

> the world fell apart when 3,000 people died on 11 September 2001. No one blinked an eye when aid agencies warned that even the threat of bombing imperiled 7.5 million starving Afghans, and when US bombing subsequently claimed more than 3,000 civilian lives. In January 2002, the American media analyst Edward Herman reported that the first US combat casualty in Afghanistan had received more coverage in the US media than all the Afghan casualties combined.[52]

There are no global knowledges that can 'explain' or 'justify' this discrepancy. Imposing a standard university curriculum and pedagogy across the world – thereby deskilling academics, dividing teaching from research and demeaning the importance of educational qualifications – undermines thought, creativity, difference and critical literacy. After September 11, even more than before, we require highly skilled teachers to monitor, write, negotiate and theorize our curriculum. There is a paradox in John Tiffin and Lalita Rajasingham's book title. Their new educational institution may be global. It may be virtual. But it is not a university.

Definitions of the real have real consequences. More attention should be placed on definitions. For example, the word 'virtual' is defined as 'almost'. Therefore virtual learning is an odd combination of words. Those of us involved in education must decide if almost is good enough for our students, educational system and nations.

52 Edwards and Cromwell, *op. cit.*

Conclusion

The gift: why education matters

> More and more students either work for cash or do volunteer work in the community and, compared with 20 years ago, students are forced to manage their time better. Students also have much less structured time, with more learning done via the internet. I think there is more pressure on them because they are still expected to do just as well, even though they are learning many of the subjects by themselves.[1]
>
> Diana Green

Professor Green was Vice Chancellor of Sheffield Hallam University when she made this comment. When I read her statement – and kept returning to her words assuming I had missed a phrase – I realized why I wrote this book and why I continue to teach. That a Vice Chancellor would doom a generation of students to learn 'by themselves' in full conscience and awareness, justifying this irresponsible pedagogy to the notion that 'learning [is] done via the internet', confirms why this book is needed. Every technological application, hardware invention or software innovation has its marketers and public relations consultants employed to sell its value. There are few such celebrations for the small victories in reading, writing and thinking. Good teachers must transgress and transform this digital diatribe to stretch ourselves and aim for high standards. Learning is not 'done' via the internet. Learning is not 'done' in a classroom. All learning is conducted in a context that constructs a scholarly and structured relationship between data, information and knowledge. It is the relationship between teachers and students that configures an interpretative matrix around and through data. No one learns anything 'by themselves' or in isolation. The best scholars value the intellectuals that precede them, and demonstrate this intellectual allegiance and inheritance through research and dense footnotage. We as teachers need not accept the structures imposed by human resource managers and educational administrators who attempt to place a lifetime of learning and expertise into a weekly spreadsheet. The replacement of educational revelation with technological competency is a product of the managerial transformation of universities. In such an environment, education – not skill development – is even more important.

---

1 D. Green, interviewed by Sophie Borland, 'The campus question', *The Independent*, Education and Careers, 7 April 2005, p. 5.

Sorting out the images and ideas, facts and interpretations, educators have a responsibility to teach how arguments are formed and evidence mobilized. Unfortunately, the crumbling institution of the university can barely help itself at the moment, let alone assist the society that it is meant to serve. The system is tracing a broader crisis in meaning, value and truth. Universities remain the most important institution in late capitalism as they can change manage the ageing workforce, the relationship between public and private funding, and map and teach the shifting definitions of reading, writing and thinking. While there is much talk about 'radicals' or 'lefties' teaching propaganda rather than knowledge, there are few qualms raised by the corporatization of the academy, or the impact of non-government income on academic standards and research projects. At their independent best and working through the spaces between education and culture, universities transcend the banality and mediocrity of policy makers.

Teaching biographies are important. To write about teaching not only transforms theoreticians into storytellers, but gives a texture to educational experiences. Classrooms, cyberspaces – all spaces – are improved by the narratives woven around and through them. Such stories integrate on and offline lives. The point of this book is to connect pedagogy with technology in a productive, rigorous and applied fashion. There is far too much babble and utopic posturing about the 'inevitability' of education's technofuture. In recognizing what is working effectively in the current system, we can ascertain what can be improved and how the internet may assist or undermine this process.

Since Ancient Greece, education has held a pivotal symbolic value. Our era selects the tropes of choice, skills and flexibility as the basis of an education system, rather than diversity, scholarship and challenge. The question must be shifted from what citizens/consumers/students want to why choice is the primary imperative. More attention is needed on what lessons students are implicitly discovering by teachers and administrators dismissing commitment and discipline in favour of flexibility and lifestyle learning. B.M. Gourley outlined the consequences of this new environment.

> Universities exist in a highly competitive climate where they are putting greater and greater pressure on the public purse. What they do is no longer (if it ever was) regarded as automatically a social good. Calls for accountability and relevance give clear notice that universities can no longer rely on public opinion being on their side.[2]

While I am in favour of universities – and all public institutions – being scrutinized, regulated and monitored, there are costs when the government of the day offers too great an influence. The modern university emerged through the Enlightenment to serve the needs of the nation state. As our understandings of space and time have changed, so must the purpose of education. But the globalizing market is not an

2 B. M. Gourley, 'The Council Lecture, 21 September 2001: Diversity and change in a global context', *The International Journal of Humanities and Peace*, 2002, p. 10.

adequate replacement for the regulatory matrix of the nation. The short-term benefits of shareholders are not sufficient foundations on which to build an educational sector in an environment when nationalized governments privatize health, welfare and disability services. John Tiffin and Lalita Rajasingham stated with great confidence that 'Universities desperately need the efficiency and common sense that is inherent in good business practice'.[3] Their statement is absolutely correct in the management of educational administration, through the auditing of budgets, public accountability of money spent and transparent procedures. But good business practice is not enough for the development of teaching and research innovation, scholarly brilliance and risk-taking excellence. To enact research at the edge of knowledge requires a relentless *attack* on commonsense, on those ideas that are too easily accepted without thought or question. Assumed knowledge and dominant ideologies deaden the lightning sparks of possibilities that illuminate the path to new thinking. As to teaching, their claims are even more irrelevant. The best of education is not efficient like corporate banking. It is emotionally draining and physically exhausting, often requiring an elastic timetable so that staff can sit with students explaining and re-explaining, confirming and testing, encouraging and motivating. Good business practice cannot countenance such inefficiencies. Education bubbles through culture and society in odd and unexpected ways. Teachers can never know the consequences of our actions in the long term. Our bottom line is not reconcilable at the end of a financial year.

One final example from my teaching biography captures the long-term influence of education that confirms its distance from a market economy and yearly budgets. On 1 November 2004, my 100 first year students gave me a gift. At the end of my final lecture, they stood and cheered for two minutes. It was unexpected. I was gathering up my course materials for the last time to head back to the office, tired but satisfied. As I looked up from my folders, energy erupted from the auditorium. It never happened before or since. By the standards of e-university marketing consultants, I had done everything wrong throughout the semester. I had conducted all the lectures and tutorials,[4] working way over workload because I was not prepared for ill-qualified staff to baffle students with generic competences rather than specific knowledge. There was no website attached to the course, and I did not record my lectures in any form. I did not even use PowerPoint.

---

3 J. Tiffin and L. Rajasingham, *The Global Virtual University* (London: RoutledgeFalmer, 2003), p. 139.

4 The college tutorial, with its origins in Oxbridge, is a crucial venue for the development of knowledge. It asks students to defend their positions and encourages a flexibility of the mind. To this day – and even with 20 students in a room – I maintain this role of the tutorial in encouraging debate and critical interpretation of scholarship. For an evocative analysis of how and why the Oxbridge tutorial was formed – and its value in education – please refer to Ted Tapper and David Palfreyman's evocative monograph, *Oxford and the Decline of the Collegiate Tradition* (London: Woburn Press, 2000), particularly pp. 98–123.

If the students missed a session, there was no way for them to 'catch up'. I was inflexible, disciplined and demanding. I embedded the information scaffold that I discussed in the first chapter of this book into the course and insisted that they mobilized scholarly monographs, refereed articles and carefully scrutinized websites to conduct their research. Google was not enough. I transgressed all the dogmatic rules for flexibility established by educational managers. Yet the students stood and cheered at the end. It was stunning.

There was a context for their response. It had been a harrowing semester. The programme in which I worked and they were enrolled was under economic threat. My teaching methods were attacked. Every morning, I woke to wonder what challenges, arguments and conflicts would jab from my inbox during the day. I had done my best to protect these students from the worst excesses of this system, wanting to finish this soon-to-be cancelled course with dignity, to honour all the great academics who had taught this material before me and all the extraordinary students who had changed my life through their participation. It made the teaching and learning during the semester emotionally volatile. During that two minutes, we shared something important. Not only were we a community that had bonded in the educational trenches, but we had shared an intellectual journey. The waves of belief and respect in the room were like nothing I have experienced. Such a moment cannot be presented to promotion committees or discussed in an annual professional development review. It cannot be captured in language. Yet the best education is based on gifts such as this – of experience and sharing ideas – rather than a determination of profit and loss, productivity and efficiency.

Four months later, I paid the penalty for these transgressions. On the same day that I received two university teaching awards, for undergraduate and postgraduate education, my courses were cancelled by the university. This dark tale of institutional failure amid teaching success was not caused by the internet, the web or Google. The long-term reduction in funding and the social standing of educators, librarians, schools and universities had a dense and tragic consequence. Within 18 months, I had not only left this institution but the country. There was nothing left to say, write or teach. I had lost. A soft and silent departure ensured that the students were not disrupted in their goals and future. Learning goes on even when the teacher does not.

From:
Sent: Saturday, 8 July 2006 5:09 AM
To: Tara Brabazon
Subject: Farewell Tara

Tara, this is XXXX here. I wish to thank you for all the crazy antics and amazings things you taught us throughout the course. Life would have

> been boring without you. It is also a sad thing that you are leaving for Pommy land (pardon the pun). I guess i won't be the only person who misses you. You have shed light unto places which were once covered with darkness. All the best in your future endeavours and don't forget that there is one chinese dude from Penang, Malaysia that thinks you're one of the best lecturers he has ever had. Hope to visit you one day.

Through despair and failure, cancellation and migration, this book remains a testament – a memory text – to these transformative courses and transgressive students who have shed light in the darkness and will continue to do so. *The University of Google* is an affirmation of the need to teach a broad range of literacies so that multiple sources in many media can be accessed, balanced, assessed, discarded or used. Yet – in a Marshall McLuhan dystopic nightmare – the medium (the internet) has become the message (economic rationalism). Intervention and interpretation are no longer required. The consequences of this sloganized 'learning strategy' are that cutting and pasting displace reading critically. Paraphrasing (at best) and plagiarism (at worst) scratch out evocative writing. Speed searching wipes away considered thought and planned research strategies.

Google is an outstanding search engine, with problems that all search engines reveal. Their addition of Google Scholar and Google Book Search is important, even though many of the articles referenced cannot be read in fulltext because of commercial aggregators buying the rights.[5] The decision by Google to digitize millions of books and put them online is also important, a digital gift. But being able to digitize a book does not confirm that it will be read. Access does not confirm use. This is the point of confusion for critics such as Stephen Matchett. Finding a website does not equate with understanding it.

---

5 This lack of access to scholarly works has major consequences for universities. Polly Curtis, for example, reported that 'Scottish universities sign open access deal', *The Guardian*, 14 March 2005, http://education.guardian.co.uk/elearning/story/0,10577,1437377,00.html, accessed on 15 March 2005. Scottish universities, having recognized the fees involved in journal publishing, have signed a Declaration on Open Access which commits the signatories to the formulation of online libraries of research findings and doctoral papers which all academics can mobilize and use. Sheila Cannell, the Director of Library Services at the University of Edinburgh, was quoted by Curtis as stating that 'we would like to see publicly funded research being publicly available rather than locked up in academic journals'. Similarly, Derek Law, the University Librarian at the University of Strathclyde, confirmed that 'there is now clear evidence that open access articles are more frequently cited. If Scottish-based research is made available through open access it will be cited more, which means it will by definition be read more'.

> This scheme will create the world's biggest library universally accessible. Out of print is now out of date. And with everything from historic archives to increasing numbers of academic journals online, knowledge is not just instantly available, vast swags are effectively free. But just as we are determined never to appear impressed, many of us are also deeply suspicious of anything that looks like it may improve the human condition ... there are as many maps of the library as there are people with passions for their own special interests who know how to build a website. And this makes for endless associations of ordinary folk around the world who learn from each other online.[6]

The flaws of the Google discourse emerge through this passage: Google makes information easy to find and there are benevolent cyber-wizards in the matrix that will gift their knowledge to the newbie. Let us unravel these assumptions. The books being digitized are the complete collection from Michigan and Stanford Universities, selected shelves from Harvard and New York Public Libraries and a million books held in Oxford's Bodleian. All are English-speaking campuses and libraries, and elite universities at that. Significantly, the transatlantic domination of information on the web is increased once more. These conservative, elite universities do not have a reputation for their popular cultural collections or non-print based materials. Another point raised by Stephen Matchett is the most troubling one. It is simply too convenient, as education systems around the world are starved of funding and scholars are dismissed as relics of an earlier age, to argue that experts are everywhere and everyone supposedly is online. Education matters. Expertise matters. Reading and thinking matters. Scholarship matters. Google has provided an infrastructure. We now need a social system to give it a context and meaning.

The blinking cursor of Google demands a response, an answer. Before we next enter Google.com, thought and preparation are needed. Living a life of the mind grants the pleasure and joy of challenge, effort, confusion and reward. The gift of education is understanding, awareness and consciousness and it pays dividends in the long term. The outcomes of a university education cannot be listed like the outcomes of a business model, through overheads and shareholder dividends. At their best, universities teach us to pay, not bills, but attention to details. In being humble to the scholars who preceded us, in moderating our experiences to truly hear and contextualize the words of others, we see ourselves as part of a society, a community on a thinking journey to feel more.

In moving beyond in/difference, the task of this book is to ask teachers, students and citizens to lift, to reach, to extend beyond the mediocre, the banal, the stupid and the ordinary. The loss of public oratory through celebrity culture and dog whistle politics has been accompanied by tabloidized news and current affairs reporting. Through such national conversations by proxy, we must manage the gothic almost pre-industrial tragedies around us. The Tsunami, the second Iraq War, the bombing of the London

6 S. Matchett, 'Babel takes back seat', *The Weekend Australian*, 22–23 January 2005, p. 40.

Underground and the muddy relics of the once-vibrant New Orleans prompt jagged grief and pain. While the 'war' on terrorism created us and them based on knee-jerk responses to skin, religion and politics, the nightmarish row of body bags on beaches in South-East Asia reordered our mind furniture. Stinging tears blur our view of the new world. The pseudo events and enemies that construct our contemporary reality required a tragedy on the scale of the Tsunami to finally remind us that we have to discriminate between the real and the illusion. We must not let transient news cycles wear away our humility and humanity. Google helps us find information. Education helps us build knowledge. But teaching must be different. With discipline and grace, we recognize the final, gritty truth: we teach what we need to learn.

Select bibliography

Altbach, P., 'Globalization and the university: myths and realities in an unequal world', *Tertiary Education and Management*, Vol. 10, 2004, pp. 254–6.

Aronowitz, S., *The Knowledge Factory* (Boston: Beacon Press, 2000).

Aronowitz, S., *How Class Works* (New Haven: Yale University Press, 2003).

Aronowitz, S., Martinsons, B. and Menser, M. (eds), *Techno Science and Cyberculture* (New York: Routledge, 1996).

Askling, B. and Stensaker, B., 'Academic leadership: prescriptions, practices and paradoxes', *Tertiary Education and Management*, Vol. 8, 2002, pp. 113–29.

Barrell, B., 'Literacy theory in the age of the internet', *Interchange*, Vol. 31, No. 4, 2000, pp. 447–56.

Bastedo, M. and Gumport, P., 'Access to what? Mission differentiation and academic stratification in U.S. public higher education', *Higher Education*, Vol. 46, 2003, pp. 341–59.

Beard, L. and Harper, C., 'Student perceptions of online versus on campus instruction', *Education*, Vol. 122, No. 4, 2002, pp. 658–64.

Bello, W., *Deglobalization: Ideas for a New World Economy* (New York: Palgrave, 2002).

Christie, F. and Mission, R. (eds), *Literacy and Schooling* (London: Routledge, 1998).

Clarke, J. and Willis, P., *Schooling for the Dole? The New Vocationalism* (Houndmills: Macmillan, 1984).

Cuban, L., *Oversold and Underused: Computers in the Classroom* (Cambridge: Harvard University Press, 2001).

Englund, T., 'Higher education, democracy and citizenship – the democratic potential of the university', *Studies in Philosophy and Education*, Vol. 21, 2000, pp. 281–7.

Halliday, J., 'Who wants to learn forever? Hyperbole and difficulty with lifelong learning', *Studies in Philosophy and Education*, Vol. 22, 2003, pp. 195–211.

Hunter, M. and Carr, P., 'Technology in distance education: a global perspective to alternative delivery mechanisms', *Journal of Global Information Management*, April–June 2000, pp. 50–55.

Husu, J., 'Constructing ethical representations from the teacher's pedagogical practice: a case of prolonged reflection', *Interchange*, Vol. 34, No. 1, 2003, pp. 1–21.

Johnson, R., 'Talking of students: tensions and contradictions for the manager-academic and the university in contemporary higher education', *Higher Education*, Vol. 46, 2003, pp. 289–314.

Kapitzke, C., 'Information literacy: the changing library', *Journal of Adolescent and Adult Literacy*, Vol. 44, No. 5, February 2001, pp. 450–56.

Keightley, K., 'Low television, high fidelity: taste and the gendering of home entertainment technologies', *Journal of Broadcasting and Electronic Media*, June 2003, pp. 236–60.

Leu, D. and Kinzer, C., 'The convergence of literacy instruction with networked technologies of information and communication', *Reading Research Quarterly*, Vol. 35, No. 1, 2000, pp. 108–27.

Lewison, M., Seely Flint, A. and Van Sluys, K., 'Taking on critical literacy', *Language Arts*, Vol. 79, No. 5, May 2002, pp. 382–92.

Liedman, S., 'Democracy, knowledge, and imagination', *Studies in Philosophy and Education*, Vol. 23, 2002, pp. 353–9.

Lyon, D. (ed.), *Surveillance as Social Sorting: Privacy, Risk and Automated Discrimination* (London: Routledge, 2003).

Marvin, C., *When Old Technologies were New* (New York: Oxford University Press, 1988).

Maycroft, N., 'Cultural consumption and the myth of life-style', *Capital and Class*, No. 84, Winter 2004, pp. 61–76.

Meister-Scheytt, C. and Scheytt, T., 'The complexity of change in universities', *Higher Education Quarterly*, Vol. 59, No. 1, 2005, pp. 76–100.

Postman, N., *The End of Education* (New York: Vintage Books, 1996).

Pugh, G., Coates, G. and Adnett, N., 'Performance indicators and widening participation in UK higher education', *Higher Education Quarterly*, Vol. 59, No. 1, January 2005, pp. 19–40.

Robertson, H. 'Toward a theory of negativity', *Journal of Teacher Education*, Vol. 54, No. 4, September/October 2003, pp. 280–97.

Robertson, J. 'Stepping out of the box: rethinking the failure of ICT to transform schools', *Journal of Educational Change*, Vol. 4, 2003, pp. 323–44.

Schwarz, G. 'Media literacy prepares teachers for diversity', *Academic Exchange*, Spring 2004, pp. 224–8.

Smith, A. and Webster, F. (eds) *The Postmodern University? Contested Visions of Higher Education in Society* (Buckingham: Open University Press, 1997).

Taylor, T. and Ward, I. (eds), *Literacy Theory in the Age of the Internet* (New York: Columbia University Press, 1998).

Tiffin, J. and Rajasingham, L. *The Global Virtual University* (London: RoutledgeFalmer, 2003).

Weissberg, R., 'Technology evolution and citizen activism', *The Policy Studies Journal*, Vol. 31, No. 3, 2003, pp. 385–96.

Index

Abram, Stephen 142
Adnett, Nick 8, 95, 224
Agre, Phil 59
Albright, Alan 116
Alessi, Stephen 87
Computer-based Instruction 87
Allen, David 7
Allen, Katherine 139
Allon, Fiona 187
AltaVista 17–18
Altbach, Philip 189–90, 223
Anderson, Benedict 179
Imagined Communities 179
Anderson, Gary L. 209
Critical Literacy: Political Praxis and the Postmodern 209
Anderson, Jon 188
Anderson, Melissa 120
Appadurai, Arjun 179
Armitage, Catherine 62
Aronowitz, Stanley 24, 30, 72, 89, 132, 160, 163, 165–66, 169, 182, 186–87, 224
Education Under Siege 89
How Class Works 24, 166, 187
Implicating Empire: Globalization and Resistance in the 21st Century World Order 182
Postmodern Education 132
Roll Over Beethoven 169
Techno Science and Cyberculture 24
The debate about globalization 182
The Jobless Future 165
The Knowledge Factory 72, 160, 163
The Politics of Identity 24
Arthur, Charles 18, 46
Ashton, David 161
Askling, Berit 190, 223
Asselin, Marlene 203
Assoc. of Heads of University Administration (UK)7

Badger, Lynne 205
Ball, Christopher 93
Higher Education into the 1990s 93
Barke, Mike 23
Students in the Labour Market 23
Barnett, Jenny 205
Barrell, Barrie 114, 223
Bash, Lee 166–67
Bastedo, Michael 123, 223
Bates, A.W. (Tony) 106, 114–15
Battelle, John 17
The Search 17
Bauman, Zygmunt 10, 60, 131, 176
Globalization: The Human Consequences 60
Liquid Modernity 10
Beard, Lawrence 80, 117, 223
Beaumont, John 2
Beeson, Mark 184
Bellamy, Alex 184
Bello, Walden 184, 208, 223
Bennett, John 123–24
Bereiter, Carl 95
Must we Educate? 95
bibliography (annotated) 21, 30–34, 43–45
Billing, David 81, 96
Course Design and Student Learning 81, 96

Bindley, Lynne 111
Blair Government, the 2, 93
Blair, Tony 25, 28, 63, 172, 176–78
blogs 35, 40, 57, 142–43, 169, 197–98
see also bloggers 59, 142–43
blogging 59
Bloom, Allan 149, 184
Blunkett, David 2
Boal, Iain 164
Bok, Derek 170
Booth, Alan 104
History in Higher Education 104
Booth, Nick 53
Bowring, Finn 25, 166
Boyce, Angie 139
Brackett, K. 119
Brass, James 171
Bray-Crawford, Kekula 188
Brennan, Teresa 10
Exhausting Modernity 10
Brin, Sergey 17
Britt, Judy 42
Brook, James 164
Brookfield, Stephen 9, 85, 89
Becoming a Critically Reflective Teacher 9, 85, 89
Brown, Gordon 28, 178
Brown, Russell 18, 133, 142–43
Bryant, Scott 25
Buchanan, Pat 149
Burge, Liz 110
Listening to Learn 110
Burman, Eva 86
Values in Education 86
Burniston, Stephen 171
Busse, Reinhard 158

Cannell, Sheila 219
Cannadine, David 54
The Rise and Fall of Class in Britain 54
Carr, Peter 122, 223
Carroll, Mary 158
Caves, Richard 168–69
Creative Industries 169
Centre for the Study of Higher Education (Melbourne University) 55
Chen, Kuan-Hsing 68
Critical Dialogues in Cultural Studies 68
Christie, Francis 29, 203–04, 223
Literacy and Schooling 29
Cisco 53
Clarke, John 172, 223
Schooling for the Dole? The New Vocationalism 172, 223
Coates, Gwen 8, 95, 224
Coates, Tim 37–38
Cohen, Elisia 200
Coleman, Simon 124
Comber, Barbara 27, 150, 205, 209–10
Comer, James 97
Waiting for a Miracle: Why Schools Can't Solve Our Problems – and How We Can 97
Connell, R.W. (Bob) 97
Teachers' Work 97
Connor, Helen 93
Cooper, Maxine 86
Values in Education 86
Cope, Bill 203
copyright 19, 46, 113, 116–21, 127, 169, 172, 176
Coupland, Douglas 1
Microserfs 1
Coyle, Diane 25, 161, 207, 209
Crawford, Scott 188
creative industries 8–9, 40–41, 82, 168–70, 172–77, 180
Cromwell, David 196, 213
Cross, Michael 63
Cuban, Larry 28, 223
Oversold and Underused: Computers in the Classroom 28, 223
Cubitt, Sean 144
cultural difference and diversity 3, 31–32, 128, 193

cultural studies 8, 21, 32–33, 35, 40, 66, 68, 78, 135–38, 148–50, 161, 170, 193, 206, 208, 211
Cumming, Joy 29, 147
Cunningham, Stuart 172–73, 175–76
curriculum 8–11, 27, 29–32, 36, 40–43, 48, 53, 62, 66, 79, 90–91, 93–95, 109, 113, 128, 133, 136, 138, 147–48, 151, 155, 167–68, 171, 176, 193–94, 198, 203–05, 208–10, 212–13
  see also enacted curriculum 29–30, 147
Currie, Jan 96
Curtin University 89, 121–22
Curtis, Polly 38, 54, 219

Daley, John 163
Davis, Hilarie 36
Davis, Mike 122
Dewson, Sara 93
DiFazio, William 165
  The Jobless Future 165
Digital Hemlock 1–3, 6, 83
Docker, John 133–34, 146
Doig, Shani 29, 147
Dowling, Tim 16
Drucker, Peter 10
  Post-Capitalist Society 10
Dudfield, Angela 22
Duke University 113
Duncum, Paul 103
Durrant, Cal 28, 145
  Literacy and the New Technologies in School Education 28, 145
Dyer, Thomas 116

Edwards, David 196, 213
Edwards, Viv 26, 207
Eggins, Heather 93
  Higher Education into the 1990s 93
EHE [The Enterprise in Higher Education Initiative] 171
Elliott, Robert 159
Englund, Tomas 66, 223
Expanded Academic Database 20, 31
Ezzy, Douglas 166

Faigley, Lester 51
Falk, Ian 27, 204–05
Fallows, Deborah 197
  Fast Capitalism 29, 48, 186
Fazackerley, Anna 7
Fernekes, William 36
Field, John 167–68
  Lifelong Learning and the New Educational Order 168
Finders, Margaret 137
Flannery, D.D. 123
Flew, Terry 173–74
flexible learning 2, 9, 71–72, 75, 77–82, 84–85, 90, 96, 98, 101, 119, 148, 209
Flexner, Abraham 92
  Universities: American, English, German 92
Florida, Richard 24, 170–71, 176
  Cities and the Creative Class 24, 170
  The Flight of the Creative Class 24
  The Rise of the Creative Class 24, 170
Ford, Liz 3
Foster, Hal 183
  Postmodern Culture 183
Fox, Susannah, 139, 196–97
Freebody, Peter 29
  Constructing Critical Literacies 29

Galvin, Michael 195
Gascoigne, Toss 39
Gates, Gary 171
Gautney, Heather 182
  Implicating Empire: Globalization and Resistance in the 21st Century World Order 182
Gee, James Paul 27
Gibbs, Graham 81
Gidden, Anthony 10
  The Consequences of Modernity 10
Gilman, Sander 190

Giroux, Henry 89, 132, 137, 147, 149
Education Under Siege 89
Postmodern Education 132
Global Virtual University, The 211–12, 217, 224
globalization 9, 24, 59–60, 149, 156, 163, 172, 179, 182–85, 187–89, 191, 203, 208, 211, 223
Google Book Search 46, 219
Google Ranking 42, 142, 162
Google Scholar 45–46, 219
Googlers 56
Googlescape 8, 48, 51, 182
googling 16, 19, 49, 59, 68
Gordon, June 54
Gould, Alice 19
Gourley, Brenda 216
Graham, Steve 52–53
Gray, John 193–94, 196
Green, Bill 25, 28, 145, 209
Literacy and the New Technologies in School Education 28, 145
Green, Diana 215
Greer, Germaine 77
Gumport, Patricia 123, 223

Habermas, Jurgen 26
Legitimation Crisis 26
Hall, Stuart 68
Halliday, John 56, 177, 210, 223
Hammond, Jennifer 24
Harper, Cynthia 80, 117, 223
Harris, Cheryl 48
Hartley, John 136, 173
Harvard University 99, 170
Hawthorne, Susan 15
CyberFeminism: Connectivity, Critique and Creativity 15
Healy, Kieran 169
Hearn, James 120
Hearnshaw, David 87
Hebdige, Dick 1, 11
Hiding in the Light 1
Heinz Endowments 170–71
see also University and the Creative Economy, the 170–71
Held, David 183, 208
Globalization/Anti-Globalization 183, 208
Henry, Miriam 94
An Introductory Sociology of Australian Education 94
Hertel, Shareen 187
Hewison, Robert 8, 136
Future Tense 8, 136
Higher Education Funding Council for England (HEFCE) 2
Hirsch, Edward 149
Hladky, Christine 36
Hoare, Stephen 60
Hobsbawm, Eric 156
Hodgens, John 25, 209
Debating literacy in Australia 25
Hoffman, Donna 63
Hoggart, Richard 51, 132, 136
The Uses of Literacy 132, 136
Holloway, Darren 96
Holmes, Georgina et al. 120
Holt, Margaret 122
Hong Xu, Shelly 148
Hoogveld, Ankie 208
Globalization and the Postcolonial World 208
Hookham, John 174
Horrigan, John 139, 199
Houston, Douglas 185
Howkins, John 169–70
The Creative Economy: How People Make Money from Ideas 170
Hunter, M. Gordon 122, 223
Husu, Jukka 128, 223
Hutnyk, John 139
Hyland, Paul 104
History in Higher Education 104

iLecture 85, 105, 116–19, 121–22, 126–27
Illich, Ivan 95
Alternatives to Schooling 95
Illing, Dorothy 93, 176
information age 12, 25, 29, 49, 51, 53, 101, 144, 157, 161, 172, 178, 188, 207
information society 63, 161, 181
intellectual property 46, 116–22, 124–25, 169–70, 172
Internet Corporation for Assigned Names and Numbers 181
internet education 10, 48, 99, 114
iPod 72, 109, 113, 116, 121, 141, 144–45, 163
Irvine, Patricia 209
Critical Literacy: Political Praxis and the Postmodern 209

Jacoby, Russell 62–63
Jameson, Fredric 183
Jenson, Jane 177

Kalantzis, Mary 203
Kapitzke, Cushia 125, 224
Keightley, Keir 141, 165, 224
Kekale, Jouni 29
Conceptions of quality in four different disciplines 29
Kellner, Douglas 191
Kinzer, Charles K. 148, 224
Klein, Naomi 17
No Logo 17
Klein, Renate 15
CyberFeminism: Connectivity, Critique and Creativity 15
Kling, Rob 163
Computerization and Controversy 163
Knight, John 94
Knights, Sue 96
Knudsen, Brian 171
Kroker, Arthur 24
Kumar, Krishan 51
Kureishi, Hanif 180
Kuzma, Lynn 43

Lanchester, John 17
Lang, Morgan 56
Lankshear, Colin 24
Lash, Scott 149, 156
Lau, Donald J. 148, 224
Law, Derek 219
Lawson, Jennifer 200
Leadbeater, Charles 72, 140, 172, 176
Living on Thin Air 72, 172
lectures/lecturers 3–6, 15, 44, 64–66, 71–79, 85–89, 97–131,151, 162, 174–75, 208–19
see also iLectures
Lee, Elizabeth 203
Leeds Metropolitan University 2
Lenhart, Amanda et al 22, 38, 139, 197
Leonardo, Zeus 29, 54
Lewis, Jon 151
Lewis, Tania 77, 85
Lewison, Mitzi 16, 224
librarians 17–18, 20, 37–39, 46–47, 55, 78, 83, 100, 144–45, 148, 159, 162, 218
library studies 8, 46, 95
Liedman, Sven-Eric 66, 224
Liefner, Ingo 61
lifelong learning 6–7, 25, 38, 56, 159, 167–68, 171–74, 177–78, 210, 223
Ling, Lorraine 86
Values in Education 86
Lingard, Robert 94
An Introductory Sociology of Australian Education 94

literacy 6, 8, 13, 20, 23–27, 29, 39, 48, 53, 60, 77, 97–98, 132, 136, 144–49, 186, 197–212
adult literacy 24, 27, 98, 126, 137–38, 205, 224

contemporary literacy theory 16, 171
critical literacy 16, 27–30, 33, 36, 137–38, 176, 193–99, 202–4, 207–213, 224
cultural literacy 28, 148, 194, 202
declining standards 25–26
definitions 25, 28, 148
development of 27, 148
digitization of 28, 60, 162, 176
education of 25–27, 29, 42, 97, 137–38, 142, 147–50, 174,178, 180, 185, 203–212, 223
encoding and decoding of 24–25, 27, 30, 48, 197, 205, 209, 212
information literacy 15, 33, 39, 125, 203, 224
media literacy 23, 141, 148–49, 151, 176, 224
multi literacy 103, 142, 144, 176
operational literacy 28–30, 199
technologies 28, 145 174
theories of literacy 16, 30, 51, 114, 194–95, 209, 223–24
web literacy 9, 60, 63, 115–16, 125, 223
Loertscher, David 17
Lomax, Pamela 20
Lord of the Rings Trilogy, the 133
Luddites, the 57–58
Luke, Allan 25–27, 29, 203, 205, 207, 209
Constructing Critical Literacies: Teaching and Learning Textual Practices 27
Luther, Judy 142
Lyon, David 53, 224
Surveillance as Social Sorting: Privacy, Risk and Automated Discrimination 53, 224

MacCabe, Colin 58, 156
Macdonald, Catherine 8
Mackay, Hugh 30
Reinventing Australia 30
Macken-Horarik, Mary 29, 203–4, 212
MacLennan, Gary 174
MacLeod, Donald 2–3, 111
Macquarie University 80, 117–19
Madden, Mary 139, 196–97
Marable, Manning 182
Marginson, Simon 77, 85
Martin, Adrian 131
Martin, Bill 164–65
Martino, Wayne 44
What about Boys? 44
Boy's Stuff 44
Martinsons, Barbara 24, 223
Techno Science and Cyberculture 24, 223
Marvin, Carolyn 145, 224
When Old Technologies were New 145
Maslen, Geoff 55
Mason, Geoff 171
Massey, David 59
Masterman, Len 146
Matchett, Stephen 219–20
mature-aged 11, 78, 96, 100, 194, 208
Maycroft, Neil 167
McDonald, Ron 96
McGrew, Anthony 183, 208
Globalization/Anti-Globalization 183, 208
McLaren, Peter 123, 137
McLuhan, Marshall 219
Meikle, James 108
Meister-Scheytt, Claudia 160, 224
Menser, Michael 24, 223
Techno Science and Cyberculture 24, 223
Meyenn, Bob 44
What about Boys? 44
Meyrowitz, Joshua 22
No Sense of Place 22
Mission, Ray 29, 203–04, 223
Mitchell, Candace 27
Rewriting Literacy 27
Modgil, Celia 26, 207
Educational Dilemma: Debate and Diversity 26, 207

Modgil, Sohan 26, 207
Educational Dilemma: Debate and Diversity 26, 207
Morley, David 68
Critical Dialogues in Cultural Studies 68
Morley, Paul 19
Words and Music 19
Moss, Stephen 57
motivation 55, 60, 63–66, 75, 80, 86, 88, 96, 99, 157, 160, 167–68, 174, 212
Mundt, Mary 116
Murdoch University 21, 31, 85, 96, 116, 118–19
Muspratt, Sandy 29
Constructing Critical Literacies 29

National Union of Students 108
Nelson, Brendan 133, 157, 207
Higher Education at the Crossroads 207
Neville, M 118
New Zealand 133, 140, 143, 181–82, 188, 200
Newlands, David 97–98
Newman, John Henry 91–92
The Idea of the University 91
Niranjana, Tejaswini 185
Nixon, Helen 205
Norquay, Margaret 110
Listening to Learn 110
Novak, Thomas 63

O'Donnell, James 99
Avatars of the World: From Papyrus to Cyberspace 99
O'Grady, Erinn 139
Oberman, Cerise 37, 47
Orlowski, Andrew 37
Orwell, George 51–53, 56, 68
The Road to Wigan Pier 51–52, 54, 56
see also Richard Hoggart 51
outcomes-based education system 198

Page, Larry 17
page rank 17–18
Palfreyman, David 190, 217
Oxford and the Decline of the Collegiate Tradition 217
Pallotta-Chiarolli, Maria 44
Boy's Stuff 44
Pearce, Terry 99
Clicks and Mortar: Passion Driven Growth in an Internet Driven World 99
Pelikan, Jaroslav 147
The Idea of the University: A Reexamination 147
PEW Internet and American Life project, the 22, 38, 125, 139, 197, 199
Phillips, Rob 86
Pietrykowski, Bruce 120
Pike, Gary 61
Pillay, Hitendra 159
Pitt, Jane 205
plagiarism 28–29, 186, 219
popular culture 6, 9, 45, 56, 113, 131–34, 136–41, 143–49, 181, 193, 196, 199
Porter, Lynnette 79, 99
Creating the Virtual Classroom 79, 99
Postman, Neil 67, 224
The End of Education 67, 224
postmodernism 146, 149, 156, 183, 199
postmodernity 156, 198–99
Pottruck, David 99
Clicks and Mortar: Passion Driven Growth in an Internet Driven World 99
PowerPoint 83–84, 97–98, 107–110, 126–27, 175, 218
Pugh, Geoff 8, 95, 224
Putnam, Robert 61
Bowling Alone 61

Queensland University of Technology, the 174, 176

Rainie, Lee 139, 196–97, 199
Rajasingham, Lalita 211–13, 217, 224

The Global Virtual University 211
Redhead, Steve 2, 31, 139, 168, 195
Repetitive Beat Generation 30–31, 168, 195
refereed articles 15, 20, 30, 35–36, 45–46, 143, 162, 218
online refereed articles 45–46, 219
Reilly, Susan 136–37
Rivalland, Judith 29, 137
Roberts, Judy 110
Listening to Learn 110
Robertson, Heather-Jane 23, 28, 224
Robertson, John 120, 224
Robinson, Eric 95
The New Polytechnics 95
Rodger, John 171
Rohl, Mary 29, 137
Ronan, Jana 20
Ross, Jonathan 112
Royal National Institute for the Blind 110
Ryan, Jill 29, 147

Said, Edward 62
Saint-Martin, Denis 177
Salmon, Gilly 99
Sanger, Larry 144
Santos, Sergio M. 189
Saupe, Joseph 61
Sayers, Richard 38
Scalmer, Sean 185
Schell, Jonathon 195
The Unconquerable World 195
Scheytt, Tobias 160, 224
Schiller, Dan 201
Schiller, Herbert 57, 98,
Information Inequality 57, 98
Schneider, Troy 187
Schrag, Robert 119
Schrock, Kathy 22–23
Schuetze, Hans 7
Higher Education and Lifelong Learners 7
Schultz, Robert 112
Schwarz, Gretchen 148–49, 224
Schwartz, J. 196
Schwoch, James 136–37
Scott, Peter 93
search engine 16–20, 25, 36–39, 45–46, 142, 219
Search Engine Optimisation (SEO) 142
Seely Flint, Amy 16, 224
Sen, Abhijit 187
Shapiro, Sherry 90
Pedagogy and the Politics of the Body: A Critical Praxis 90
Sharp, Stephen 124
Sherin, Miriam 10
Shreeve, Jimmy Lee 116
Sillitoe, Alan 56
Saturday Night and Sunday Morning 56
Simon, Roger 147
Simpson, Ronald 67, 117
Singletary, Russ 20
Slattery, Luke 198
Slaughter, Anne-Marie 201
Slowey, Maria 7
Higher Education and Lifelong Learners 7
Smith, Coralee 42
Smithers, Rebecca 54
Snyder, Ilana 77, 85
Soloway, Elliot 78
sound (sonic media) 9, 22, 28, 78, 103–04, 109–15, 121, 126–27, 141, 147, 169, 187, 199, 207
Sparrow, Ryan 113
Stafford, Beth 15
Stanford University 17, 220
Stearns, Peter 104
Stensaker, Bjorn 190, 223
Stephenson, Joan 86
Values in Education 86
Stevens, Lisa Patel 138
Stoffle, Carla 162
Stolarick, Kevin 171
Stratta, Erica 8
Strauss, Peter 10
Street, Brian 24

Literacy in Theory and Practice 24
Street-Porter, Janet 134, 149, 158
Studt, Tim 38
Subramani 179–80
Sumner, Robert 166
Sunal, Cynthia Szymanski 42
Sunal, Dennis 42
Swartz, Nikki 162

Tait, Alan 106, 114–5
Key Issues in Open Learning – A Reader 106
Tapper, Ted 171, 190, 217
Fee-paying Schools and Educational Change in Britain 171
Oxford and the Decline of the Collegiate Tradition 217
Taylor, Sandra 94
An Introductory Sociology of Australian Education 94
Taylor, Todd 51, 224
Literacy Theory in the Age of the Internet 51, 114, 223–24
Te Ara, Encyclopedia of New Zealand 133, 143
Teichler, Ulrich 28
Tepper, Steven Jay 171
textual (topics)
analysis 32–33
composition 39
contextual 9, 27, 57, 122, 138, 150, 161–62, 199, 209, 220
digital 39
diversity 21, 141, 144
environment 28, 148
habitat 27
movement 28
practice 29, 145
Thompson, E.P. 62, 160
Threadgold, Terry 29
Tiffin, John 11, 211–13, 217, 224
The Global Virtual University 211
Time magazine 41
Topping, Earle 110
Touraine, Alain 165
Critique of Modernity 165
Toynbee, Polly 57
Hard Work 57
Tranter Deborah 166
Trend, David 149
Trollip, Stanley 87
Computer-based Instruction: Methods and Developments 87
tutorials 4, 28, 31–34, 44, 48, 64, 78–80, 85, 88, 100–01, 106–11, 117, 124–25, 129, 150–51, 175, 191, 194, 208, 217
Twin Towers 184, 193–95

UKeU 2
Beaumont, John Chief Executive 2
University and the Creative Economy, the 170–71
see also Heinz Endowments 170–71
University of Aberdeen 98
University of Central Lancashire 2
University of Edinburgh 219
University of Exeter 7
University of Hull 132
University of Liverpool 2
University of London 76
University of Middlesex 87
University of New South Wales 118
University of Nottingham 2
University of Queensland 112–13
University of Strathclyde 219
University of Surrey 81
University of Sydney 28
University of Ulster 2
University of Western Australia 106–7, 115, 118, 123, 125–27
Unsworth, Len 27, 202–03, 205, 210
Literacy Learning and Teaching Language 27, 205
Teaching Multiliteracies across the School Curriculum 27

Vandenberg, A. 62
van Es, Elizabeth 10
Van Sluys, Katie 16, 224
Vargas, Lucile 55
Vattimo, Gianni 8
The End of Modernity 8
Veblen, Thorstein 172
Virilio, Paul 139, 195
virtual capitalism 24
Vise, David 17
The Google story 17

Wajcman, Judy 164–65
Walby, Sylvia 185
Wallace, Raven 78
Ward, Irene 51, 224
Literacy Theory in the Age of the Internet 51, 114, 223–24
Ward, Melanie 97, 98
Weiler, Kathleen 27
Rewriting Literacy 27
Weissberg, Robert 22, 224
Welsh, Irvine 56, 168, 195
Trainspotting 56, 168,
West, Jessamyn 54–55
White, Mimi 136, 37
Whitehead, Alfred North 109
The Aims of Education and Other Essays 109
Wikipedia 133,143–44
Willis, Paul 172, 223
Schooling for the Dole? The New Vocationalism 172
Wills, John 161
Wilson, Glen 76
Wilton, Janis 128
Winsbeck, D. 53
Wittgenstein, Ludwig 208
The Blue and Brown Books 208
Wood, David 52–53
Wooldridge, Adrian 184
World Trade Organization 185
World Wide Web 16–17, 19, 24, 37, 39, 43, 46, 87, 99, 112, 115, 127, 134, 137, 139, 175, 180–81, 186–88
Wurzburg, Gregory 158
Wyatt-Smith, Claire 29, 147

Yorke, M 8
Young, Jerome 96

Zapatero, Jose Luis Rodriguez 196
Zappacosta, Mario 158
Zurawski, Nils 188